RETAIL MANAGEMENT

Third Edition

Roger Cox

Bsc (Econ), MA, MCIM
Visiting Lecturer, London Guildhall University

Paul Brittain

BSc, MA, DMS, MCIM
*Senior Lecturer in Retailing and Marketing,
Nottingham Business School, Nottingham Trent University*

M&E
PITMAN
PUBLISHING

London • Hong Kong • Johannesburg • Melbourne • Singapore • Washington DC

PITMAN PUBLISHING
128 Long Acre, London WC2E 9AN
Tel: +44 (0)171 447 2000
Fax: +44 (0)171 240 5771

A Division of Pearson Professional Limited

Third edition published in Great Britain 1996

© Pearson Professional Limited 1996

A CIP catalogue record for this book can be obtained from the British Library.

ISBN 0 7121 1061 5

10 9 8 7 6 5 4 3

Typeset by WestKey Limited, Falmouth, Cornwall
Printed and bound in Great Britain by Bell & Bain, Glasgow

The Publishers' policy is to use paper manufactured from sustainable forests.

CONTENTS

Preface   ix

Part One
RETAILING AND THE CONSUMER

1 **The retail industry**   3
Introduction; Trends in retailing; Theories of retail change

2 **Retail organizations**   8
Classification of retail firms; Independent traders; Multiple or
chain stores; Co-operative societies; Department stores; Discount
stores; Superstores and hypermarkets; Franchising; Mail order;
Service retailing; Other forms of retail selling; Wholesale
organisations

3 **International retailing**   23

4 **Retail planning and strategy**   32
Planning; What business am I in?; Where do I want to go?; How
do I get there?; General retail strategies; Specific retail strategies

5 **Retailing research**   40
Information; The retailing research process; Sources of
information; Collecting the information; Questionnaire design;
Sampling; Analysing the information and presenting the
findings. Types of retailing research

6 **The retailing environments**   50
Levels of environment; The retailing macro-environment; The
micro-environment

7 **Consumer buying behaviour**   58
The buying process; The buying participants; Factors influencing
choice: internal variables; external variables

8 **Segmentation**   68
Differing customer needs; Bases for segmentation; Advantages
and disadvantages of segmentation; Segmentation strategy

Part Two
THE RETAIL MIX

9 Store location   79

The importance of location; Store location and the customer; Determining the general area in which to locate; Catchment area analysis; Determining the sales potential of different catchment/trading areas; Choosing a specific site: types of site; the specific site; Profit appraisal

10 Product decisions   96

Merchandise; Own branding; Stock turnover/gross margins; Sales forecasting

11 Buying   106

Merchandise buying; Who buys?; The buying plan; What to buy; How much to buy; From whom to buy; When to buy

12 Stock management   117

Stock control; Stock shortages; Merchandise receipt and return; Marketing; Storage

13 Pricing   131

Terminology; Factors influencing pricing decisions; Setting prices; Pricing tactics; Price adjustments; Margins

14 Advertising   142

Communication; Retail advertising; How much to spend; What media to use; What message to use

15 Personal selling   150

The sales force; Customers; The progress of the sale; Importance of the salesperson

16 Sales promotion and public relations   157

Definition and objectives; Supplier-originated sales promotions; Retailer-originated sales promotions; Public relations

17 Atmosphere and layout   165

Store image and atmosphere; Store exterior; Store interior; Layout; Laying out a store; Display; Allocation of selling area space

18 Customer service decisions   179

Service and level of service; Credit; Alternative service offerings; Handling complaints

Part Three
ADMINISTRATION

19 Financial planning   189
Profit planning; Budgetary control; Financial statements; Ratio
analysis; Other retail performance measures

20 Human resources   202
Organization; The personnel department; Training

21 Property and location development   215
The property function; The cost of sites; Location development

22 Unit management   231
The store manager; Measuring a manager's performance; Other
aspects of branch management; Security; The introduction of
new technology

23 Retailing and the law   245
Consumer protection; Employee legislation

Appendix 1 Bibliography   259

Appendix 2 Case studies   260

Index   267

PREFACE

You may have heard people talk of the 'High Street revolution', but is this description justified? Surely shops have always been a part of civilized society? So what is different about today's retailers?

We have written this book because we believe there has been something of a revolution in the world of retailing which started in about 1980 and is still continuing. This has resulted in the balance of power shifting, in many cases, from the manufacturer to the retailer. Food retailing is a prime example, where the consumer's major decision is not which brand to buy, but which retail outlet to choose for the weekly grocery shopping.

In addition, the pace of sociological and technological change has increased and the retailer is in a far better position to keep in touch with these changes (interacting as he does on a daily basis with consumers) than the manufacturer, who is two or three steps away in this distribution chain. The manufacturer however is now fighting back, for example by utilising direct marketing techniques to communicate directly with customers. Also the retailer is under threat with the development of home shopping through the Internet.

This book is intended not only for students of retailing, but also for those in marketing who require more knowledge of the way retailing works. There will also be a large number of retail managers who have received little formal training on the subject who will appreciate the aim of this text, which is to describe the essential elements of retail management.

The book is divided into three major parts. Part one is concerned with the structure of retailing, the relationship between the consumer and retailer, and the methods of researching that interaction. Part two is devoted to the retail mix – that special blend of strategies that a retailer can use to appeal to target customers. Part three deals with the administrative side of retailing, demonstrating that planning, particularly financial planning, and the measurement of performance are just as vital in retailing as in any other business enterprise.

Acknowledgements

Our sincere thanks are due to many people who have assisted in the preparation of this book. Especially helpful comments and criticisms were made by Dr Paul Whysall, Mr Steve Marlow and Mr Rob Bradgate, Senior Lecturers at Nottingham Trent University. We also thank Dr David Pearson, Principal Lecturer in Marketing at Nottingham Business School, Mr Graham Beaver, Principal Lecturer at Nottingham Business School, and Doyne North of the Chartered Institute of Marketing, for the illuminating case studies presented in the Appendix.

Thanks are also due to Diana Tunney of Marketing Focus UK Ltd. for help with Chapter 5 and to David Salako and James Cox for help in word processing part of the manuscript.

We also acknowledge the assistance of Kings Town Photocodes Limited for supplying examples of bar codes, and the Chartered Institute of Marketing for permission to reprint the Westerhams case study.

We hope the reader will find this book stimulating, and that it provides encouragement to seek new challenges in the fascinating world of retailing.

Roger Cox
Paul Brittain

Note
A reference such as (*see* **32**) refers to numbered section 32 in that same chapter. A reference such as (*see* 2: **2–5**) refers to numbered sections 2–5 of Chapter 2.

Part One

RETAILING AND THE CONSUMER

1

THE RETAIL INDUSTRY

INTRODUCTION

1. Definition

Retailing is one of the most important industries in this country. Napoleon Bonaparte's jibe about 'a nation of shop-keepers' still has a ring of truth. Historically retailing has been viewed as the sale of goods to the consumer through retail shops. However, retailing today should be viewed as being rather broader.

Retailing is the sale of goods and services to the ultimate consumer for personal, family or household use. Thus retailing involves more than selling tangible products. The purchase of a service such as a haircut or dry cleaning is also a retail transaction. Purchases for business or industrial use are not retail transactions.

2. Place of the retail stores sector in the economy

Despite the wider definition of retailing suggested above the retail stores sector is particularly important because

(a) It is the final link in the chain of production which begins at the extractive stages, moves through the manufacturing processes and ends by the distribution of goods (and services) to the final consumer.

(b) It is the second largest employer in the UK with 2.3 million workers involved.

(c) It accounts for 24 per cent of the Gross Domestic Product.

(d) It accounts for about 37 per cent of consumer expenditure

(e) It is an important tax collection point, e.g. value added tax.

3. Functions of retailing

The retail outlet may provide some or all of the following services to its customers:

(a) Convenient location.

3

(b) An assortment of merchandise appropriate to the particular market (i.e. allows choice).

(c) Breaking of bulk so that small quantities can be sold.

(d) Processing of merchandise to more acceptable forms.

(e) Holding of stock for instant availability at relatively stable prices.

(f) Helping to effect change in ownership of goods.

(g) Causing goods to move through the distribution system, e.g. from manufacturer to retailer to consumer.

(h) Providing information not only to the consumer but to suppliers.

(i) Providing product guarantees, after-sales service and dealing with customer complaints.

(j) Providing credit and hire-purchase facilities.

(k) Providing some facility for social intercourse.

TRENDS IN RETAILING

4. Demand for retail products and services

There is a trend showing consumer expenditure shifting from spending on goods to services. For example, catering (meals and accommodation), hairdressing and beauty care, and financial services have all performed well during the period from 1980. Food expenditure has remained relatively buoyant after taking inflation into account, whilst expenditure on clothing and footwear has shown less positive growth. These shifts can, in part, be explained by pressure on consumers' disposable income as a result of the recession in the late 80s and early 90s.

5. Number of shops

In 1971 the Census of Distribution showed that there were 504,781 retail outlets in Britain. This number has now declined to 320,000 outlets, although the rate of decline has dropped markedly in the period from 1980. The reasons for the decline in the number of retail outlets are as follows:

(a) Competition from multiples who with their tremendous buying power and economies of scale make it increasingly difficult for many independent traders to stay in business.

(b) Multiples and co-operatives rationalizing their businesses, closing down smaller units and opening fewer, larger ones.

(c) Large supermarkets and superstores with a wide range of goods on offer

4

have led to increasingly large quantities of merchandise being handled by a comparatively small number of outlets.

A similar tendency towards reduction in the number of retail outlets may be observed both in Western Europe and the USA.

6. Retail polarization

This is the trend towards both larger and smaller retailers with medium-sized retailers encountering the greatest difficulty. The larger stores are offering the customer 'one-stop' shopping and the smaller retailer can be successful through specialization (e.g. Benetton).

7. Mergers and acquisitions

Many store groups have combined to form even larger groups. This trend has been particularly prevalent in food retailing but is by no means confined to it. Dixons' acquisition of Currys and Boots' acquisition of Halfords illustrate how successful retailers feel they can bring their formula for success to bear on less successful groups and achieve improved operating efficiencies.

THEORIES OF RETAIL CHANGE

Four theories of retail institutional change have originated in North America, but they are equally applicable in the UK.

8. Natural selection in retailing

Charles Darwin's biological theory of natural selection has been plagiarized and paraphrased to 'retail types (or units), which best adjust to their environment, are most likely to survive'. The department store is often cited as an example of a retail type failing to adapt quickly to changes in external condition like suburban growth and congestion in town centres. These very factors have, of course, helped the out-of-town stores.

The major environmental factors affecting retailing are:

(a) Changes in the consumer character:

   (*i*) demographic, e.g. population age changes
   (*ii*) social, e.g. product and service preferences
   (*iii*) economic, e.g. changes in real incomes.

(b) Changes in technology, e.g. greater ownership, use of motor cars, food freezers, and microwave ovens.

(c) Changes in competition, i.e. changes in the levels of competitive strength within the areas of influence. It will be seen that these factors may react upon the environment in both a friendly and unfriendly way depending on the type of retail organization.

9. The wheel of retailing

This theory, first championed by Professor McNair of Harvard, postulates that an efficient innovatory form of retailing (such as discounting) enters the market and attracts the public by its new appeal. Growth and maturation occur during which market shares are increased, but trading-up occurs and finally the firms become high cost, high price retailers once again vulnerable to the next innovator. Reasons for its occurrence include:

(a) Organizational deterioration. As young innovators age they become more conservative and may seek greater social acceptableness. Again, they may be unable to recruit management capable of extending the life of the innovation.

(b) Economic factors. The popularity of non-price competition produces higher gross margin requirements as an institution matures. It suggests that non-price competition is less ruinous than price competition.

10. General-specific-general cycle or accordion theory

This describes the tendency for retail business to become dominated (alternatively) by generalists, then specialists and then generalists again. The switch to the specialist store from the old time 'general' store occurred because:

(a) The greater variety of customer goods available could not be accommodated in the old general store

(b) Growth of cities meant that consumer markets allowed profitable segmentation

(c) It provided a social content to the shopping trip which was required as society became more complex and impersonal.

The tendencies helping to create the new 'general' store (superstore or hypermarket) include:

(a) Joining complementary lines, e.g. meat, groceries and produce

(b) *Creaming,* i.e. taking the most popular lines from other retail outlets' ranges, e.g. paperbacks, confectionery, to create small but sure profits

(c) *Scrambling,* i.e. the taking of risky merchandise from other outlets means buying high margin, lower stockturn lines, e.g. unit audio, expensive toys

(d) Adding complete ranges 'borrowed' from other institutions, e.g. Marks & Spencer selling food to increase the physical density of shoppers in their stores

(e) The growth of shopping centres. Large modern air-conditioned centres, particularly those with a substantial food complement, are somewhat like huge general stores. Note also the return to small convenience stores which are now competing successfully primarily by staying open for long hours.

11. The retail life-cycle

The retail life-cycle theory is based on the product life-cycle theory – details of which may be found in any standard marketing text. The retail life-cycle theory suggests that retail institutions also have a life-cycle which can be divided into four phases: innovation, growth, maturity and decline.

In the innovation stage, the new retailer will have few competitors, rapid growth in sales but low profitability due to start-up costs, etc.

In the growth phase, sales growth is still rapid and profitability is high due to the economies of scale now possible. However competitors will spot this and begin to encroach on this market.

At the maturity stage, there are many competitors, sales growth has declined and profitability moderates.

In the final decline phase, sales and profits fall and new, more innovatory retailers are developing and growing.

It has also been suggested that the life-cycle of retail institutions is getting shorter.

Progress test 1

1. Describe the position that retailing holds in the economy.

2. What functions does the retailer carry out?

3. What have been the main trends in retailing over the last ten years?

4. Summarize three theories of retail change.

5. Aldi, the German supermarket chain, has decided the time is right to expand its retail concept in the UK. Their style of operation is 'no frills' – minimal decor, secondary locations, small-medium sized units of 10–15,000 square feet and restricted product ranges but very low prices.

   On the other hand, Sainsbury, Tesco, and Safeway have all been adding extra customer services to achieve competitive advantage. Making reference to retailing theory examine the viability of Aldi's price-led approach.

2

RETAIL ORGANIZATIONS

CLASSIFICATION OF RETAIL FIRMS

The retail industry is extremely diverse and, because there are so many different kinds of retail firms, classifying them all into one neat system has proved difficult.

1. Bases for classification

Retail firms can be classified into a number of categories by:

(a) Legal form. The three basic legal forms of ownership are sole proprietorship, partnership and limited liability company (private or public).

(b) Operational structure. There are three operational structures: the independent trader (usually operating only one retail outlet); the multiple or chain store; and the consumer co-operative.

(c) Range of merchandise. Some retail businesses offer a wide range of goods. Examples of these include variety stores like Marks & Spencer or department stores like Harrods. Others concentrate on narrow ranges like health foods, leather goods, greetings cards and these are called speciality stores or niche retailers.

(d) Degree of service. Although many retail outlets have been converted or built to self-service or self-selection standards, there are others which offer their consumers services such as delivery, credit, gift wrapping, repairs, etc. It is interesting to note that many former self-service retailers are now looking at ways of gaining competitive advantage by adding new customer services.

(e) Pricing policy. Some retailers choose to emphasize low price rather than the service element of their retailing mix. Aldi, the German food retailer, expanded very rapidly in the late 1980s by pricing below the competition. Others choose to price above the competition knowing that they will generate business on the basis of some other attribute such as convenient location or exclusive image.

(f) Location. Another way to classify retailers is according to geographic location. With the increasing cost of town centre sites and traffic congestion, many retailers have sought edge-of-town locations, whilst others have preferred to stay in 'cluster' locations in town centres.

(g) Size of outlet. The average size of many multiples' branches has increased quite markedly over the past few years as more and more firms become large and medium-space users. The term 'superstore' has been used to define outlets between 25,000 and 50,000 sq ft and hypermarkets are those stores over 50,000 sq ft. Many outlets are now being built in the 50,000–100,000 sq ft range. The number of superstores and hypermarkets increased from two in 1963 to 400 in 1986 and reached 1,000 in 1995.

(h) Method of customer contact. Most retail transactions are conducted by face-to-face contact in retail stores. However, a significant proportion of retail sales is generated by non-store retailing operations such as mail order catalogues, telephone selling, vending machines, door-to-door selling or mobile shops.

It will be seen that some of these categories overlap but they are all important in specific marketing situations. The conventional and most common classification of retail organizations is based primarily on operational structure and range of merchandise.

Having attempted a classification scheme for retail organizations and noted the degree of overlap between categories which continue to blur as firms diversify and respond to the changing environment, it is now appropriate to consider the main types of retail organization in more detail.

INDEPENDENT TRADERS

2. Definition

The great majority of shops in Britain are owned by a single individual or sole trader. Independents are defined as retail organizations (other than co-operative societies) with less than ten branches. The usual number of branches controlled by the sole trader is one or at the most two. The market share of the independent, particularly in the food trades, has been falling for some years and the number of independently-owned shops in most trades has diminished.

3. Disadvantages of the sole trader

These may be summarized as follows:

(a) Price competition from retail multiples who can reduce their costs through bulk buying and other economies of scale.

(b) Lack of specialist expertise in retail functions, e.g. buying, instore merchandising, accounting, or possibly lack of time to carry them out adequately.

(c) Lack of capital to expand and improve the business.

(d) Inertia – the small trader may not wish to expand because of the extra problems expansion brings.

(e) Due to high accommodation costs the independent often lacks the advantage of being in a large shopping centre with heavy pedestrian traffic generation.

(f) Changing shopping habits brought about by increased car usage has concentrated purchases in large well-located 'one-stop' stores.

4. Advantages of the sole trader

Although the multiple usually has the edge over the small trader in price competition, the latter often wins in terms of service competition as the following advantages, which the small trader can offer the customer, show:

(a) Personal relationship with customers.

(b) Convenient locations for 'walk-in' trade from customers' houses or places of work.

(c) More flexible merchandising policy, allowing for individual tastes.

(d) Longer and more convenient opening hours.

(e) Overheads can be kept low because of cheap sites, use of family assistance, etc.

(f) Some of the advantages of the multiple can be gained by membership of a voluntary group (*see* **32**), e.g. bulk-buying, national advertising, specialist services, etc.

5. Future prospects

The independent traders' share of the retail market has now fallen well below the 40 per cent level (down from 54% in 1961). However, there are now signs that the continual decline in the independent sector is not irreversible and, for example, in the grocery sector the independent is fighting back by adopting a convenience store format with longer hours of trading and personalized services to a local community.

MULTIPLE OR CHAIN STORES

6. Organization

The large multiple retail organization is invariably of the joint-stock company type (either private or public) and therefore in common ownership with a degree of centralized control. A large multiple is defined as an organization (other than a co-operative) with ten or more branches. The chain is often made up of speciality shops, i.e. those selling a related range of merchandise (for example furniture, clothing or books and periodicals). Variety chains like Marks & Spencer, and some branches of the larger food multiples like Asda, are exceptions to the rule on related merchandise, however, and stock a very wide range of foods and non-foods. The multiple, by opening many branches, is able to attract a larger market. Multiples currently take nearly 60% of all retail sales (up from 32.5% in 1961).

7. Characteristics

The characteristics of many multiples are bound up with economies of scale and are:

(a) Centralized buying

(b) Concentration on fast-moving lines – manufacturers' brand leaders or own-labels

(c) Merchandise largely pre-sold or self-sold through a mixture of national advertising and open instore displays

(d) Located in major shopping centres alongside other multiples (giving them the advantage of associated sales)

(e) Relatively low prices

(f) Strong corporate identity most noticeable in shopfronts, fascias, in-store fittings and advertising

(g) Centralization of many other functions such as advertising, personnel recruitment and training, operating policies, etc.

Whilst the above is true for general line multiples, many specialist multiple chains are now becoming prominent through targeting a well-defined consumer group and providing a range of merchandise to suit the needs of that target group. The Next chain is such an example, and although centralized buying is a characteristic of this chain, low pricing is not and the service element is stressed to a greater degree than other multiples. Similarly, many general line multiples formerly very strong in the high street are moving out to larger, lower cost, edge-of-town locations.

CO-OPERATIVE SOCIETIES

8. Origins

The Co-operative Movement began in Rochdale in 1844. A co-operative society is defined as a co-operative retailing organization trading on co-operative principles, affiliated to the National Co-operative Movement (through the Co-operative Union) and registered under the Industrial and Provident Societies Acts. Because many retail co-operative societies operate branches they are in this respect similar to multiple chains, but in the form of organization and control they are in many ways quite different. In 1995 the Co-operative movement as an entity was still one of Britain's biggest retailers.

9. The principles of the Movement

The principles of the Movement applicable to retailing are:

(a) Voluntary and open membership

(b) Democratic control; one member, one vote

(c) Payment of limited interest on capital

(d) Surplus allocated for co-operative development, the common good or in proportion to the members' transactions.

One big problem has been the conflict between principle **(b)** and the need to fight the growing power of the multiple retailers. Co-operative market shares have declined substantially since the last war and, in an effort to counter this, attempts have been made to merge societies into larger, more powerful units.

10. Problems

The main problems facing the co-operatives have been as follows:

(a) Poor management. Although some successful societies have attracted high calibre management, many of the smaller less successful societies have not. This largely stems from the inexperience and inefficiency of lay boards of directors and the lack of promotion opportunities and financial incentives for executives in some societies.

(b) Unco-ordinated marketing. Sometimes two or even three buying groups attempt to cover merchandise in some society areas.

(c) Too much decentralization. Local society boards of directors sometimes wish to remain in office and this reluctance to merge with other societies has reduced opportunities for scale economies.

(d) Too many societies. Strenuous efforts have been made to reduce the number of societies by merging them into regional societies. In 1960 there were 875 societies and this fell to just over 200 by 1977. Today there are just 50 societies.

(e) Too many shops. One aim of the Co-operative Movement has been to provide shopping in the most convenient places for 'walk-in' shoppers. Shop numbers fell by over half to 14,000 between 1961 and 1973. Today the total stands at fewer than 4,500 outlets but there has been a significant increase in the number of Co-op superstores.

(f) Lack of an up-to-date image. Co-operative stores are often regarded as old-fashioned whilst the typical customer is slightly older and of a slightly lower socio-economic group than multiple shop customers.

(g) Financing. The main source of funds for development has been members' savings and profit retentions but these are insufficient. The movement has therefore often found it necessary to borrow money at commercial rates. However, it is itself involved in finance through both the Co-operative Bank and Co-operative Insurance Society.

11. Solutions

The Co-operative Movement has tackled these problems in the following ways:

(a) Professional management. Better managers are being recruited at all levels, but most particularly in the larger, more successful societies.

(b) Marketing. In theory, there is nothing to stop individual retail societies negotiating separate agreements with manufacturers, but in practice over 60 per cent of all packaged food and groceries are bought through the Co-operative Wholesale Society (CWS). The CWS also carries out national negotiations in respect of a much wider range of goods especially for the national advertising programme of promoted lines.

(c) Warehousing. This has been streamlined to eight regional distribution centres in the UK.

(d) New development. Some societies are pushing ahead with extensive super-store openings and, in line with the retail polarization trend, medium-sized units are being closed whilst the smaller units are being converted to the convenience store format with later opening hours.

12. Present trends

Although co-operative societies have declined seriously in trade share from the late 1950s, recent results show a slight reversal of the trend. Comparison with experience abroad is largely impossible due to the fact that historical factors have caused shares to vary from country to country, e.g. in Sweden co-ops take about 20 per cent of retail trade compared with very little trade in the USA.

DEPARTMENT STORES

13. Definition

A department store is defined as a large store selling, under one roof but in physically separate departments, four or more different classes of consumer goods, one of which is women's and girls' clothing. Some large departmental store groups like House of Fraser and Debenhams own up to 100 branches and these chains are called multiple department stores. There are also a number of much smaller chains of department stores, e.g. Bentalls, and also a few autono-mous units. Within the larger groups some central buying is attempted but normally the accent is on customer service with each department carrying out its own buying, merchandising and stock control. Scope for economies of scale in buying is therefore narrow. Department stores have seen a gradual erosion of market share as the large supermarket groups have added non-food merchandise to their retail offer. General modernization of city centre stores and the quality of management will be the key to the future success of department stores.

14. The general principles of operation

The general principles of operation of department stores are:

(a) Siting in major shopping centres or locations supported by potentially large catchments.

(b) Freedom for the customer to move around the store and view.

(c) Relatively high prices with margins large enough to cover heavy staffing, the range of services offered and high accommodation costs.

(d) Provision of a large number of specialised goods in one location which allows some associated sales. (However, many of the larger groups have been carrying out range pruning.)

(e) Special staff expertise in particular products.

(f) Wide range of customer services such as delivery, credit, the making-up of soft furnishings and the provision of restaurants, cloakrooms, telephones, etc.

(g) Space concessions offered to 'shop-within-shop' operations (often manufacturers) like Wedgwood or Berkertex.

15. Future trends

Department stores are expected to maintain their proportion of trade. This implies that their ability to withstand the dynamic trading of the leading multiple shops will continue. Movement towards new shopping centres, new centres of population and to the suburbs is expected to continue. In both Europe and the USA department stores have been one of the most successful types of retailing. (It has been suggested that variety stores such as Marks & Spencer in the UK have helped to hinder departmental growth here; this former type of retailing is not quite as popular abroad.)

DISCOUNT STORES

16. Characteristics

Cut-price retailing has been common in the UK since the abolition of retail price maintenance in 1964. Every retail trade (with the exception, until 1995, of bookselling) indulges in it, some firms to a greater extent than others. Discount stores tend to have characteristics such as:

(a) Very low prices

(b) Low gross margins

(c) High degree of self-service

(d) Low-cost fittings

(e) No free services, such as delivery

(f) Reliance on heavy advertising in nearby large population centres

(g) Relative isolation of locations from conventional shopping areas with consequently low rents predominantly in 'edge-of-town' sites. The dependence is therefore on shoppers requiring:

    (*i*) good communications
    (*ii*) plenty of car parking
    (*iii*) visibility of the site from some distance.

Pure discount stores (such as the original Comet electrical operation) became very successful in the late 1960s and early 1970s on the basis of the discount concept. However, the 'wheel of retailing' has turned and distinctions between Comet and other electrical retailers are no longer marked. Similarly, Asda, which started as a food discount chain, now has a substantial number of own-label products and is similar in trading style to the other large supermarket groups.

Out of the various discount sectors, DIY retailers are the largest. These are closely followed by food discounters and carpets and furniture retailers. A new wave of limited-range food discount retailers such as Aldi entered the market in the late 1980s when the UK recession began to bite and customers were again increasingly looking for the lowest possible prices; their success however has been limited and are not now thought to pose a major threat to the major grocery retailers.

SUPERSTORES AND HYPERMARKETS

17. Superstores and hypermarkets

The development of very large retail units grafting substantial non-food sales to a supermarket operation started in the early 1960s in the UK. Applying the basic principles of discount stores, low prices and minimum service, growth has been spectacular. From two stores in 1963 to 210 in 1978, the current total is over a thousand.

Superstores have a sales area of 25,000–50,000 sq ft, whilst the term 'hypermarket' is reserved for units over 50,000 sq ft of selling area. Their characteristics are:

(a) Substantial surface car parking spaces under the control of the superstore retailer and serving the superstore largely or exclusively.

(b) A range of 25,000–30,000 individual items, covering most foods and many non-foods (the latter may take up 40 per cent of the total selling area).

(c) A broadly similar pricing, service and general marketing strategy to the discount store.

(d) The provision of often cut-price petrol retailing adjacent to the store and its car park.

(e) The comprehensive in-store use of information technology such as electronic point-of-sale equipment, and advanced food preparation equipment, e.g. for in-store bakeries.

Many planning problems have been encountered by retailers eager to open these very large stores. Now, many local authorities are reluctant to give permission to units which they believe might help to blight town centres and put many small independent retailers out of business.

The proportion of retail sales captured by this sector has increased from 2.7 per cent in 1980 to over 7 per cent in 1986 and in 1995 some 50 per cent of grocery sales was transacted by superstores.

FRANCHISING

18. Franchising

Franchising is the granting of sole selling rights within a given geographical area. The franchising company (the franchisor) supplies equipment and/or raw materials for a licensee who either pays a franchise fee or a percentage of turnover, or contracts to buy supplies from the franchisor (or a mixture of these methods of payment). The licensee is also helped in finding a location and is trained in all aspects of the business. Franchising is most frequently found in retail catering (Wimpy, Kentucky Fried Chicken), car maintenance and launderettes, but also in many other trades such as electrical retailing and bridal wear.

Despite the recession, franchising accounted for 24% of retail sales in 1995 and is expected to grow to 30% by the year 2000.

Franchising really took off in the USA in the 1960s and now accounts for well over a third of all retail sales there – it is not difficult therefore to see why many retailers feel there is a lot more potential in the franchise business format in the UK.

MAIL ORDER

Mail order retailing – using the mail to get orders and/or facilitate delivery – takes several forms as follows:

19. Mail order catalogues

This category involves two types – the general merchandise catalogue, and the specialist catalogue. Examples of the latter are the specialist seed, bulb and plant catalogues. But the general merchandise catalogue is by far the more important in this sector and is dominated by Great Universal Stores' companies with 40 percent of the market. Other houses include Littlewoods, Freemans, Grattan and

Empire Stores. Much of the selling is done through a network of part-time agents who are paid 10 per cent commission on the things they sell.

Mail order catalogue retailing currently accounts for 2.9 per cent of all retail sales as compared to 4.7 per cent in 1976. However, the last few years have seen a reversal of the downward trend with the introduction of several new specialist catalogues, most notably the Next Directory.

From the agency mail order operators' point of view, the advantages and disadvantages of the system are as follows:

(a) The advantages are:

(*i*) no conventional retail overheads
(*ii*) lower buying costs possible
(*iii*) less under-employment of staff than in conventional retail outlets (i.e. no peaks and troughs in the daily sales volume)
(*iv*) relatively high margins for the retail sector.

(b) The disadvantages are:

(*i*) high working capital ratio (which means that a higher proportion than normal of net assets are earning less than average returns)
(*ii*) fixed prices (the catalogue is prepared many months beforehand)
(*iii*) high commission, credit and carriage costs (particularly for returned goods)
(*iv*) inflexibility in sales administration (e.g. the numbers of agents cannot be altered quickly to take account of new situations).

The advantages of the general merchandise mail order catalogue to the customer are:

(a) 'Free' credit

(b) Price stability over the lifetime of the catalogue

(c) Savings in transport fares and petrol

(d) Wide selection of merchandise

(e) Approval facility

(f) 'Armchair shopping' for mothers, old people and families living some way from shopping centres (i.e. convenience).

Free credit, it is said, far outweighs the advantages to customers of lower prices obtainable elsewhere but in any case the structure of mail order trading is not conducive to competition in terms of price.

Mail order catalogue retailing has been stimulated by the launch of mail order catalogues by mainstream retailers such as Marks & Spencer with their home furnishings catalogue and the Next chain's launch of the Next Directory.

20. Direct response advertising

This is the use of advertising in newspapers or magazines to describe a product and stimulate the customer to write or telephone for it. Firms such as Innovations or Kaleidoscope have used this method successfully to sell anything from silk blouses to home copying machines. Most national newspapers have a Saturday bargain squares section advertising all manner of postal bargains.

21. Direct mail

This is the use of advertising literature sent directly to the potential customer for the purpose of selling goods or services. The Reader's Digest have been particularly successful in selling books in this manner and records, tapes and collectors' pieces are also sold via direct mail.

SERVICE RETAILING

22. Service retailing

As disposable incomes rise, so consumer spending has shifted from purchasing essential items to goods and services which increase the consumer's quality of life. There has been a marked increase in the provision of primary services as the focal point for retail transactions. In the same way as a product satisfies the needs and wants of consumers, so can a service. The prime difference between products and services is the intangible nature of the service (i.e. you cannot touch it).

Service retailers have existed for many years – shoe repairers, travel agents and dry cleaners being some examples. However, many new service retailers are now being established and are thriving. Examples are the amusement or 'theme' parks, dance studios, health spas and gyms.

As well as increasing disposable incomes, the growth of service retailing has been fuelled by:

(a) An increasing number of working women

(b) Changing lifestyles with increasing emphasis on leisure activity and personal care

(c) New service offerings – for example, private health screening.

OTHER FORMS OF RETAIL SELLING

23. Markets

Although traditional markets account for less than 1 per cent of total retail turnover, they affect general retail sales wherever they are held because of their attraction. Many of the older provincial markets like Bury and the Bull Ring in Birmingham have been successfully accommodated in new shopping centre schemes.

24. Mobile shops

These are travelling shops and are distinct from roundsmen's vehicles from which milk, bread and certain other goods are delivered regularly to an established list of customers.

25. Automatic vending

Selling out of machines has been part of the retail scene for many years (particularly for cigarettes and confectionery) and there has been something of a recent boom in auto-vending, notably in closed, relatively vandal-proof areas such as sports centres and airports. This possible limitation reduces the main advantage of the machine in that they can be in operation for twenty-four hours a day, seven days a week.

26. Door-to-door trading

Selling by travelling salesmen has declined since pre-war days but brushes (Betterware), cosmetics (Avon) and encyclopedias (Britannica) are still sold in this way. A variety of foodstuffs is also regularly delivered in Britain to the doorstep, e.g. milk and bread.

27. Party selling

This idea, which originated in the USA, has been quite successful in the selling of the Tupperware brand of plastic containers and in children's clothing. It involves a local person organizing a party demonstration in his or her own home.

28. Club trading

Some retailers encourage people to join a club, paying a weekly sum for the article they wish to buy. This is still a popular method for the purchase of large items especially for Christmas.

WHOLESALE ORGANIZATIONS

29. Definition of the wholesaler

The wholesaler is an organization, independent of producer and retailer, which undertakes the classic functions of distribution. These functions are:

(a) Merchandise selection

(b) Forward buying

(c) Warehousing

(d) Breaking bulk

(e) Financing, i.e. credit

(f) Presentation, e.g. preparation, packaging

(g) Levelling out of price variations.

30. Basic types of traditional wholesaler

(a) General. This involves the stocking of a wide range of merchandise.

(b) Specialist. This type keeps stocks of particular categories of goods, e.g. toys, electrical goods, etc.

Both of these types of wholesaler may operate nationally and may employ staff to call on retailers, either to sell or to deliver goods or to do both.

31. Changes in wholesale patterns

The wholesaler in the traditional mould has been declining due to changes in the structure of retail distribution, e.g. fewer, larger multiple-owned shops with direct deliveries from manufacturers. New types of wholesaler have arisen, namely voluntary groups, cash-and-carry warehouses, and warehouse clubs.

32. Wholesale sponsored voluntary groups

These are often large organizations like Spar and Happy Shopper which sell to the group's retail members.
    The advantages to the member of the 'symbol' group are as follows:

(a) Bulk-buying by the group means bigger discounts and thus the possibility of lower prices to compete with the multiple.

(b) The problems of administration of buying and so on are largely taken from the group member.

(c) Group 'own-brand' products help to give a corporate multiple-type image; this is boosted by national group advertising, sales promotion and display cards.

(d) In larger group wholesale chains, financial assistance and advice on development are available to the member.

The disadvantages of being a member are as follows:

(a) A minimum weekly order must be placed with the local warehouse.

(b) A member may be asked to keep special accounts.

(c) For the larger member with very big stores, membership is less advantageous because the local warehouses often do not stock the very broad ranges needed for modern superstore operation.

33. Cash and carry wholesalers

The basic elements of cash and carry are:

(a) A wholesale warehouse

(b) Customers are traders

(c) Complete or partial self-service

(d) Payment always in cash

(e) Customers carry their own goods away.

The advantages to the retailers are:

(a) Lower buying prices

(b) The ability to purchase as necessary, i.e. the retailer can use the cash and carry as a stockroom

(c) Time saved in dealing with representatives, receiving and checking goods, invoices, etc.

(d) A better knowledge of what is available

(e) Greater contact with the wholesaler in connection with exchange of views, etc.

The advantages to the wholesaler are:

(a) Better net margins

(b) Greater contact with retailers.

34. Significance of cash and carry

Although there was a great upsurge in cash and carry development up until the early 1990s this seems to have stabilized at near saturation point in some areas. Many of the large groups have rationalized their chains by closing down badly sited branches and extending those outlets that have proved to be profitable. Others such as Costco have followed the US warehouse club format which targets the small business customer, but also serves an increasing number of non-business customers.

Progress test 2

1. What are the main bases for classifying retail firms?

2. What problems face the independent trader and how has he tried to overcome them?

3. What are the characteristics of a multiple?

4. How has the Co-operative Movement attempted to regain its position in UK retailing?

5. Describe the characteristics of a department store and compare them with discount stores.

6. What are the three forms of mail order retailing?

7. What functions does the wholesaler carry out?

8. How do voluntary groups operate? Do they have any disadvantages?

9. Multiple retailing has assumed a dominance over consumer channels of distribution that is becoming increasingly difficult to break. How do you account for this dominance and what are the implications of this situation for other distributive organisations?

10. Recent advances in IT have resulted in the possibility of new advances in home shopping and the delivery of services direct to the consumer on an information 'super highway'. Do these advances spell the death knell for the traditional store-based retailer?

3

INTERNATIONAL RETAILING

1. Introduction

Retailing, which is one of the world's biggest but most localised industries, is undergoing a change which many observers would have dismissed twenty years ago. The recent explosion in international or cross-border retailing belies the bad experiences of retail companies like the Burton Group in France or Carrefour in Britain during the 1970s. Of course there have been well-established international retailers such as Woolworth and C & A for many years but they were the exception rather than the rule. Political, legal, economic and socio-cultural factors militated together against any mass migration of retail brands over international boundaries. This was largely true of most products and services which had to be extensively modified or re-branded for export. The costs of such effort were often seen as largely non-productive and the failure rates were seen as too high. In any case there was no need to attempt to operate in cross-border fashion except for large consumer packaged goods manufacturers like Heinz, Unilever, Coca-Cola and Nestlé. But as was observed as early as 1985 in Britain the retail sector was showing signs of maturity in falling returns on capital in investment, increased price competition and greater advertising expenditure; 'there are too many stores in the wrong place and/or in the wrong hands. The present epidemic of take-overs reflects this. . . .' This maturation of the market is one of the so-called 'push' or threat factors causing retailers to look overseas. These push factors as well as 'pull' factors are discussed in the next two sections.

2. Push factors

(a) Saturation. The biggest 'push' factor is saturation of domestic markets. While there is room for expansion at home, retailers have no need to look abroad but that option is fast disappearing.

In the UK for example retail chain's share of the grocery retailing market increased from under half in 1973 to over 80 per cent by 1995. A similar pattern can be seen in such countries as France, Germany, Belgium and the Netherlands.

With such levels of concentration at home, companies are moving into countries with less developed retail markets like Spain or buying existing chains in developed markets. In Britain this latter option is no longer possible for grocery supermarket chains. After the acquisition of Hillards (Yorkshire) and Wm. Low (Scotland) by Tesco there is only one regional grocery chain left in the UK.

(b) Recession. Another threat or push factor has been the severity of the 1990–92 recession which began in the US in 1989 and was only ending in Japan around 1995. This followed the 1980–81 downturn and, clearly, retailers like other sectors see the need for a portfolio of assets covering economies which offer contra-cyclical advantages, i.e. when your own economy is down other nations' economies could be booming.

The strategic need to maintain and enhance growth in a fast-changing set of environments is a paramount objective for retail managers in all sectors. If one door closes then another has to be found. In this case the door is abroad.

(c) Planning restrictions. Growing aversion to the spread of hypermarkets and retail parks has taken hold in several European countries. In Britain the Department of Environment published new planning guidelines in 1993 called PPG6, calling for town centre development to be favoured over out-of-town localities. After two years it became apparent that the guidelines had produced a decisive shift away from out-of-town shopping. As a result J. Sainsbury the grocery supermarket chain was building only 12 new stores in 1995 out of an original 20 planned. Sainsbury says it is now winning only one in 10 planning appeals against seven in 10 previously.

In France, inventor of the hypermarket, restrictions were introduced in 1973 when the number of hypermarkets soared to more than 200. Paris alone was surrounded by eight giant regional centres. Controls were toughened in 1993 and now every centre needs permission from a government body composed of local mayors, trade and consumer groups. France's Promodès says that because of planning restrictions it can only open one hypermarket a year at home and that is why it has become a major player in Spain. As a result some Spanish local authorities are becoming worried and Catalonia for example has banned developments of more than 2,500 sq. metres.

Controls of some sort are also applied in Germany, Denmark, Finland, Belgium and Holland.

In the US with the greatest number of shopping malls in the world, growth has slowed since 1989 not so much because of planning problems but the recessional conditions in North America.

3. Pull factors

There are several factors which can be seen as opportunities rather than threats.

(a) Falling barriers to market entry. The European Union now offers a more standardised environment for retailers in terms of the movement of goods for example. The creation of a single European market of 320 million consumers has also made Europe a much more attractive market for US retailers. The crumbling of the Berlin Wall and the collapse of Communism has opened up not only Eastern Europe but the countries of the CIS (the old USSR).

Trade blocs elsewhere such as NAFTA (the North America Trade Free Area) have encouraged American retailers to look next door at Mexico and Canada. Japanese department stores spread across Asia in the 1980s and in the 1990s are gaining a foothold in London.

(b) Supplier strategies. Manufacturers of goods for retail distribution are becoming more international themselves. Groups such as Unilever are restructuring manufacturing operations on a pan-European basis and are adopting international marketing campaigns. A sign of this is the growing importance of internationally recognised brand names ('global brands') in consumer goods. Nestlé for example has re-branded all the Rowntree products since that confectionery company was taken over, using the Nestlé logo.

(c) Strategic retail alliances. Since 1988 some European food retailers have formed joint ventures, forming eight loose alliances. This could lead to joint buying and greater pressure on food manufacturers to sell at common prices.

(d) Identification of less developed markets. From the 1970s the Southern European markets of Spain, Italy and Portugal were invaded from the North. Four of Spain's top five food retailers are now French-owned, for example.

(e) Converging consumer tastes. Increasing foreign travel by consumers and the spread of cross-border mass media such as satellite television are creating 'common denominations in consumer tastes.'

4. Cross-border trends

If we were to list half a dozen key retailing issues of the 1990's, internationalism would be near the top. Cross-border moves by retailers have increased substantially since the 1970s and the trends have been tracked by Corporate Intelligence, a UK retail consultancy. Table 3.1 shows the situation for European retailers over the past forty years or so.

The table shows that the pace of internationalism, particularly for European retailers, is quickening.

US retailers are also on the move; the number of US store groups operating in Europe rose from 15 in 1991 to 45 in 1994.

However, the 'heady atmosphere' of the late 1980s encouraged many smaller retailers, especially in the clothing sector, to announce plans for expansion into foreign markets. Much of this activity had been either cancelled or postponed by the middle of the 1990s, including the plans of several US retailers which had intended to open in Europe. Again, certain large retail groups have had to restructure dramatically because of poor trading conditions, including the

Table 3.1 Cross-border moves by European retailers

Decade	Number
1950s and earlier	11
1960s	24
1970s	157
1980s	611
1990 to end of 1993	610

Source: Corporate Intelligence Research.

shedding of some of their foreign operations. In the UK, for example, Storehouse have withdrawn from most of its direct overseas activity, and has sold Habitat to IKEA, the Swedish furniture retailer.

5. Strategic methods

The word strategy is from the Greek for 'general' and this suggests a plan which will support a major directional move by a corporation. We see in Chapter 4 that a retail company like Marks & Spencer can adopt a market development strategy and move into overseas markets for the reasons discussed earlier in this chapter.

Having decided, after due research and analysis to carry out a cross- border move the retail company has three broad methods by which such a strategy can be implemented. These are organic growth, acquisition or joint venturing. We examine each option along with its benefits and problems and give examples of success and failure in each category.

(a) **Organic growth.** This involves a company starting from scratch in a new market. Also termed internal development, a firm buys in the basic resources needed to set up its own operations, in this case, abroad. Given the perceived differences in tastes and cultures in each country it may seem strange that organic growth has been a popular method of implementing cross-border strategies. Even stranger, much organic growth has been seen in the retail food sector. One has only to look at the entry of German food retailers Aldi and Lidl & Schwarz into the UK. Differences in food tastes between the UK and elsewhere was underlined by the failure of Campbells Foods when it first entered the UK market with its own US range of soups which proved a failure in Britain. Things are clearly changing when Toys 'R' Us (US) and IKEA (Sweden), retailing toys and furniture respectively, can develop organically not only in Britain but across the world.

(b) **Acquisition growth.** Here companies buy up local firms. Whereas organic growth can be time-consuming, growth by take-over can be fast, with the added advantage of buying local knowledge (the problems of 'cultural shock' have to be managed in advance for success).

Examples of successful acquisition include Tesco and its purchase of Catteau, a French supermarket chain, and Kingfisher also buying a French electrical retailer, Darty.

Some retailers have had well publicised problems with their international ventures. They include Dixons, the electrical stores group with its acquisition of the US Silo chain, Marks & Spencer which made a costly entry into the Canadian market, and Britain's Signet (formally Ratners) which bought into the US retail jewellery market.

(c) **Joint ventures.** These are also called strategic alliances and include franchising as well as other looser affiliations. The two leading retail franchise groups are McDonalds (US) and Benetton (Italy). The advantage of this type of joint venture is that the entrepreneurial skills of local business people can be harnessed to the pull of a proven international brand so that a 'symbiotic' relationship can be developed. Joint venturing reduces the risks of investment in overseas markets.

6. Country preferences

Up to 1990–91 strong preferences were shown for and between certain countries. Although some retailers attempted pan-European coverage (German mail order operations and Italian fashion chains such as Stefanel and Benetton) it was more common for activity to flow within set areas. Scandinavia and the Benelux countries were similar in that the considerable activity within their borders rarely spilled over their borders.

Other identifiable flows were more unilateral in nature. These included France to Spain, Germany to Austria, from the UK to the Irish Republic. Most of these flows are clearly understandable for cultural and similar reasons, as was the tendency of the UK to look readily at the US and, starting in the mid-1980s, vice versa. Even Italian and Portuguese retailing is characterized by the presence of multiple chains in most sectors. A significant number of these have ventured abroad with varying degrees of success but the 1990-92 recession saw an abrupt decline in overseas investment by retailers after their extravaganza of the late 1980s. However the tide has started to turn, albeit slowly. In 1993, Kingfisher announced the acquisition of Darty, a major electrical chain in France. Wickes is pursuing further expansion in Benelux and Northern France. Eastern Europe has attracted some adventurous operators – but nothing like the extent that German and Austrian retailers are moving in, although Tesco now has a major stake in the Hungarian supermarket chain, Global. For a number of other organizations in foreign markets, retrenchment has continued.

7. UK retailers in the USA

North America remains the focus of attention for many UK retailers' overseas aspirations, but the recent recession there has resulted in mixed experiences with a number of important investments turning sour. Equally though, others have continued expanding. Examples include:

- *Laura Ashley*   Down to 155 stores in 1994, with turnover declining over the last 3 years.

- *The Body Shop*   189 outlets by 1994, approaching 50 more than the previous year.

- *C & J Clark* (shoes)   Small decline in outlets in 1994. Trades as Hanover, Bostonian and Outlets, totalling 238.

- *Dixons*   Dixons expanded Silo from 119 outlets at acquisition in 1987 to 233 by early 1992, but a year later was down to 185. Trading continued to be weak and a new format, YES, was being tried immediately prior to the chain's disposal in September 1993 to US competitor Fretter.

•	*Grand Metropolitan*	Pearle Health Services is a US-based opticians business with over 1,000 outlets world-wide, but Grand Met no longer has any retail operations in the UK.
•	*Hanson*	Some 430 Endicott Johnson shoe shops in the USA.
•	*Marks & Spencer*	Brooks Brothers has opened outlets in a number of factory shop malls of late, and now has 83 in total. The Kings Supermarket chain now has 19 stores in the New Jersey area.
•	*Signet*	From its first US acquisition in 1987, Signet (formally Ratners) built up to a 1,100 strong chain by 1991. A subsequent rationalisation brought the 1994 total down to about 920.
•	*J. Sainsbury*	Shaws Supermarkets' sales in 1993–94 were £1.3bn. By 1994 there were 87 stores, an increase of 8 in one year. Sixteen percent of the Giant Foods chain was acquired in 1995.
•	*Thorn EMI*	Thorn EMI Rental Americas comprises the Remco and Rent-A-Center operations with close to 1,100 stores. Remco was acquired in early 1992. HMV has 65 stores in Canada and is now expanding in the USA.
•	*W.H. Smith*	USA operations continue to be expanded. More news and gift shops have opened – the total is over 300, and the addition of 80 more music outlets helped sales nearly double; there are now some 170 outlets. A third Waterstone's bookshop has been opened.

Source: The Corporate Intelligence Group: *Cross Border Retailing in Europe*; 1994 Edition.

8. UK retailers in Western Europe

Despite the Single Market coming in officially on 1 January 1993, there remains little evidence of large-scale reorientation of UK retailer investment towards continental Europe and away from North America.

•	*Laura Ashley*	60 stores in 1994, including France (26), Germany (16), Italy (9), Netherlands (7).
•	*The Body Shop*	The company's European presence continues to increase and includes Belgium (12), Denmark (15), France (26), Germany (43), Greece (33), Netherlands (48), Italy (40), Spain (55) and Portugal (8).
•	*Iceland*	Having acquired full control of the Au Gel chain in Northern France and introduced its own name to the region, the company subsequently closed the operation in June 1994.

- *Granada*　　Retains a strong position in German TV rental market with Telerent.

- *Marks & Spencer*　　Continuing with ambitious but cautious expansion plans particularly in France, the Netherlands and Spain. By 1994 the company had 48 European outlets and plans to double its floor space before the year 2000.

- *MFI*　　Expanded Hygena-Cuisine chain to 46 outlets in France and many more were scheduled for 1995.

- *Storehouse*　　Storehouse European interests have contracted with the sale of Habitat and are now confined to Mothercare franchises, 15 of them in Switzerland, plus a smaller number of BhS franchises, including Greece and Spain.

- *Tesco*　　At end-1992, Tesco announced the acquisition of Catteau, a regional supermarket chain in Northern France, completing the purchase in June 1993 at a value of £106m. In mid-1994 Tesco took a controlling interest in the Hungarian supermarket operator Global. By 1996 it had moved into Poland, the Czech Republic and Slovakia.

- *Thorn EMI*　　The company has rental businesses in Benelux, France, Sweden, Ireland, Norway, Finland, Spain, Switzerland and Denmark. In Denmark it also owns the Fona electronics chain. Meanwhile more HMV shops are opening – but outside Europe.

- *Tie Rack*　　61 outlets in 11 European countries with the highest number in France. Also present in North America, Australia and the Far East.

- *Wickes*　　Wickes is an important player in the Benelux DIY market with 34 outlets plus 2 in Northern France. It has raised funds for a new of phase of European expansion.

Source: The Corporate Intelligence Group: *Cross Border Retailing in Europe*; 1994 Edition.

9. US retailers in the UK

Until the 1980s with the notable exception of Woolworths, few US retailers had ventured into Europe. Now a new wave is crossing the Atlantic, often using the UK as a convenient stepping stone to continental Europe, as well as it having profitable potential in its own right to a degree not common elsewhere. These US operations mostly have either a new format – warehouse club, 'category killer'; or a fresh approach to an existing market – leisure clothing, entertainment merchandising. Toys 'R' Us was the predecessor, and the new examples include:

- *Blockbuster*   Video superstores and indoor adventure playgrounds.

- *Walt Disney*   Character merchandising stores.

- *The Gap*   Leisure clothing.

- *Lands' End*   Direct mail leisure clothing.

- *Bath & Body Works*   The Limited's distinctive toiletries format in a joint venture with Next.

- *Costco*   Warehouse clubs.

- *QVC*   TV home shopping by cable/satellite.

- *Sunglass Hut*   Specialist sunglasses outfit.

- *Staples*   Office products superstores in joint venture with Kingfisher.

- *Talbots*   Classic womanswear superstores plus mail order.

- *T.J. Maxx*   Discount clothing.

- *Tower Records and Sam Goody*   Recorded music.

Source: The Corporate Intelligence Group: *US Retailers in Europe – The New Wave*.

Greece which had received little attention earlier were experiencing cross-border forays from other nations although the latter suffered through the 1990s with the ex-Yugoslavia wars which restricted distribution channels.

10. Cross-border strategy guidelines

Frank Woolworth opened his first store outside the US in 1909. The Brenninkmeyers who founded the C & A empire in Holland opened their first foreign outlet in Germany in 1911 and in Britain in the 1920s. A lull then occurred which was only broken decisively during the 1980s. The world has now become borderless for many more retail companies.

Despite all the difficulties, more and more retailers will enter foreign markets over the next decade. Some guidelines on how to do it have begun to emerge.

(a) Study the market. Toys 'R' Us says that it looks at new markets for several years before taking the plunge. It has considered Mexico for 5 years, and 'three times we decided not to go in', says Larry Bouts, the firm's international director.

(b) Decide on your pace. After observing Australia for 4 years, Toys 'R' Us has opened 17 stores in its first 18 months. A slow build-up 'gives less leverage with suppliers and real-estate developers, and means less customer awareness', Mr Bouts says. But others, including Wal-Mart and Marks & Spencer, start with small pilot investments in new markets, allowing fine-tuning before any full-scale commitment.

(c) Think about local partners. Many international retailers use joint ventures to help them deal with local politics, regulations and suppliers. Picking the right partner can be crucial: Wal-Mart's success in Mexico owes much to its alliance with Cifra, the country's top retailer. Conversely, Carrefour blames the failure of its hypermarkets in Britain on the shortcomings of its local partner, an investment company.

(d) Adapt to local conditions. This may mean local sourcing, or adjusting ranges to fit local tastes and constraints. For example in Marks & Spencer's shops in Hong Kong food accounts for only 10% of sales compared with 40% in Britain, because the company found it could not get local supplies of acceptable quality.

(e) Stick to core skills. Newcomers must ensure that their logistics and computer systems can be made to work in new markets, and that they can maintain their reputation for quality, low prices or service. This means that exporting single-format businesses has proved easier than, for example, department stores.

(f) Develop local management. This is the key to understanding new markets, and the biggest constraint on international expansion. Transferring a retailer's corporate culture across borders is perhaps the trickiest part of internationalisation.

Ignore some or all of these rules if they clash with your corporate culture or business methods. IKEA jumps into new markets without local partners and with only cursory research. The firm says it needs to be in a market to understand it, and needs to have achieved a high volume of sales before it can profitably adapt its products to local tastes.

Despite the complexities, venturing abroad will be a main source of growth for both European and American retailers in the next few years. But even as they stride out, American retailers in particular are looking anxiously over their shoulders at a new threat in their own backyard. What if new technology allows their customers to dispense with stores altogether? What if consumers find they can do their shopping from home? (The potential threats from computer shopping are discussed in Chapter 22.)

Progress test 3

1. The phrase 'push and pull' is commonly used in marketing. Explain, with examples, what it means in the context of cross-border retailing.

2. In moving into overseas countries describe the various entry methods used by retailers. Discuss their relative advantages and disadvantages.

3. Outline the broad reasons for retail companies choosing one country or countries rather than others.

4. Discuss the risks inherent in cross-border retailing and offer some prescriptions for success.

4

RETAIL PLANNING AND STRATEGY

PLANNING

1. Introduction

Until fairly recently many retail companies have grown in a largely unplanned way, but before a company can begin to suggest to itself the sort of policies it should be pursuing to reach its corporate goals, it must decide what sort of company it is today and where it wants to get to within a finite time-scale. Many retail companies now use corporate planning techniques or variants thereof. Corporate planning has been described as the total planning of a company's entire resources for the achievement of both long and short-term objectives. Although the term 'corporate planning' may sound rather grand, the techniques of corporate planning are just as applicable to the corner shop as they are to the multiple.

2. The process

The retail planning process can be divided into three discrete yet interlinked steps. The first step is a statement of the retail mission which answers the fundamental question, 'What business am I in?' From this, objectives are established to answer the question, 'Where do I want to go?'

The statement of objectives will naturally lead to a series of strategies for achieving those objectives. Thus answering the third question, 'How do I get there?' These strategies will relate firstly to target markets (for example to serve the total market or only a specialized part of it). Once it has been decided who the target customer is, retail mix strategies are developed to meet the needs of those customers in terms of merchandise, price, location, promotion, level of service, etc.

WHAT BUSINESS AM I IN?

The answer to this question is often far less obvious than would at first appear. For example, what business is a florist in – the flower business or the gift business? The definition chosen will materially affect how that retailer interprets such aspects as customer requirements and competitors.

3. The retail mission

The precise retail mission statement will evolve from a close study of the environment in which the retailer sees himself or herself operating.

4. Situation analysis

The situation analysis will involve investigation of the defined market in terms of market size and market trends as well as looking closely at the competition, their strengths and weaknesses and market shares. The potential customers should also be studied to determine their motivations, how, why, what and where they buy, and if there are needs which are not being totally satisfied. The larger forces in society should also be studied to detect social and economic trends and the effects of technology and government. Finally, in the situation analysis the retail organisation must look at itself, determine its strengths and weaknesses and build on those strengths to exploit gaps unfilled due to the weakness of competition or simply not identified as yet (*see* Figure 4.1).

5. SWOT

A SWOT analysis should then be produced defining S (strengths), W (weaknesses), O (opportunities), and T (threats) for both the retailer's own organization and also that of the competition in relation to those factors already identified through the situation analysis.

For example, factors to be considered in determining strengths and weaknesses will include location, merchandise, personnel, store layout, management capability, financial aspects and market share position.

Figure 4.1 Situation analysis factors

6. Level of generalization

The question to be addressed now is, 'At what level of generalization should this situation analysis be carried out?', and the apparently rather unhelpful answer is at a level that is meaningful to the individual retail organization. Thus the multiple retail organization may well be concerned at a national or even international level, whereas the corner shop may only be interested in an area of a few hundred households. It is suggested, however, that the analysis, even for the smallest operator, starts off with an investigation of the national picture through which identifiable trends can be detailed which can then be revisited within the contexts of the local catchment area.

For example, it is unlikely that the size of the market in cash and unit terms for pizzas in the Nottingham area is immediately accessible. However, national data are available which can then be extrapolated to the local level on a consumption per capita basis.

WHERE DO I WANT TO GO?

7. Objectives

After completing the situation analysis, objectives (goals or targets) need to be set so it is clear what job has to be done and whether the goals have been reached at a specified point in time; and to ensure the organization is moving in a direction consistent with the corporate mission.

The variety of objectives the retailer seeks to achieve varies widely but generally falls within four broad areas: corporate, financial, marketing and organizational.

Corporate objectives are an extention of the personal beliefs of the most senior executives. Thus, for example, corporate objectives are often stated in terms of growth, profitability and prestige as: 'To increase our net sales area by one million sq ft and investment in new stores of over £1 billion over the next five years.' Marketing objectives should be defined in terms of sales, market share, communications, customer service, etc. Financial objectives would include targets for profit and return on investment, whilst organizational objectives might specify employee turnover and quality of labour force.

HOW DO I GET THERE?

8. Strategy

Having identified a direction through the objectives, it is now time to consider alternative ways (strategies) of achieving those objectives.

Once again, the concept of the appropriate level of generalization in developing strategies is met. It is therefore useful to develop strategy at the general level and the specific level.

GENERAL RETAIL STRATEGIES

These will focus upon growth, selectivity and productivity.

9. Growth strategies

No business can stand still as it needs to adapt to change. Growth can be achieved by pursuing a number of different routes. These may be described in terms of the merchandise offered and customers chosen as the target market (*see* Figure 4.2).

(a) The penetration strategy. This relies on the retailer aggressively seeking to increase his or her market share. This strategy has been pursued very success-fully by Sainsbury in the grocery retailing field where increase in market share has been won at the expense of direct competitors such as the small grocer and the Co-ops.

(b) Merchandise development. There is a limit to the growth which can be achieved by penetrative strategies and most retailers pursuing growth will look to add new merchandise to appeal to their customers and thus generate extra sales. This merchandise development strategy has been successfully pursued by Marks & Spencer, moving into food retailing, and more recently into furniture and financial services. Next have also been successful in offering their prime target customer – the 25–40 year old fashion-conscious female – a greater range of merchandise which now also includes jewellery.

(c) Market development. This strategy can be pursued in two ways:

(*i*) New customers can be sought in geographic areas not presently served, for example Asda's move south, or Marks & Spencer's move into overseas markets.

(*ii*) Alternatively, market development may involve attracting new customers

Figure 4.2 Growth strategies

in the same geographical area. This approach has been used by a number of retailers with varying degrees of success, for example Curry's attempt to appeal to the discount-orientated customer with their out-of-town electrical discount stores. The difficulty is that if the merchandise remains the same but a new group of customers is being sought, some other element of the retail mix has to change to appeal to them. As in the example above, price can be the variable which is changed. Location may also be changed and the image of the store could be modified as for example with MFI's attempts to move up-market.

(d) Diversification. New merchandise for new target customer groups is the most expansive of the growth strategies. It is possibly the riskiest of the growth strategies but can bring the highest rewards. Woolworth's purchase of B & Q and Comet was an example of a diversification strategy, as was the purchase of Halfords by Boots.

10. Integration

An alternative strategy for retailers is to seek to minimize conflict in the channel of distribution by ownership of channel members, acquisition or merger. Thus, Thorntons, for example, manufacture quality chocolate and confectionery products and also sell them through their own retail outlets. MFI, the flatpack furniture retailers, acquired the Hygena furniture manufacturing business in order to cut out the middleman's profits and derive the benefits of assured continuity of supply and economies of scale.

11. Selectivity strategies

Next is a good example of a retail organization which had lost its direction – trying to meet the needs of too many markets. In the late 1980s a new strategy was devised, which laid down a strategy for reducing the range of merchandise in order to appeal to a more well-defined target group of customers. This strategy resulted not only in a reduction of merchandise lines, but in some cases also, in order to be consistent with this strategy, a reduced geographical scope – pulling out of certain geographical areas.

12. Productivity strategies

Productivity strategies concentrate on producing better results with the same mixture of resources or the same (or better) results with fewer resources. Thus, as in many areas of business, the 80/20 rule applies – 80 per cent of profit is generated from 20 per cent of the merchandise offered, and if those high turnover lines are identified increasing inventory turnover can be achieved. Productivity strategies also involve closely monitoring costs and identifying ways of reducing costs, for example in staff, energy usage, etc.

Whilst much of the emphasis in productivity strategies is directed towards improving operating efficiency, managerial efficiency is also an important element. Training of managers is an expensive business and thus it is essential that an organization reduces its managerial turnover and drop-out rate to maximize its managerial training resources.

SPECIFIC RETAIL STRATEGIES

The retailing concept proposes that the most critical factor in determining the success of a store is the identification and satisfaction of customer needs. Thus specific retail strategies should address this objective requiring the retailer, first, to identify the target customers and then to satisfy their needs through an appropriate retail mix strategy – considering location, merchandise, price, communication, store atmosphere and layout, and customer service.

13. Segmentation strategy

Segmentation is concerned with identifying subsets within a market, groups which have something in common which will differentiate their needs and wants from other groups. Following the identification of these subsets, three strategic alternatives are available. An *undifferentiated* strategy where group differences are ignored and a standardized retail mix is developed to suffice for the whole market. The *differentiated* approach entails developing different retail mixes for different segments and the *concentrated* strategy focuses on one segment as the target market and develops a distinct retail mix to satisfy that discrete segment. Segmentation strategy is examined more fully in Chapter 8.

14. Location strategy

Where the retail organization chooses to locate can make the difference between success and failure. Additionally a location that is right for one type of retailer (e.g. a discount furniture warehouse) could be totally wrong for another (e.g. an exclusive high class fashion retailer). Location strategy is examined more fully in Chapter 9.

15. Merchandise strategy

Arguably the most important strategic choice is what product to offer. However, a product is much more than a tangible good. The consumer's perception of a product is anything that satisfies a particular need or want and as such the retailer must consider much more than a physical offering or technical specification. (More depth on merchandise strategy will be found in Chapter 10.)

16. Pricing strategy

Price is often considered a surrogate indicator of quality and the consumer often makes judgement on products or indeed on the store as a result of his or her response to the prices of merchandise. Thus for example a retailer could adopt a strategy of offering goods at relatively high prices in order to be consistent with a general strategy of appealing to consumers who are wanting exclusivity. Pricing strategies are considered in more detail in Chapter 13.

17. Communication strategy

The retailer has to communicate with customers, initially to make them aware of his or her offerings and then to stimulate interest and desire. The techniques available to the retailer include advertising, personal selling, sales promotions and public relations. Through the use of these communication tools the retailer establishes a position in the consumer's mind which hopefully will move the consumer to choose that store in preference to competitors. (*See* Chapters 14–16.)

18. Store image and customer service strategy

In addition to the four communication tools listed above, it can be seen that everything the retailer does communicates something to the consumer. Thus the exterior of the store, window displays, the interior design and layout, all combine to communicate a store's personality and to add to the image that the consumer has of that store. This image is further modified by the number and quality of services that are available to the customer and the basis on which they are offered.

Chapter 17 explains store image further and Chapter 18 deals with customer services.

It is important that the strategies adopted are consistent with the defined objectives, and as such each strategy is integrated within the framework of the others. Thus for example a discount pricing strategy would not be consistent with an objective of establishing an up-market image for the store. Similarly, the location of the store should be chosen to reflect the needs of the defined customer group, and although there are always exceptions to every rule the consumer has come to expect lower prices out of town.

19. Control and continuity

Success cannot be achieved without a reliable feedback mechanism. This will allow modifications to the plan on a rolling basis to fit in with changes in the external environment. It will also show how actual progress matches the plan so that extra throttle or a touch on the brakes can be administered. The plan should be thoroughly reviewed:

(a) Annually to take account of the company's progress

(b) Whenever there is a distinct change in the company's market, e.g. the merger of two large competitors

(c) Every five years to modify basic objectives and to make out a new checklist of strengths and weaknesses.

Progress test 4

1. What are the three interlinked steps in the retail planning process?

2. What is a SWOT analysis?

3. Describe the three general retail strategies of growth, selectivity and productivity.

4. What is the function of the feedback mechanism in retail planning?

5. What is meant by the retail mix? Describe the retail mix of a retailer of your own choice and analyse whether it is appropriate or not.

5

RETAILING RESEARCH

INFORMATION

1. Management

Management is essentially concerned with planning, decision making and control.

As has been seen, the planning process has been described as an attempt to answer three fundamental questions:

(a) What business am I in?

(b) Where do I want to go?

(c) How do I get there?

2. Retailing research defined

In order to answer questions, information is required, and the way this information is provided is through the use of research. This involves the systematic design, collection, analysis and reporting of data and findings relevant to a specific retailing situation. In order to focus our attention on the retail situation the term 'retailing research' will henceforth be used to mean marketing research within the retailing context.

3. Importance of information

Information and information management is important to the retailer because of the increasing pace of environmental change to which the retailer must adapt. Changes in the age profile of the population, more single-parent households, increasing disposable income amongst a myriad of changes all have implications for retailers. Additionally, new technology in retailing, new products and new types of store all go to produce an extremely complex environment which the retailer must monitor and react to.

4. The retail information system

The retailer should set up a system to organize and retrieve information. This should set out well-defined procedures and practices by which people and equipment generate information in a form that, and at a time when, retail decision makers require it.

THE RETAILING RESEARCH PROCESS

Effective retailing research involves six steps:

(1) Define the problem

(2) Define the research objectives

(3) Determine the sources of information

(4) Collect the information

(5) Analyse the information

(6) Present the findings.

5. Define the problem

For example, a large furniture retailer wishes to find out whether providing a play area for children within the store will be worthwhile. A definition of this problem could be, 'Will offering a play area create enough incremental business to justify the initial cost and loss of selling space?'

6. Research objectives

The research objectives could then be to determine:

(a) The type of customer who would make use of the service

(b) How valuable this type of customer sees the service

(c) Whether this customer would spend more time in-store if the children could be left

(d) Whether spending more time in-store would lead to increased expenditure.

SOURCES OF INFORMATION

The next stage of retailing research is to develop a procedure for gathering the required information in the most efficient manner.

7. Four sources

There are four sources of information acquisition:

(a) Internal sources – within the company

(b) External sources – outside the company

(c) Secondary data – gathered originally for another purpose

(d) Primary data – gathered to solve the specific problems at hand.

8. Order

Remembering that the information must be obtained in the most cost-effective manner, the order in which attempts are made to access information from the four sources is important. This would therefore normally be:

(1) First, internal secondary sources

(2) Second, internal primary sources

(3) Third, external secondary sources

(4) Fourth, external primary sources.

The task is of course completed when we have the information required which would ideally be as early in the above sequence as possible in order to minimize cost.

9. Internal secondary sources

Particularly with the advent of electronic point-of-sale systems (EPOS), retailers are gathering large quantities of data internally which may be invaluable for research purposes.

EPOS systems can provide information on sales of products by units and value and much more besides. Customer order forms contain information about the location of customers. Credit records too may have location details and frequency of purchase. Accounting records will be useful for sales history and forecasting trends whilst previous research (primary) may now be used as internal secondary data for the purposes of the new search.

The use of EPOS is now well established and can provide detailed information on items sold, price, when sold, inventory and also promotion evaluation; in fact the challenge now is not just to provide information but to present it in the most useful manner.

10. Internal primary sources

Employees of the retail organization can also be a useful source of information. Sales assistants, checkout operators and delivery people all come into contact with customers and receive comments about the store, price, service, etc.

11. External secondary sources

There is a tremendous range of external secondary data available. This can be divided into three main types:

(a) Government statistics, for example:

(*i*) Census of Retail Trade
(*ii*) Retail Inquiries
(*iii*) Census of Population 1991
(*iv*) Business Monitors (SPD 25)
(*v*) Family Expenditure Surveys
(*vi*) General Household Surveys
(*vii*) Economic Trends, Regional Trends, Social Trends.

(b) Periodicals and books, for example, *Retail Business, Retail Intelligence, Market Research Great Britain, Kompass, International Journal of Retail & Distribution Management.* Also specialist publications such as *The Grocer, Electrical Retailing*, etc.

(c) Reports from specialist retail research organisations such as Corporate Intelligence, Verdict, Mintel, Neilson Retail Audits and AGB.

12. External primary sources

Suppliers and competitors may be sources of information but consumers are the most common source of external primary data.

13. Advantages and disadvantages

The advantages of secondary data are essentially low cost and speed of access. The disadvantages can be numerous, including data being out of date, different units of measurement, different definitions, etc.

Primary data offer the retailer the advantage of timeliness but the disadvantage is the cost and the time involved in collecting the data.

COLLECTING THE INFORMATION

Internal data are obviously available in-house and external secondary data should be relatively easy to access through public libraries or, in the case of commercial data, through the company concerned. However, gathering external primary data will require more time and effort. External primary data can be gathered in three main ways: observation, experiments and surveys.

14. Observation

The observation technique simply involves the observation and recording of behaviour. The advantage of this method is that respondent co-operation is not required and therefore the results obtained are more likely to be a true reflection of the facts than if a questioning technique is used. Observation of the consumer can be carried out either by an individual or through the use of mechanical devices such as video cameras.

Personal observation is often employed in-store to determine customer flow patterns and general shopping behaviour. Customer traffic counts may also be done this way. Mechanical observation can also be used for traffic counts as well as more sophisticated observation such as customer/sales assistant interaction.

15. Experiments

Experimental research uses the scientific methodology of selecting a matched group of subjects, subjecting them to different treatments, controlling extraneous variables and then measuring the observed differences. An example of experimental research would be to reduce the price of a merchandise item and to monitor the effect on sales. All other factors such as promotion, shelf location, etc., should be kept constant and sales in one week could be compared with sales in the experimental week at a reduced price. The difficulty with this type of research is ensuring that the only factor that changed is the price or the variable which is to be changed. Similar experiments can be carried out with different promotions, shelf locations, displays, etc.

16. Surveys

The survey method is perhaps the most common way of generating external primary data. It essentially uses some type of questionnaire as the mechanism for gathering information, and this questionnaire can be administered personally, over the telephone, or via the mail.

(a) **The personal interview** or face-to-face method allows a lot of detailed data to be gathered because people quite often like to be asked their opinions and to offer it to another person who is interested! High response rates are therefore achieved by this method but there is a danger of the results being inaccurate due to interviewer bias, that is the interviewer may in some way (perhaps unconsciously) influence the answers given.

(b) **The telephone survey** offers a quick and relatively inexpensive method of administering a questionnaire. It allows person-to-person contact which facilitates probing and explanation but respondents soon tire of a telephone administered questionnaire and therefore it is only suitable for short, simple information gathering. There is also the problem that information can only be gathered from respondents who have a phone!

(c) **The postal survey** – the questionnaire – is mailed to respondents, thus offering the retailer the opportunity of reaching many potential respondents over a wide geographical area. The greatest difficulty with mailed questionnaires is the low response rates, which are often well below 25 per cent. This leads on to the problem of non-response bias, that is bias against those *not* answering the questionnaire. It is highly probable that those answering a mailed questionnaire do so because they are interested in the subject, or are perhaps more educated or articulate. Thus they may not be wholly representative of the total number of people who received the questionnaire. None the less, mailed questionnaires are popular with retailers because they are seen to be economical and versatile.

The survey technique is most useful for obtaining information about customers' knowledge, beliefs, attitudes, preferences and so on, but because the methodology deals with these qualitative or subjective areas, it is vitally important that the questionnaire is designed properly.

QUESTIONNAIRE DESIGN

17. Structured or unstructured

The design of the questionnaire must be such as to provide the appropriate information in a form most suitable for interpretation. Thus the major design issue is to choose between a structured or an unstructured questionnaire.

The highly structured questionnaire consists of a series of questions and a predetermined set of answers set by the researcher (closed questions). The other extreme is the highly unstructured questionnaire where the general area for scrutiny is predetermined but the questions are allowed to develop during the information gathering process and the respondent is allowed to answer in his or her own words (open-ended questions).

Each type is appropriate to a particular situation: structured when the expected answers are known; unstructured when the researcher cannot predetermine answers or wants to research the widest possible interpretation of issues.

18. Wording and sequence

In preparing the questionnaire the researcher must also carefully choose the questions asked and the wording and sequence in which questions are asked.

Thus each question must provide data which contributes to the research objectives. The wording of questions should be simple, direct and unbiased. The questionnaire should start with a question which will create interest, whilst difficult, personal or classificatory questions should be reserved for the end.

SAMPLING

The retailer must select respondents to answer the questionnaire. He or she will usually choose a sampling procedure, since administering the questionnaire to the total population (a census) would be far too expensive and time-consuming.

19. Random sampling

The technique of random (or probability) sampling gives each member of the population a chance of being selected but in practice is difficult to conduct.

20. Non-probability samples

As a matter of course many retailers resort to talking to customers at a store or shopping centre. This is a form of non-probability sampling known as a convenience sample (i.e. convenient to the retailer). Other forms of non-probability sample which aim to be somewhat more scientific in approach are the judgement sample and the quota sample.

The judgement sample is based on the judgement (expertise) of the retailer. For example, he may describe a typical customer as a 25-45 year old female. Thus respondents who answer this description may be selected.

In the quota sample the sample is selected in proportion to characteristics in the population considered to be important discriminants (e.g. by income, age and sex).

ANALYSING THE INFORMATION AND PRESENTING THE FINDINGS

21. Analysis

The next step is to analyse the data and extract pertinent information. Data are tabulated and averages and measures of dispersion calculated.

22. Presentation

Since the purpose of acquiring information is to enable the retail decision-maker to choose the best alternative solution to a retailing problem, it is incumbent upon the researcher to present the research findings in a form suitable for that purpose. Thus the presentation of findings should concentrate on the major issues that are relevant to the retailing decisions facing management. Too many numbers, charts and sophisticated statistical techniques will only lose them and lessen the import of good research.

TYPES OF RETAILING RESEARCH

Many research techniques have now been developed to meet the specific needs of retailers, for example

(*i*) Store audits
(*ii*) Pricing checks
(*iii*) Exit surveys
(*iv*) Diaries
(*v*) Mystery shopping
(*vi*) Accompanied shopping
(*vii*) Discussion groups
(*viii*) Observation

23. Store audits

Conducted in the store, store audits involve checking stock on the shelves – usually with the retailers permission, but sometimes 'incognito'. Store audits provide information on:

(*i*) Stock movement
(*ii*) Market share
(*iii*) Shelf facings
(*iv*) Prices

24. Pricing checks

In addition to store audits, prices can also be checked with consumers. The process involves structured interviews and provides information on:

(*i*) What consumers are prepared to pay
(*ii*) Opinions of prices charged.
(*iii*) Thresholds at which consumers would switch to an alternative product or brand
(*iv*) Perceptions of value for money.

25. Exit surveys

These involve stopping shoppers as they leave a store and conducting a short structured interview. Exit surveys provide information on:

(*i*) Profiles of shoppers
(*ii*) Where they live
(*iii*) Where else they shop
(*iv*) What they intended to buy and what they actually bought on this trip
(*v*) Their opinions of the store.

26. Diaries

These are usually self-completion and involve consumers recording their shopping activities for a week or a month. They provide information on:

(*i*) Where they have shopped
(*ii*) When they shopped
(*iii*) What they bought
(*iv*) How much they spent
(*v*) How quickly the product was used.

27. Mystery shopping

This technique involves mystery shoppers visiting outlets pretending to be genuine consumers. Visits involve observation, interaction with staff, and going through the purchase process. Immediately after the visit, a questionnaire is completed as a record of the trip. It provides information on:

(*i*) Staff and the service they offer
(*ii*) General appearance of the store
(*iii*) Quality of displays
(*iv*) Customer care

28. Accompanied shopping

Shoppers are accompanied by an interviewer whilst on a shopping trip. The technique involves the interviewer observing, talking to the consumer and possibly taping the discussion. After the shopping trip is completed a written report is prepared which provides information on:

(*i*) Shopping behaviour
(*ii*) Store layout
(*iii*) Product displays
(*iv*) In-store promotions
(*v*) Staff and service
(*iv*) Factors influencing consumer choice.

29. Discussion groups

These may be conducted in-store or away from the store, and involve a skilled moderator talking with consumers for anything between one and three hours. The group size can range from three to nine respondents and the discussion provides an opportunity to go into more depth when gathering information. Discussion groups are more flexible than using a questionnaire format and allow consumers to express their views in their own words. The discussions are taped, transcribed and a content analysis is carried out; then the findings are reported, often supported by verbatim quotations from the consumers in the discussion groups.

30. Observation

Consumer behaviour is 'observed' usually without their knowledge and often with the use of film or video equipment. Records are made of:

(*i*) The direction shoppers are moving in
(*ii*) Products browsed
(*iii*) Products purchased
(*iv*) The order in which products are browsed/purchased
(*v*) Time spent at displays

The observation method can be combined with other research techniques to provide more information about the shopper.

Progress test 5

1. What is retailing research?

2. Describe the retailing research process.

3. What are the four general sources of information acquisition?

4. Describe the three ways of gathering external primary data.

5. Under what circumstances would you consider using an unstructured questionnaire?

6. What is random sampling? How useful is it in retailing research?

7. What are the main sources of information available to a small business-man wishing to start his first specialized lighting shop? What information is it essential to have before he invests any money and how would he access this information?

8. What particular problems are faced when doing marketing research within the retail sector? What techniques are available to overcome them?

9. As deputy manager of a large department store you have been asked to assist in the training of Eddie, an 18-year-old trainee. As part of his training programme you are asked to briefly explain the value of marketing research to the retailer.

10. Eddie and Rita Robertson have decided to open a new menswear shop in Chester. They believe there is potential for a retail outlet serving the busy businessman who wants a little more than a 'Marks and Sparks pinstripe suit' but is not sufficiently fashion oriented ('poserish' as Eddie describes it) to find 'Next for Men' attractive. They wish to be business-like in their approach and they have decided to check out their hunch by carrying out marketing research.
    Identify the *sources of information* that are available to them and how they might go about gathering information.

11. A leading chain of CTNs with over 750 shops located primarily in tertiary trading locations is coming under heavy pressure from supermarkets, petrol forecourt shops and others taking increasing shares in its main merchandise areas. A consultant to the company has suggested abandoning the strategy of remaining a CTN and has suggested the company should focus on its prime benefit to the customer – convenience. Make recommendations for suitable forms of retailing research to evaluate the viability of this suggestion.

6

THE RETAILING ENVIRONMENTS

LEVELS OF ENVIRONMENT

1. Environmental change

The retailer is part of the larger environment and must therefore monitor changes and adapt in such a manner as to thrive in the new environment. Additionally, forecasting changes in the environment will then allow the retailer

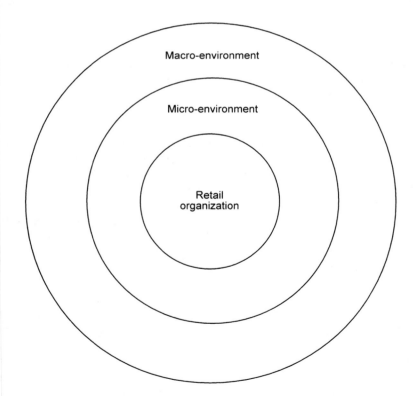

Figure 6.1 Retailing environments

to plan the adaptation process. The retailing environment can be thought of as having two levels – the micro-environment and the macro-environment (*see* Figure 6.1).

2. The retailing micro-environment

This consists of those elements within the environment that immediately impinge upon the retailer on a day-to-day basis and which require immediate responses. Customers, competition and other distribution channel members can be defined as the members of the micro-environment.

3. The retailing macro-environment

This is made up of those elements within the environment which are not controllable by the retail organization and which consist of the larger societal forces such as demographic, economic, cultural and social, political, legal, technological and natural factors.

The process of monitoring and gathering information on the retail environments can be seen as part of the retailing research function and many of the sources of information on environmental change are those described in the previous chapter.

THE RETAILING MACRO-ENVIRONMENT

4. Demographic factors

The retailer must scrutinize demographic data to determine what is happening to his or her customers and the implications for the business. At present in the UK there is a static population but in terms of age distribution there is a very marked increase in the older age groups (people are living longer). Women are delaying having their first child and are having fewer children. There is an increasing number of households but this increase is primarily of the one person or one parent type.

There is an increasing number of working women (up from 8.4 million in 1971 to 10.6 million in 1995) and their profile is changing. They are now likely to be married and have children, often working for personal satisfaction rather than simply for the money. Therefore, with less time for shopping and the preparation of meals, there has been an increase in one-stop shopping and the purchase of convenience foods.

There has also been a geographical shift away from inner cities to the suburbs and also to some extent from the North to the South.

5. Economic factors

The standard of living of the population is increasing and can be measured by a number of criteria. Real personal disposable income per head is increasing and is reflected in the increasing penetration of consumer durables in UK homes. Most householders now have a television and refrigerator but sales of dish-washing machines are now increasing as other needs are satisfied. The percentage of owner-occupied dwellings has also increased significantly over the past 20 years.

Other economic factors which the retailer must monitor are the rate of inflation and the cost of credit.

6. Cultural and social factors

Individuals are becoming more self-centred and show a greater need for self-expression. This is reflected in the growth of designer labels and specialist clothing shops. People are paying more attention to their quality of life, and healthy living and concern for the environment are current issues. There is a growing 'consumer movement' which requires business to operate in the best interests of the consumer. Lifestyles are changing which can, in part, be explained by the increasing number of people travelling abroad and introducing foreign ways of life, food and goods into their own lifestyles. There is a greater amount of design and a greater emphasis on quality rather than price. These changes in society will be reflected in the wants and needs of customers and the retailer must be aware of these changes in order to fulfil the primary role (to anticipate and satisfy these wants and needs).

7. Political factors

Differing political philosophies can have a major effect on retail organizations. The problems of inflation, foreign competition and unemployment will be tackled in different ways according to which political party is in power. For example, Conservative policy is to lean towards a *laissez-faire* attitude with market forces determining the course of events and a minimum of political intervention. Privatization of British Telecom, British Gas, etc. has led to new opportunities for retailers.

A government's economic policy can also have a major effect on interest rates, taxation – either direct or indirect – credit, and a host of other factors which will affect the retailer, the volume of business and profitability.

8. Legal factors

Closely associated with political philosophy is the role of the law and regulating authorities set up to administer and enforce the law.

The Office of Fair Trading, the Equal Opportunities Commission, the Health and Safety Executive, amongst others, are bodies which have been set up by the government which can and do bring retailers to task when appropriate. In addition many laws relating to the management of a retail establishment exist and are constantly being modified. For example, the law as it relates to labelling requirements, pricing, credit, hours of trading are constantly being updated and therefore changing the way in which the retailer operates.

9. Technological factors

Changes in technology not only affect the products that retailers sell but also the way they sell them. Most particularly the influence of computerization and the development of sophisticated data capture facilities has led to the revolutionizing of certain sectors of the retail industry.

For example, the introduction of electronic point-of-sale (EPOS) equipment has provided retailers with detailed information which allows for extremely efficient stock control systems, price change procedures and up-to-the-minute sales reports.

The introduction of electronic funds transfer at point of sale (EFTPOS) systems, allowing transfer of funds from a customer's account to the retailer's account without the need for paperwork, is seen as a further beneficial measure of efficiency to both parties.

Many believe that teleshopping is about to take off in the UK; the facilities exist and will be increasingly used, via television, telephone and the Internet, to shop from home.

10. Natural factors

Environmental groups have brought to the public's attention the problems of pollution, energy shortage and the diminution of limited natural resources. This public awareness of environmental issues has resulted not only in the creation of a new political party but also led to shifts in consumer buying, for example the establishment of the Body Shop chain on the basis of providing cosmetics made entirely of natural ingredients – no money wasted on fancy packaging, no animal testing of products, and refillable bottles.

THE MICRO-ENVIRONMENT

The elements of the micro-environment – competitors, distribution channel members and customers – influence retail decisions on a daily basis so it is important to monitor changes in the micro-environment and also how it interacts with the larger societal forces of the macro-environments.

11. Competitors

Within any market there will be competition to satisfy the needs and wants of the participating customer. Wherever there is an opportunity, someone will spot it and attempt to capitalize on it. No retailer can afford to rest, even if he or she has a commanding market share, because his or her very success will signal to the others that there are opportunities within that market place which are just too tempting to resist. The retail market place has been likened to a battleground with retailers competing with each other to win the favours of the customer.

12. Who are the competitors?

The first step in formulating a competitive strategy is to define the competition. This can be accomplished by looking at the two variables of the store and the product. Competition can be between two retail store of the same type, e.g. Tesco and Sainsbury, or between different types of retail store selling the same product, e.g. Tesco competes with Boots in the toiletries market.

Retailers often define their competition as similar retail stores but this is not necessarily the most appropriate approach. For the consumer the starting point in the purchase process is an awareness of a need or a want. This leads in a series of steps to the final purchase of a product or service to satisfy the need/want. Along this route the consumer will ask the question, 'Where can I go to purchase this product or service?' and at this point will have a set of possibilities. This set of stores ('the evoked set') will then be considered and a choice made on which to go to.

This concept is important to the retailer because it implies that the retailer cannot simply rely on a consumer instinctively knowing that particular goods are available from a particular store, but that the objective of the retailer must be to figure in the consumer's awareness and this is achieved by communication.

13. The perceptual map

Within the set of possible stores the consumer will have an image of each and will be comparing attributes of one against the other within the framework of a *perceptual map*. That is, consumers can be asked to rate attributes of different stores along a number of dimensions, e.g. quality and value for money, and different stores are then plotted on this graph to determine their position on the perceptual map, i.e. how close they are together. By adopting this approach the retailer can not only determine the competition but also the closest competitors (*see* 8:13).

14. Market shares

Another way of measuring the strength of the competition is to determine their share of the market. It is a reasonable assumption that the market leaders are doing something right or they would not be in the leading position. However, this analysis can be taken a stage further by looking into the market shares not only by the type of retail store but also by the product type, and in this way identification of weaknesses can come to light.

15. Competitors' retail mix

Other elements of competitors' retail mixes should also be monitored to detect strengths and weaknesses. Location, price and communications, as well as product, may prove to be a retailer's Achilles heel and provide an opportunity for exploitation.

16. Competitive strategy

Through this competitor analysis will come an understanding of the competition which will allow forecasting of their behaviour and anticipation of how competitors will react to the retailer's own strategy. This leads to evolving the most appropriate strategy to counter the competition. There have been many interesting competitive battles on the British retailing scene and none more so than in the field of grocery retailing. It is fascinating to observe the strategies being adopted by Tesco and Sainsbury in their battle for market leadership. In the late 1970s the battleground shifted from an emphasis on price to quality. In the 1990s choice and additional customer services have been highlighted. Safeway's growth through acquisition has also put them in the big league and their decision to convert larger Presto stores to the Safeway fascia is in response to the increasing customer demand for quality, choice and additional services.

17. Other channel members

The retailer, by definition, is the final link in the distribution chain. Products may well pass from the original manufacturers through several intermediaries (agents, wholesalers, etc.) before reaching the retailer. If anything goes wrong with a single link in the chain the retailer, being the last link, suffers. For this reason it is imperative that the retail organization approaches channel decisions in an informed and systematic way. The basis on which each link in the chain operates is that they receive some benefit (usually financial) for some service performed (e.g. breaking bulk, transport, storage, etc.).

18. Co-operation and conflict

The ideal situation is established where there is complete co-operation between channel members and they all work together for mutual benefit. However, conflict may arise when one channel member feels that another is gaining at their expense or is getting an unfairly large cut of the rewards.

19. Power

At this stage the concept of power within the channel is raised because the exertion of power can reduce conflict and/or raise co-operation. Within a number of retail sectors, for example grocery retailing, the balance of power has now shifted from the manufacturer to the large multiple who can now dictate terms. This has implications both for manufacturers who plead that they are not making sufficient profit to invest in research for new products, and for consumers who may, as a result, get a reduced choice. The small retailer also complains that he or she is not able to compete with the very low prices offered by the large supermarkets.

20. Vertical marketing systems

What then are the responses of retailers to this channel evolution? One has been the growth of vertical marketing systems (VMS) whereby channel members forge formal links, for example by contract, to enable maximum co-operation between channel members, thus acting as a unified system. There are three types:

(a) A corporate VMS. All stages from manufacturing to retailing are under one ownership, e.g. Thorntons, CWS.

(b) An administered VMS occurs when each channel member is independent but responds to a dominant member's efforts to effect co-ordination, e.g. Marks & Spencer.

(c) A contractual VMS has shown the greatest growth through the legal or contractual basis for co-operation. There are three types of contractual VMS:

(*i*) The retailer-sponsored VMS, such as the Londis group of grocery retailers, consists of a group of independent retailers who join together to gain buying economies. Participating members are required to purchase a proportion of their stock (usually 30–50 per cent) through the group.

(*ii*) The wholesale-sponsored VMS, such as Spar, is similar to the retailer-sponsored VMS but is initiated and sponsored by a wholesaler. In addition to the economies of bulk buying, participating members receive assistance with merchandising, layout, pricing, etc. and are perceived by the customer to be part of a larger group which carries out national advertising.

(*iii*) The manufacturer-sponsored VMS, also known as Franchising, involves two parties – the franchisor and the franchisee. The franchisor has developed a successful business format which is made available to the franchisee for a financial consideration (usually an initial lump sum plus a continuing percentage commission on turnover). Explosive growth has been experienced by some franchise operations whilst others have been less successful. Benetton, Wimpy and Prontaprint among many others are household names in the field of franchise.

The final element of the micro-environment is the customer and forms the basis of the following chapter.

Progress test 6

1. What are the two levels of the retailing environment?

2. Describe the main demographic trends of interest to retailers.

3. What are the major technological factors affecting retailing?

4. What are the elements of the micro-environment?

5. What is the significance of the concept of power within the channels of distribution?

6. How does the formation of a VMS help the retailer?

7. Analyse the changes occurring in the retail environment and discuss the possible implications of such changes for retailers in the next decade.

8. Mike Johnson is a successful retailer of mid- to high-priced furniture in Grantham. He realizes, however, that the retail environment has changed a great deal since he began in the furniture trade in 1965. He thinks he needs to conduct an analysis of the retail environment but does not know where or how to begin.

   (*i*)   What factors in the external environment should Mike monitor?
   (*ii*)   How can he get information on these factors?
   (*iii*) If Mike finds that most of his customers are two-income families, how might he wish to react to this information?

9. A vertical marketing system (VMS) operates when manufacturer, wholesaler and retailer act as a unified system to achieve operating economies and maximum market impact. Illustrate by reference to two examples how operating within a VMS may give a competitive advantage.

7

CONSUMER BUYING BEHAVIOUR

The consumer is the focus of all retail decisions. It is therefore important to appreciate how consumers go about making their buying decisions. How do they decide upon what product to buy, the brand, and the store to buy them from? What are the factors influencing these choices?

THE BUYING PROCESS

1. The decision process

The buying process is essentially a decision process designed to provide solutions to problems. The first stage in the process is the awareness of a need or a want; this is followed by an information processing stage prior to the purchase decision. But the buying process should not be considered complete until the product/service has been used and resulted in satisfaction or dissatisfaction in the original need or want (*see* Figure 7.1).

Figure 7.1 The stages of the buying process

2. The felt need/want

Human beings have certain fundamental needs for survival: food, water, shelter (warmth) and security. These may be satisfied in quite simple ways or through the expression of more complex requirements – wants. For example, the need for water is as a result of a basic biological requirement. However, this water may be delivered as water, or the human being (consumer) may express a preference for Coca Cola or lemonade or a myriad of other products designed to satisfy the want for more than just plain water. This felt need or want can be considered as a problem. The natural response of the human being to this problem state is to seek a solution, and the process of seeking a solution leads naturally to the search for information and the exploration of alternative ways of resolving the problems.

It should also be stated that this problem state may be expressed in a vague way, for example, 'I am bored', or in a specific way, 'I want to go to Alton Towers'.

3. Pre-purchase activity

This stage is concerned with gathering information and processing it to allow the consumer to move towards a purchase decision. The mnemonic AIDA simply describes the stages of pre-purchase activity. Firstly, the consumer becomes *A*ware of products or services which may satisfy his or her requirements. *I*nterest is generated which becomes more intense as more information is gathered, resulting in a *D*esire to obtain the item, and finally *A*ction – the decision to purchase. This same process has been described as Awareness→ Knowledge→ Liking→ Preference→ Conviction→ Purchase. It is clear that there are two key elements to this – firstly, the information search and, secondly, the evaluation of alternatives.

The extent of the information search is dependent upon the perceived difficulty in resolving the problem. For routine grocery purchase, the consumer evolves an automatic pattern of behaviour which requires minimal information search and alternative evaluation. However, for a high involvement purchase (i.e. where the risk of making the wrong decision is great, e.g. financial outlay for a new car), the information search will be extensive.

The generation and evaluation of alternatives centres around the product, the specific brand and the store, and which of these three takes precedence will again depend on the nature and extent of the perceived problem.

Therefore, the sequence for the weekly grocery trip will probably be store-product-brand. However, for purchase of a new motor vehicle it will probably be product-brand-store.

The implications for the retailer are clear. He or she must attempt to make the problem-solving process easier by ensuring that the customer includes his or her store in the list of alternatives and has a positive image of the store as being the place which will stock the customer's preferred product/brand. Successful retailers have realized that the key lies in targeting a well defined group of customers and then offering them the type of product or service they require. In turn this customer will come to regard the store in precisely that light – i.e. 'My kind of store'. Repeated satisfaction will generate loyalty to the store, so that in any decision relating to 'Where can I obtain that product?', the same store will be at the top of the list. The authors of this book even have experience of people who would not move to a new area unless there was a particular grocery store there – so loyal were they in the belief that only that store (Sainsbury) could satisfy their particular grocery requirements.

4. The purchase decision

The purchase decision is not a single decision but a bundle of decisions, any one of which can result in a change of mind and an alternative route being followed. Thus, for example, a consumer may have decided on a product, brand and store but is finally persuaded that this is in fact the wrong choice because the price in that store is not as competitive or because the sales staff have not been helpful.

So the actual time of purchase is important as it can either help or hinder the decision process. Helpful, courteous and attentive sales assistants are essential. Information provided in-store can lead to additional purchases or trading up. In-store promotions and store design and layout will provide the right incentives and atmosphere for purchasing.

Finally, the purchase transaction is important as it is the last impression the customer has of that purchase situation. Ease of purchase, lack of queues, credit facilities, treatment by sales personnel and efficient handling of problems, comments or complaints, can make a lasting impression. Difficulty in these areas can lose a sale or even lose a customer permanently.

5. Use behaviour

As was stated previously, the product is not purchased for its own sake but for its ability to satisfy a need. For example, the PC is not purchased because it is a computer but because with it the customer can manipulate information and play games! Much is to be learnt by understanding why consumers buy products. For example, a customer buys a typewriter and brings it back two weeks later demanding a refund because 'it is not up to the job'. A little questioning reveals that the purpose for the purchase was as a method of typing standard letters for use in a direct mail shot. Knowing this the retailer is able to save the day by offering the customer, for very little extra outlay, a simple word processor.

Other questions the retailer can ask about the product in use are: Who uses the product? When and where is it used? and What other products is it used with? The answers can provide opportunities for ensuring customer satisfaction, and additional sales.

Once again the satisfaction of customer needs is paramount. There is little point in making a sale but losing a customer. That customer talks to other people and bad news spreads very quickly. The sales assistant should determine the use the product is going to be put to, and then guide the customer to the right product. Often it is not possible to question customers in this informal way;

therefore surveys should be carried out periodically to monitor customer satisfaction with the store and products purchased from the store.

6. Post-purchase feelings

Dissatisfaction with a product can be as a result of a genuinely disappointing performance of the product due to faulty manufacture, inappropriate use, etc. Sometimes, however, dissatisfaction is due more to psychological factors such as the tension created by wondering if the right choice has been made – particularly if the alternatives were also attractive. Also, even if the product appears to be performing well, adverse information provided by friends or neighbours may reduce satisfaction or cause the consumer to fear failure of the product so causing him or her to return it and demand a refund.

Recognition of this phenomenon, known as post-cognitive dissonance, will lead the retailer to provide mechanisms for reducing this tension either at the time of purchase or shortly afterwards. A liberal returns policy will allow the customer to feel that even if the product is not quite right when they get it home, they are still able to get a refund without a problem. This reassurance actually makes it easier for the consumer to make the purchase decision. Also, the fear of product failure can be lessened by the retailer providing extended guarantees or offering products which offer a manufacturer's extended guarantee. Reassurance can also be offered that the customer has made the right choice by offering information on the number of other satisfied customers or the popularity of that particular product, e.g. 'The best selling car in Europe', 'The No.1 best seller', 'Brand leader', etc.

To reiterate, the importance of post-purchase feelings is not only their relevance to post-purchase satisfaction but also because they affect the consumer at the point of purchase and fear of making a wrong decision can result in a lost sale – or a lost customer. Consider your feelings if you had been persuaded by a retailer to purchase a product which proved to be unsatisfactory. What would your attitude be towards that store? Many customers do not like the hassle of returning goods but would simply choose not to shop in that store again.

THE BUYING PARTICIPANTS

The buying process has been described as a problem-solving exercise, designed to result in the satisfaction of a need or want. However, it should not be forgotten that the consumer does not live in a vacuum and there are many factors which will influence consumer behaviour in a particular buying situation. The four possible roles of the actors in the buying process are considered below – the buying participants.

7. Influencers

These are the people who encourage, inform or persuade at any stage in the buying process. For example, a TV personality used in a commercial may influence choice, a prominent member of society, e.g. doctor, or simply a neighbour or friend, will influence the buyer's thought processes. Retailers can use this concept most effectively in their promotion efforts, either using TV personalities to open new stores or through advertising. Also, the targetting of local opinion leaders as recipients of promotion messages or to generate publicity is an efficient way of influencing a larger audience.

8. Deciders

The actual purchase decision maker is clearly the prime target for promotional messages but quite often the purchase decision is not made by an individual but by a group of individuals. For example, the family may be considered the decision-making unit (DMU) for a new family car, the husband and wife team will be the DMU for domestic durables such as lounge and dining room furniture. It is therefore important for the retailer to reach the DMU with promotional messages, particularly where more than one individual is involved in the buying process.

9. The buyer

The significance of the DMU is highlighted when the buyer is considered as the individual who makes the actual purchase. Consider the case of the husband with the shopping list. Has he really had a significant say in which products/ brands are on the list and which store is chosen? Perhaps this is an extreme but there will be many occasions where the buyer will merely be acting as a purchasing agent on behalf of another individual. The retailer should take care not to be misled into believing that the target market consists solely of those people who are seen in the store. Many retailers carry out in-store market research surveys asking detailed questions on standards of customer service, quality of merchandise, etc. Many of the responses will be irrelevant to the objective of determining factors for store choice if that shopper is merely acting on behalf of someone else who may hold totally different views!

10. Users

The final buying participant is the end user. The user of a product may have had no role in the initial product/store/brand choice but being the user of the product will either be satisfied or dissatisfied with it. This will usually be communicated to the purchaser who will react appropriately. How will user dissatisfaction influence future store choice? It may be a dissatisfaction with a product which results in a dissatisfaction with the store for selling such an inferior product. Or it may be dissatisfaction with the way the store handled the sale, e.g. by not providing the user with sufficient information to enable him or her to make the best use of the product, or by offering inadequate post-purchase support, e.g. delivery, installation or after-sales service. Once again the implications for the retailer are clear. The user of the product must also be satisfied and this can best be achieved by determining who the user will be and providing services appropriate to the user's need. A situation has now been described where the *satisfaction of customer needs* can be seen as rather more complex than the simple phrase suggests. Who is the customer? Is it the decider, the buyer or user? The answer will vary according to the specific buying situation but the retailer should know in order to maximize the chances of future sales.

FACTORS INFLUENCING CHOICE

In the previous section (*see* 7) the role of the influencer was briefly described. However, the consumer is influenced by many factors in choosing the product/store/brand complex. These factors may be perceived as internal variables – needs, motivation, personality, perception, learning and attitudes; or external – family, reference groups, social class and culture.

INTERNAL VARIABLES

11. Needs

A need can be defined as an inner force that prompts or moves the individual to behaviour. A hierarchy of needs has been described whereby there are different degrees of need, the most fundamental being food, water and shelter which have to be met before other needs are felt. Second order needs are for safety and security which in turn, when fully satisfied, will lead to the need to belong and love. Finally, satisfaction of esteem (prestige, success, etc.) and self-fulfilment needs are sought.

Thus a retail organization may adopt a strategy of appealing to the need to belong, e.g. 'Your caring, sharing Co-op', or to esteem needs, e.g. prestigious stores such as Harrods.

12. Motivation

A motive is an internal energizing force that gives rise to behaviour. The retailer motivates customers through stimulation of a need or want which will be sufficiently strong to give rise to purchasing behaviour. There are two stages to the process. Firstly, the retailer must generate awareness of the product or service as a satisfier of the need. Secondly, consumer motivation is enhanced by making the product more desirable. Both of these objectives can be achieved through communication devices: providing information, demonstrating the satisfaction of need or providing incentives to action. Advertising and personal selling are useful as methods of increasing motivation; in-store the provision of discounts, special offers, competitions, etc. can raise customer desire to the point where action (purchase) is inevitable.

13. Personality

The way in which an individual interacts with the environment is termed personality. It is a complex concept and has given rise to many theories of personality. One element of personality which has proved to be of particular value to retailers is the study of lifestyles. Lifestyles – how people lead their lives – can be measured by looking at three variables: activities, interests and opinions. Through measuring these dimensions it is possible to differentiate groups of consumers who lead their lives in a particular way.

Lifestyle retailing really started in the UK with the Next retailing group who originally defined their target customer as the fashion-conscious female, to whom price was a secondary consideration. Once this definition was available, other merchandise and indeed other stores were added to appeal to that same target customer.

14. Perception

Perception is the way in which an individual interprets the stimuli received from the environment. For retailers it is imperative that they realize that 'customer perception is reality'. In other words it is not what they are that is important but what they think they are. Thus some customers' perception of a store may be 'traditional, reliable, stable', i.e. a favourable impression. Others may interpret the same stimuli in a negative way as 'old fashioned, dowdy, unexciting', i.e. an unfavourable response.

15. Learning

Learning can be thought of as modification of behaviour as a result of experience. Two important aspects of learning for the retailer are the concepts of reward and punishment, and the enhancement of learning by repetition. Thus a customer who constantly finds satisfaction of need through visits to a particular store will build up a loyalty to that store.

Stimulus generalization occurs when a customer responds in a particular way to one stimulus but then generalizes the response to other stimuli. For example, one rude assistant in one branch of Marks and Spencer may result in a response whereby the customer vows never to shop in any branch of M & S again! Or the purchase of a single item which proves unsatisfactory may result in a response that all merchandise from that store is considered unsatisfactory. The lessons for the retailer willing to apply learning theory are devastatingly clear.

16. Attitudes

An attitude is a learned predisposition to respond in a consistently favourable or unfavourable way with regard to a particular object or idea.

The measurement of attitudes through retailing research and the way in which attitudes are formed and changed are important to the retailer. An attitude, once formed, is particularly resistant to change because it is an efficient way of operating. A predisposition to respond in a particular manner reduces the need for exhaustive evaluation of alternatives every time the consumer comes to make a decision. The retailer should therefore aim to generate a positive attitude towards the store and maintain it. It is far easier for a customer to move from a positive to a negative attitude than it is for a retailer to move the customer from a negative attitude to a positive one.

EXTERNAL VARIABLES

The degree of influence of external variables is illustrated in Figure 7.2, the family being the strongest.

17. The family

The influence of the family has been touched upon already when considering the buying participants. The degree of influence of the family will vary according

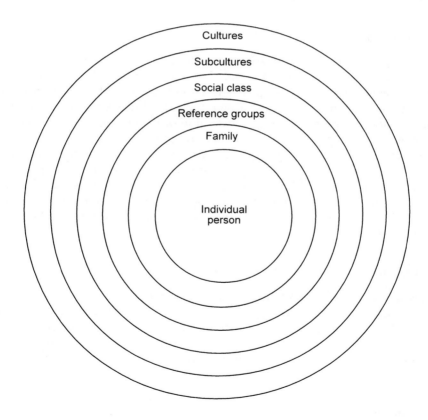

Figure 7.2 External factors influencing store choice

to the situation and the product. The degree of influence of the husband, wife, children or extended family in a purchase decision has implications for developing the retail strategy, perhaps most particularly with regard to advertising and sales promotion.

18. Reference groups

A reference group is a group with which an individual wants to be associated and whose beliefs, attitudes, values and behaviour he or she will seek to emulate. Reference groups influence decisions on store choice because members of the group are expected to adhere to group norms and act in particular ways acceptable to other members of the group. Teenagers are particularly prone to being highly influenced by reference groups, for example in their music and clothing tastes, but reference groups occur in all walks of life. Professional organizations, colleagues, neighbours, friends, may all be regarded as reference groups. The retailer can use this concept by constructing advertising to appeal to the group, for example a fashion show for the local Women's Institute, or a display of new books at the local university.

19. Social class

The system of social stratification according to socio-economic groupings provides us with definitions of social class which, although everyone agrees are not as well defined as in the past, still provide a useful classification scheme for retailers. Certain retailers will design their retail mixes to appeal to certain social classes, but perhaps the greatest value of the classification system is in the determination of appropriate media to reach target audiences. Most newspapers and magazines have information on their readers which they make available to advertisers in order to persuade them to place ads in that particular publication. Frequently this will include data on readership by social class. The retailer can then match the cost of reaching his or her target audience in terms of social class against other competing publications, and thereby choose the most cost-effective.

20. Culture

The unique pattern of behaviour and social relations that characterize a society and distinguish it from others gives rise to the concept of culture. A society's values, ideas, attitudes, traditions, symbols or technology can all form the basis of culture. Thus it is possible to describe North American cultural values as achievement, success, progress, material comfort and freedom; and this may be compared with the Chinese culture.

21. Subculture

Perhaps the greatest value of the concept of culture to the retailer is at the level of subcultures. A subculture can be defined as a distinct cultural group which exists as an identifiable segment within a larger, more complex society. For example, we can describe a primary concern of the youth subculture as entertainment, music, cinema, etc., whilst the elderly subculture is more concerned with health care and gardening! Other subcultures could be defined according to religion, racial groups, political groups, etc.

Progress test 7

1. Describe the stages of the buying process.

2. What are the four types of buying participants?

3. How has the study of personality helped retailers?

4. How can retailers use the concept of reference groups in promoting their business?

5. Is the stratification of the population into social classes still relevant?

6. Define subculture and give an example.

7. What factors are likely to be most important to customers when selecting a store? (Illustrate your answer with reference to the purchase of furniture.)

8. Briefly describe the stages of the consumer purchasing decision process. Explain and evaluate the methods used by *retailers* to influence consumer choice and actions, in this process of decision making.

8

SEGMENTATION

DIFFERING CUSTOMER NEEDS

There is an old truism that 'you can't please all of the people all of the time!' In other words, with respect to retailing it is not possible to serve all types of customer. If this is attempted none will be served adequately. This is particularly true today when consumers require a greater choice and are looking for satisfaction of their particular needs and have the spending power to demand it.

The retailer must instead look to satisfying certain groups of customers – this process is known as segmentation.

1. Definition

Segmentation is the dividing of a market into subsets of customers, any one or more of which can be selected as a target market to be satisfied with a distinct retailing mix.

2. Examples

Perhaps the best example of segmentation in action can be found in the retailing of clothing and fashion wear. Certain retailers have identified younger age groups as their target segment, e.g. Miss Selfridge. Next originally chose to serve the 25–40 year old fashion conscious female, whereas Marks & Spencer traditionally offered more conservative wear to slightly older age groups. An example of a retail organization that has learnt to its cost the lesson of segmentation is Woolworth. This company was brought to its knees in the late 1970s because it was trying to be all things to everybody, offering a vast range of merchandise and serving a wide range of customers. The company was turned around by adopting the principles of segmentation and concentrating efforts on six target markets. Operation focus, as this segmentation process was named, resulted in Woolworth stores pulling out of certain groups of merchandise, e.g. adult clothing. The six areas remaining in focus were children's clothes, toys, confectionery, records and videos, make-up and toiletries and kitchen and linen. The results were dramatic – sales per square foot of selling space increased by 40 percent. In the early to mid 90s however it was becoming clear that Woolworth was again in need of a new initiative and perhaps a new segmentation strategy.

Having illustrated the results of adopting the segmentation strategy, it is appropriate to ask, 'How can we subdivide a market?'

BASES FOR SEGMENTATION

The objective of segmenting a market is to identify segments that offer the retailer an opportunity to serve that segment and thus truly and precisely satisfy customer needs. There are five bases for segmentation: geographic, geo-demographic, demographic, psychographic and behavioural.

3. Geographic segmentation

Segmenting a market by geographic factors is a common retail practice. At the most general level many retailers restrict operation to the UK. It is only relatively recently that retailers have looked to overseas territories for growth with the same vigour as the manufacturing industry does. There are also groups of stores that restrict operation to a geographic region where they have a strong presence, e.g. Morrisons in Lancashire and Yorkshire. There are, however, many retailers who have segmented their market geographically at the level of a town or as the corner shop in the local community.

4. Geodemographic segmentation

A particularly useful scheme for classifying residential neighbourhoods has been developed by CACI which classifies every parish with a population of 50 or more into 11 groups. This scheme, known as ACORN (A Classification Of Residential Neighbourhoods), has been based on the principle that people living in similar residential areas will show certain similarities in their buying patterns. For example, people living in 'better off retirement areas' will have very different buying requirements to those in the 'poorest council estates'. A similar system marketed by CCN is known as MOSAIC.

5. Demographic segmentation

Segmenting a market by demographic variables is probably the most widely used method.

(a) **Age and life cycle stage.** Examples have already been given of retailers who target certain age groups and it is clear that consumers' requirements change with age. The teenager's requirement for cosmetics, records and cinema-going are replaced in young adulthood by home-furnishing and convenience food requirements, and so it goes on through the life cycle with older age groups preoccupied with health and filling their leisure time.

(b) **Sex.** In the area of clothing retailers, there has long been a division between menswear and ladieswear. In the 1970s the unisex trend started and the division is now less clear cut than it was. However, many retailers still target predominantly male or female customers. Consider the target markets for a fishing tackle retailer and a specialist sewing machine retailer. The composition of the target groups has a major impact on the retail mix and particularly on the ways in which the retailer communicates with the different groups.

(c) Family. Two variables are important in segmenting by family factors – the family size and the stage in the family life cycle. Larger families may be more economy minded and purchase larger pack sizes, economy brands or own labels. At the same time, the family with a youngest child under three years of age will differ in its requirements from a family with no children under 11. We recall here that the family may act as a decision-making unit in the purchasing process.

(d) Income. Segmentation by income is another long-standing retail practice. Retailers like Harrods aim to appeal to higher income groups by offering 'exclusive' products, higher than average prices and a greater range of customer service. Rising disposable income in the UK and the trend towards double income families has offered greater opportunities for retailers targetting these higher income groups. With higher incomes comes a customer orientation towards quality of merchandise and service and a lesser emphasis on price.

(e) Occupation. At one time occupation was intimately linked with income. But this relationship is breaking down with many blue collar workers earning more than others in professional and technical occupations. However, occupation can provide a useful basis for segmenting markets due to the lifestyles that individuals in that occupation will lead. For example, one might expect a book retailer to target lecturers, school teachers, and other professionals in preference to blue collar workers. It is common to feel uneasy about these distinctions and to feel an element of snobbery and undesirable class distinction or discrimination. However, it is as well to remember that the purpose of this discrimination is to serve the customer beter. Thus the transport cafe has targetted its segment and in this way serves its particular customers the way they want; so equally the Café Royal caters for another segment of the market and aims to please them with an alternative offering.

Similarly, other demographic variables which can be used as the basis for segmentation are education, religion, race and nationality.

6. Psychographic segmentation

It has been said that the retail revolution which started in the 1980s was sparked by the application of psychographics, i.e. segmenting a market according to lifestyles. Lifestyle – the way groups of people lead their lives – is determined by attitudes, opinions and interests. For example, some individuals are particularly concerned with environmental issues, they will look for economy, safety and a consideration for ecology. The Body Shop is a retail organization which had this lifestyle group particularly in mind when formulating its retail strategy.

Social class is also an important element of psychographics ranging from the

Table 8.1 Social class groupings

Social grade	Per cent of population	Social status	Occupation
A	2.7	Upper middle class	Higher managerial, administrative or professional
B	15.1	Middle class	Intermediate managerial, administrative or professional
C1	23.9	Lower middle class	Supervisory or clerical, and junior managerial, administrative or professional
C2	27.8	Skilled working class	Skilled manual workers
D	17.8	Working class	Semi and unskilled manual workers
E	12.7	Those at lowest level of subsistence	State pensioners or widows (no other earner), casual or lowest-grade workers

Source: JICNARS

A group or upper middle classes through to pensioners who make up the bulk of the E group (*see* Table 8.1).

Personality is the third element of psychographics with retailers looking for personality traits which they may use to segment the market. Individuals may be described as gregarious, ambitious, independent, self-confident, etc. and retailers may wish to appeal to individuals with one or more of these personality traits. Country Casuals would seem to be appealing to the ambitious and/or self-confident, Benetton similarly has an appeal to certain personality types. Perhaps the aim of the retailer should be to project an image which these personality types identify with and feel most at ease with. The family man may feel uncomfortable shopping in Burton and the 'fast trackers' may feel equally uncomfortable in searching for clothes in Littlewoods.

7. Behavioural segmentation

In behavioural segmentation customers are grouped according to certain aspects of their behaviour in relation to the store, rather than as previously by inferring behaviour from other factors, e.g. demographic. A market can be segmented according to occasions, benefits and loyalty status.

(a) Occasions. Customers can be segmented according to when they develop a need. For example, a convenience store can specialize in serving people who normally do their main shopping at the supermarket but find they have forgotten certain items, run out of them or need them at a time when the supermarket is closed. In this way the convenience store is able to compete with the supermarket, not on price but on convenience and providing satisfaction to 'distress purchase' buying.

(b) Benefits sought. Considered by some as the most useful method of segmentation, benefit segmentation seeks to determine the prime benefit sought by shoppers. For example, certain shoppers may patronize a department store because the prime benefits they seek are quality merchandise and the facility for charging their account at the store. Others may seek the best possible price and want a discount for cash – the discount edge-of-town superstores may well attract this type of customer.

(c) Loyalty status. Many retailers find that a high proportion of their turnover is generated by a small proportion of their customers. These individuals have developed a high degree of loyalty to that store and use it frequently. There are degrees of loyalty and retailers may attempt to identify those who are loyal to two or three stores and attempt to turn them away from competitors by provision of extra incentives (e.g store loyalty cards) and thus convert them to loyalty to the individual store.

It should be stressed that segmentation is often achieved by combining two or more of the above variables. For example, a furniture retailer may combine income, age and sex as the variables which will define its target market. Similarly the '25–40 year old fashion conscious female' defines a target market in terms of demographic and psychographic variables.

ADVANTAGES AND DISADVANTAGES OF SEGMENTATION

8. Advantages of segmentation

The purpose of segmentation is to define a group of customers that we wish to serve. By adopting this focused approach the retailer should be better able to:

(a) Spot and compare opportunities

(b) Spot different responses to different stimuli; for example, a new advertising campaign or a change in price

(c) Make fine adjustments to the retail mix.

In short the advantage of segmentation is to enable the retailer to more accurately identify customer needs and wants and satisfy them. The approach has been likened to the rifle bullet rather than the shotgun approach.

9. Disadvantages of segmentation

Targetting a well-defined segment has provided a new lease of life to many retailers who seemed to have lost their way (e.g. Woolworth, Burtons), but there is the danger of:

(a) Becoming cost inefficient – i.e. by targetting a small group the retailer will lose economies of scale.

(b) Becoming too myopic in serving only one segment and missing opportunities that may arise in others.

(c) Trying to compete in too many different segments. The process of identifying segments naturally leads to the decision of which to serve. Many retailers find it difficult to jettison some segments, hoping that they will be able to attract some business from it. This leads to the 'jack of all trades, master of none' syndrome which has been the downfall of many retail operations, particularly of the department store type.

(d) Becoming locked into a segment that is declining. Many small retail outlets have been lost because they served a segment that was in decline. For example, the changing retail environment has meant that for food purchases most people prefer to buy most items once a week at one outlet. Therefore, many fishmongers, butchers and bakers have lost out to the superstore where the convenience of one-stop shopping was the benefit sought by the customer.

SEGMENTATION STRATEGY

Having identified different segments through gathering information the stage now reached is to determine which segments to serve.

10. Deciding factors

There are many factors which will impinge upon this decision, including:

(a) The size and profit potential of the alternative segments.

(b) The objectives of the retail organization.

(c) The strengths and weaknesses of the retail organization. For example, a small company with limited resources may find it impossible to compete in many different segments.

(d) The strengths and weaknesses of the competition. It is often preferable to attract a small segment where competition is weak than a large segment which is adequately served by strong competitors.

(e) Channel relations – it may be very difficult to break into a market segment, not because of direct retail competition, but because the intermediaries provide a significant barrier to entry, e.g. newspapers and magazines.

(f) Company image – a segment may be seen to offer significant potential but does not provide consistency with the company image.

11. Alternative strategies

There are three alternative segmentation strategies which may be adopted.

(a) **Undifferentiated.** The retailer recognizes that there are different segments but focuses on the common needs of consumers rather than their differences. Thus the retailer hopes to attract a sufficient number of consumers from all segments with one retail mix. Perhaps one of the most successful adopters of this strategy is the McDonalds fast food chain which offers a highly standardized mix on a global basis.

(b) Differentiated. Here the response to the different segments is to design different retail mixes to satisfy the differing needs. For example, the Burton group operates a number of successful retail operations targetted at several different segments. The Dorothy Perkins chain is targetted at the young segment, Top Shop and Top Man at the teenager market, whilst Principles aims at an older, more style-conscious group of customers.

(c) Concentrated. The concentrated strategy is aimed at gaining a larger share of one segment and is perhaps the most appropriate segmentation strategy for the new smaller operator. Many examples of successful operation of a concentrated strategy can be cited. For example, Mothercare became hugely successful serving the needs of the mother and baby. More recently Tie Rack and Sock Shop have concentrated on providing a very wide choice of a specialist clothing item, but have run into difficulties with this strategy (*see* **9d** above).

12. Criteria for successful segmentation

It has been suggested that in order for segmentation to be most effective, the identified segments must be:

(a) Measurable. It is difficult to measure personality variables such as ambition or rebelliousness. Therefore demographic variables are often preferred as the basis of segmenting markets because, for example, it is easy to determine the population within a certain age band.

(b) Substantial. Having measured different segments it is then possible to determine which are sufficiently substantial to afford an opportunity for targetting and thence generating a profit.

(c) Accessible. There is little point in identifying a segment if it is not accessible – if it cannot be reached by communications such as advertising, personal selling, sales promotion or publicity. In order to serve a segment the retailer has to be able to communicate with it.

In addition, the retailer's segmentation strategy must be capable of being put into action. The question of action is directly linked to company objectives and of course resources.

13. Segmentation and positioning

As we have seen, the process of segmentation involves identifying different bases for segmentation and determining important characteristics of each segment. It is then necessary to evaluate the potential or commercial attractiveness of each segment and then to select one or more segments as the target markets.

Closely linked to the whole process of segmentation is 'positioning'. This is where the store is positioned in a given market in the minds of the targetted

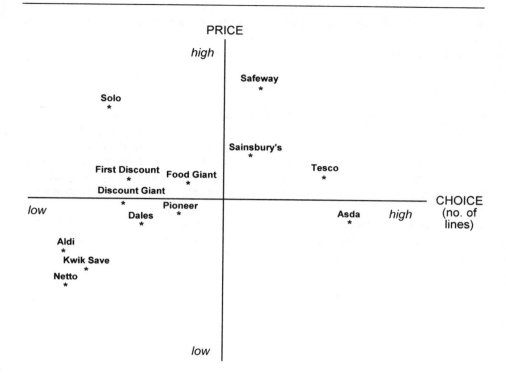

Figure 8.1 Perceptual map for grocery retailers

consumers. A 'Perceptual Map' can be drawn to show the position of the store and its competitors using important choice attributes. Thus price and range can be used to produce a perceptual map for grocery retailers (Figure 8.1).

It can be seen that on this map Asda would seem to have a satisfactory position, being perceived as providing a wide choice and lower-than-average prices. On the other hand, Safeway may be considered vulnerable since they are perceived as having higher prices and less choice. Equally there is a cluster of discounters operating within a very similar position in the market.

It is important to remember that positioning is not what you do to the store. Positioning is what you do to the mind of the customer. So you position the store in the mind of the customer.

Asda has recently completed a three-year process of repositioning – in fact to get them back to the position they used to hold as being perceived as providers of a good choice of quality merchandise at the best possible price, 'Asda-price.'

Progress test 8

1. What is meant by segmentation?

2. What are the bases for segmentation?

3. How has the ACORN classification scheme proved to be of use to retailers?

4. What are the advantages and disadvantages of segmentation?

5. Describe the criteria for successful segmentation.

6. A retailer, having conducted an extensive survey, finds that the customers most likely to patronize his store are in the 45-plus age group. He decides to mount a major effort to attract the 20–35 age-group to try to convince them to use the store. He believes there will be a higher pay-off in attempting to recruit new customers than in reinforcing attitudes of current customers. What are the arguments for and against this strategy?

7. What advantages can you suggest for a retailer who decides to segment his market using Geodemographics. What are the disadvantages of this methodology and how can they be minimised.

Part Two

THE RETAIL MIX

9
STORE LOCATION

THE IMPORTANCE OF LOCATION

1. Determining factors

It has been said that there are three criteria for success in retailing. They are location, location and location! This rather flippant remark serves to underline the importance of the location decision. Having the right location is important in terms of convenience to the customer but it is most important to the retailer because a mistake in the location decision is almost impossible to correct. If a pricing decision is wrong it can be changed, if the merchandise variety is wrong it too can be changed, but once the location is chosen the retailer is stuck with it. The store location decision should be approached bearing in mind three factors – the customer, the general area and the specific site.

STORE LOCATION AND THE CUSTOMER

2. Customers

The target market is the major determinant of the ideal store location. Thus, for example, if the target market is composed of individuals whose primary objective in selecting a store is convenience, then the store must be located conveniently for these customers. The definition of what is convenient may however differ according to customer type and merchandise required. In this way, a corner shop may be considered convenient for the purchase of a packet of sugar but may be inconvenient for the purchase of a full week's shopping if no car parking facility is available.

Similarly, an exclusive jewellery store will probably locate some considerable distance from its target market on the basis that convenience is not the major determinant of store choice for this type of merchandise but quality and service may be of greater import, and the ambience only available in a high class shopping area.

DETERMINING THE GENERAL AREA IN WHICH TO LOCATE

Once again the decision on the general area is arrived at through a stepwise process:

(a) Catchment area analysis.

(b) Determining the sales potential of different areas.

(c) Choosing the area which would fit best (retailer objectives related to needs of target market).

CATCHMENT AREA ANALYSIS

3. The catchment area

This is a term borrowed from geography which accurately describes the watershed effect which entices shoppers living within a shopping centre's sphere of influence into the centre and away from other shopping influences (*see* Figure 9.1). It may be defined as the geographical area from which a shopping centre (or large individual store) draws its custom. The main influences on catchment area size and shape are:

(a) Business attractions of the shopping centre. These consist of:

(*i*) types of major store
(*ii*) kinds and selection of merchandise offered
(*iii*) delivery, credit and other retail services
(*iv*) reputation of major retailers
(*v*) banking facilities
(*vi*) car parking facilities and restrictions.

(b) Social and amusement attractions.

(c) Population of area.

(d) Density of population.

(e) Type of consumer.

(f) Distance to travel and local 'psychology of distance'

(g) Lines of transportation (including road and rail systems, bus routes).

(h) Lines of communication. These consist of daily newspaper circulation areas, sales and readership, and other local media such as radio, TV and magazines.

(i) Car ownership in the market.

(j) Nature and competition offered by other shopping centres within or near the market.

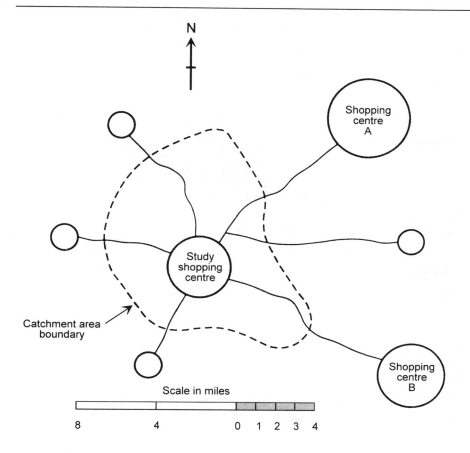

Figure 9.1   Catchment area boundary

(k) Topographical nature of market area.

4. Quantifying the catchment area

The two main approaches to determining the local catchment area are:

(a) Empirical theory. This is made up of the following methods:

(*i*) Observational methods, for example by finding natural catchment boundaries like rivers and motorways on maps or by driving round the area.
(*ii*) 'Customer spotting', based either on a shopper questionnaire or on an
analysis of customer use of credit facilities and so on. A customer 'spot map'
can be constructed from the questionnaires, etc., showing where customers
live (*see* Figure 9.2).

(b) Gravitational theory. The best known of these so-called spatial interaction
models, which is based on Reilly's Law, states that the frequency with which the

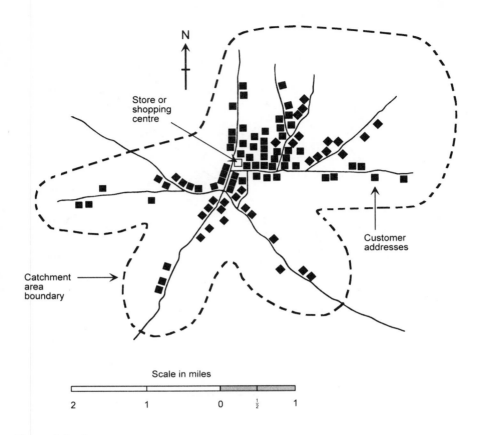

N

Store or
shopping
centre

Customer
addresses

Catchment
area
boundary

Scale in miles

2   1   0 $\frac{1}{2}$ 1

Figure 9.2 Customer spot map

residents of an intermediate settlement trade with two towns is directly proportional to the populations of the two towns and inversely proportional to the
square of the distances of the two towns to the intermediate settlement. Reilly's
Law can be modified to derive the 'breaking point' between two towns, which
is defined as the point up to which one town dominates and beyond which the
other town is dominant. This is given as:

$$\text{Breaking point (in miles from town A)} = \frac{\text{Distance A to B}}{1 + \sqrt{\dfrac{\text{Population B}}{\text{Population A}}}}$$

The following example shows how a catchment area boundary is drawn using
Reilly's method.

Example

Town A has a population of 40,000 and town B of 10,000. Town A is 6 miles from
town B. Break-points for all surrounding towns can be calculated and a line
drawn to connect these points, thus producing a catchment area boundary:

$$\text{Breaking point} \atop \text{(in miles from town A)} = \frac{6}{1 + \sqrt{\dfrac{10,000}{40,000}}} = 4 \text{ miles}$$

From either of these two basic types of catchment area appraisal, an idea of the sphere of influence of a shopping centre can be gained. This sphere of influence can be quantified by drawing a series of the break-points or a continuous line to form the catchment area boundary (*see* Figure 9.3).

5. The trading area

The trading area is the area of the market drawn upon by the individual shop or store. Most of the main influences on catchment area size would apply to the individual trading area, tempered by the localized factors affecting the site, such as:

(a) Relationship of the site to the main shopping centre and thus to the catchment area

(b) Accessibility of the site

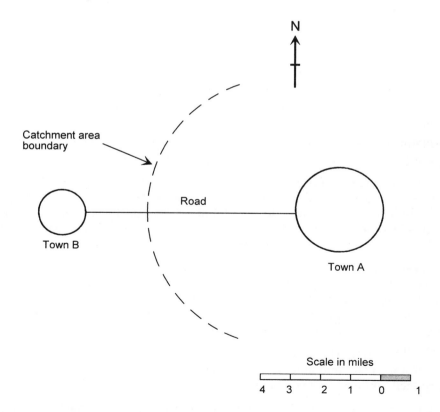

Figure 9.3 Drawing a catchment area boundary

(c) Strength of business interception, e.g. it is strong if the site is on a pedestrian walkway

(d) Cumulative attraction (amount of pull the centre has as a whole)

(e) Compatibility (amount of associated business from sympathetic trades)

(f) Competition, depending on:

  (i) location
  (ii) size and type
  (iii) character and strength,

(g) Inherent factors in the shop itself, including ability to carve out, retain and build up a viable share of available trade.

6. Sources of information

The retailer can gather much useful site and location data from the following sources:

  Local authorities
  Estate agents
  Press
  Other published data.

7. Local authorities

The local government organization in each area will provide information through various departments.

(a) Planning department. Structure plans and written statements describe the present and future shopping environment, backed by maps of relevant areas.

(b) Electoral office. Electoral rolls, which are detailed lists, show numbers and names of voters at each address in a town or city. Ward and parish maps help a researcher to make an up-to-date head count for very small geographical areas. These figures may be grossed up to include under 18 year olds by use of local data on the average number of persons per household.

(c) Rating office. Valuation registers show addresses and rateable values of all commercial properties, including shops, in an authority area. Sometimes the type of trade is included. Rateable value is a reasonable guide both to the general prosperity of the area and to that of individual shops. Some researchers have found a correlation between it and retail turnover.

(d) Clerk's office. The administrative office in each authority may be able to furnish street plans and other useful textual and statistical information (including council minutes) for the retailer.

(e) Other official sources. The local building inspectorate and the library may be able to give further information.

8. Estate agents

Shop property agents not only put vendors and potential buyers in touch with each other but can often supply local 'key' plans and research information.

9. Press

Both the local and national press can be of assistance.

(a) **Local newspapers.** These are often first with news of shopping redevelopment and they also carry advertisements for properties for sale or to let.

(b) **National property journals.** The *Estates Gazette* and *Chartered Surveyor Weekly* carry news of developments primarily for multiple traders who are particularly interested in the display and semi-display advertising for shop properties in important centres.

10. Other published data

Much information with emphasis on local and national shopping conditions has been published.

(a) **Census of Population.** This decennial count of persons in Great Britain and Northern Ireland gives much valuable demographic information including ward populations, ethnic origins, place of work and socio-economic groups. (The most recent Census of Population was carried out in 1991.)

(b) **Registrar-General's estimates.** Published annually, these show up-to-date estimates of population in the local government areas.

(c) **Family Expenditure Surveys.** Published annually these give the expenditure per family on a wide range of foods, consumer durables, semi-durables and services.

(d) **Stores and Shops Directory.** This lists retail ownership and various trade categories.

(e) **Commercial sources.** Many companies supply specialized information of interest to retailers. For example, CACI Market Analysis pioneered the use of demographic data for consumer targeting. Other companies providing specialized services to retailers are CCN Systems and Charles Goad Ltd.

11. Information required

Five main factors are of importance, namely existing shopping provision, local geography, make-up of local population, economic background and transportation.

(a) **Existing shopping provision.** This includes:

(*i*) shops that are in direct competition to the particular trade under study, with their addresses, estimated turnover and the class of the trade (e.g. 'up market' merchandise) all marked on a street plan

(*ii*) department, variety stores and major multiples that all help the area's attractive power

(*iii*) general notes on the apparent prosperity and atmosphere of the shopping 'centre' and surrounding area

(*iv*) numbers of pedestrians at various points marked in figures on the street plan (pedestrian counts)

(*v*) position of pedestrian crossings, traffic lights and crush barriers that should be marked on the town plan.

(b) Geography. This consists of :

(*i*) topography – whether any hills, rivers, etc. influence shopping flows

(*ii*) positions of motorways and other arterial roads, factories, offices and housing areas; they should be marked on the map, along with locations of competing shopping centres.

(c) Population figures. These are broken down by:

(*i*) age groups – large numbers of young or old people, for example, may put different demands on the shopping system

(*ii*) socio-economic groups – showing numbers in each type of occupational group gives a clue to spending power

(*iii*) ethnic groups – where there are concentrations of ethnic groups this shows possible requirements for different types of food and other merchandise

(*iv*) employment groups

(*v*) changes in population totals and density over the past ten years.

(d) Economic background. This comprises:

(*i*) numbers of customers per retail establishment and numbers per trade, locally, regionally and nationally;

(*ii*) average turnover per shop in the trade under study, locally, regionally and nationally

(*iii*) retail expenditure per head, per trade, regionally and nationally; this can be calculated from the Family Expenditure Survey

(*iv*) daily newspaper circulation area and readership, other local media data.

(e) Transport facilities.

(*i*) *Private.* Position and size of present and future car parking layout in the study area, with the convenience of road systems taken into account (e.g. traffic management/pedestrianisation schemes). Local car ownership per household.

(*ii*) *Public.* Lines of bus routes (marked on maps), bus stops, service frequencies, fares and any changes of route.

DETERMINING THE SALES POTENTIAL OF DIFFERENT CATCHMENT/TRADING AREAS

12. Quantifying the total market value

The steps to be taken are as follows.

(a) Assess the number of households or the total population within the area (*see* the Census of Population).

(b) Gross up the population by an expenditure factor appropriate for the trade or trades under consideration (*see* the Family Expenditure Survey).

(c) Population × expenditure factor = estimated total sales of goods and services under study.

(d) Adjust for inflation.

(e) Adjust for segmentation variable (e.g. age group, sex, etc.).

13. Index of saturation

As well as the value of the market in a given area the degree to which that market is already served will be a major factor in determining the potential for a new store. The index of saturation is a way of comparing opportunities in different areas in terms of market value and competitor activity.

$$\text{Index of saturation} = \frac{\text{(Customers in area) (Expenditure per customer)}}{\text{Retail selling space allocated to product or product group}}$$

14. Growth

Another important factor determining the potential of an area is the extent to which growth is occurring. For example, the building of new housing estates, etc.

CHOOSING THE AREA WHICH WOULD FIT BEST

15. Objectives

Having assessed a variety of catchment areas it is important to choose an area which best provides those characteristics desired by the retailer. For example, Asda has put much effort into developing stores in the South of England. They were originally strong in the North but the South was identified as the area for growth because of its relative lack of superstores.

CHOOSING A SPECIFIC SITE: TYPES OF SITE

16. City centres

Such centres in the middle of major towns offer a full range of retail outlets to the shopper, from convenience shops through durable shops to shops of a high degree of specialization in some of the most important centres. Department stores are also found in this type of shopping complex. These centres are often visited weekly by families by bus or by car. Increasing use of cars has created severe problems of congestion in these centres. These problems can be tackled in four ways as follows, by:

(a) The provision of adequate public transport and the incentive to use it

(b) Building adequate car parks and access roads

(c) Pedestrianization (excluding cars altogether from the main shopping centre)

(d) Restricting the development of a town centre and concentrating on the provision of other types of shopping (e.g. in suburban centres).

These approaches are not mutually exclusive and in particular **(b)** and **(c)** may form complementary approaches in a given situation.

City centre locations offer a variety of environments from the 'Planned Shopping Centres' which offer climatically controlled, traffic-free shopping, to the High Street locations with lower rents but problems of traffic congestion and exposure to the elements.

These centres will usually serve a population in excess of 250,000.

17. District centres

This type of centre is found in the suburbs of large cities. It is also known as a secondary shopping centre, whilst the type discussed in **16** is known as a main or primary centre. The population served might be 50,000–60,000 but could be as low as 10,000.

Successful district centres demonstrate the following attributes:

(a) A complete range of convenience goods and a choice of stores for all these goods

(b) A proportion of the more popular comparison goods shops and service outlets

(c) Sufficient support population to ensure a high level of prosperity and efficiency

(d) Easier and quicker accessibility to the district centre from every part of the catchment area than to any competing centre.

18. Neighbourhood centres

These centres are the small clusters of 2–20 shops and are found in suburbs as complements to the district and town centres. They are normally very integrated with their markets and have support populations of 2,000 –3,000 up to 10,000. As a result they are very biased towards convenience shopping and depend more on 'walk-in' trade than on car-borne shoppers. Shops in such centres are often used for 'topping-up' purchases (i.e. shopping trips made between main trips).

19. Corner shops

These are found in abundance in most urban areas of the UK and date back to a period of low personal mobility and long working hours. Today many of them have become general shops and their attributes are those of the independently owned shop (*see* 2:2–5). Urban renewal has drastically reduced their numbers but they now appear to have stabilized and are often quite successful when converted to convenience retailing with longer opening hours.

20. Factors altering shopping provision

Newer, better organized edge-of-town or out-of-town centres have taken more and more trade away from corner shops and older town centre shopping centres. The factors involved are as follows:

(a) Changing customer requirements. This is due to a shorter working week, larger real disposable incomes and higher car ownership and usage, which has made out-of-town shopping far more accessible and attractive.

(b) Redistribution of population. The demolition of inner-city areas has caused the population to move outwards to the suburbs.

(c) Redevelopment of town centres.

(d) Demolition due to road construction or slum clearance. Road and urban renewal plans have often 'blighted' shopping centres, i.e. have caused a 'no hoper' attitude on the part of shopkeepers and shoppers alike, driving both away from the doomed centre.

(e) New roads. Fast, new dual carriageway ring-roads have often cut off housing from their traditional shopping centres and made it easier for shoppers to gain access to the out-of-town centres.

21. Off-centre stores

Many discount operators have taken warehouses and old industrial buildings on the periphery of town centres. These are low-cost locations and the benefits are being passed on to consumers in the form of lower prices. Some local authorities are still wary of such practices, however.

22. Free-standing superstores

Hypermarkets and superstores are still being built in the UK on sites that are on the edges of urban areas. A great deal of antagonism from local authorities is still seen towards this type of development due primarily to problems caused by increased traffic and also the loss of green belt land. However, they are generally successful and thus the large multiples have poured money into their development. From a base of 400 in 1986 the number of superstores increased to 1,000 in 1995. Superstore operators like Tesco have suggested two points that should be particularly considered in connection with this type of retail development:

(a) Very large retail units can, through economies of scale, pass on the benefits to the customer in the form of lower prices.

(b) Superstores should be considered on at least a county planning basis and not just with regard to localized factors.

23. Out-of-town Shopping Centres

Innovated in the USA, the first being the Country Club Plaza, Kansas, which was opened in 1923. The Metrocentre (Gateshead) opened in 1986, and Meadowhall (Sheffield), Merry Hill (Dudley) and Lakeside (Thurrock) are successful British examples.

The main reasons for the development of out-of-town shopping centres are:

(a) Increasing suburban populations

(b) Increasing real income

(c) Central area decay due to:

(*i*) movement of affluent consumers to the suburbs, leaving the less-well-off consumers in the inner city areas
(*ii*) the tendency of retailers to follow purchasing power
(*iii*) the inability of successive governments to cope either politically or financially with the problems
(*iv*) the decline of public transport

(d) High level of car ownership

(e) Traffic congestion in towns and cities.

24. Advantages and disadvantages

(a) The arguments *against* out-of-town shopping centres, particularly the large regional ones, are as follows:

(*i*) The green belt or rural areas should be preserved at all costs.
(*ii*) Diversion of trade out of the towns could imperil urban renewal programmes and might seriously damage trade in smaller towns. (Local authorities, which often have a reasonable representation of small shopkeepers on their councils, sometimes plead that their rate revenues would fall.)

(b) Arguments *for* out-of-town shopping centres are:

(*i*) The green belt argument is said by some to be somewhat spurious because the belt has often already been harmed by unplanned infilling and a variety of sub-industrial uses.

(*ii*) Out-of-town centres cater specifically for those shoppers with cars who do not wish to shop in town centres because of the problems of congestion. Any restriction on out-of-town development goes against market forces which may result in the creation of more unplanned and less socially desirable features.

25. Retail parks

Another type of out-of-town shopping centre is the retail park. This is essentially a grouping of warehouse-type operators such as DIY, furniture and electrical superstores out of the town centre, often on the edge of town usually operating on discount principles.

THE SPECIFIC SITE

26. Factors in choosing a specific site

Factors which must be taken into account in choosing a specific site are as follows:

(a) **Suitability.** Whether the site or building is physically suitable for the purpose. It may be too big, oddly-shaped, lack rear-loading facilities, require extensive rebuilding or refitting and so on. Accessibility and parking facilities should also be considered.

(b) **Rent or purchase price.** High costs may make a unit quite uneconomic for certain trades or certain levels of turnover (*see* **29–31**).

(c) **Compatibility.** Whether flanking and nearby stores will help or hinder sales. Trade can be classified as

(*i*) generative – attracting business direct from shoppers' homes, or
(*ii*) shared – with other shops in an associated selling situation, or
(*iii*) suscipient – impulse attractions on trips incidental to shopping purposes, e.g. as in shops in air terminals.

(d) **Interception.** Whether the store is on a popular pedestrian route from car parks, bus stations, etc. to the shopping centre itself.

(e) **Competition.** Heavy competition nearby in certain retail sectors can be harmful, in others quite beneficial.

(f) **Planned acquisition.** Whether the site or the general area has been identified specifically by the growing company in its development plan.

27. Site research

In order to check out further the viability of a specific site the following considerations should be taken into account:

(a) Pedestrian and vehicular flow counts in the vicinity of the site for comparing with figures from apparently similar locations.

(b) Position of 'magnets' like department stores, pedestrian interruptors (vacant stores, non-retail uses) and all other influences on pedestrian flows not previously covered.

28. Estimating the turnover of a new retail unit

The most frequently used method of estimating sales of a new, enlarged or refurbished retail unit is to use the 'share of market' method.

Here an appropriate percentage of total catchment expenditure is assumed to be the potential. The percentage market share selected could be one attained at an existing store of similar size, site and location, dependent on approximately the same size and quality of the catchment area.

Competitor shares would be assessed with reference to:

(a) Size of net sales areas

(b) Number of assistants

(c) Number of checkouts/cash points

(d) Range of goods

(e) Pricing and promotional facilities.

This method is also known as the 'analogue' method when comparison is made with stores which have essential features in common with the proposed store.

PROFIT APPRAISAL

29. Gross profitability

We have seen how turnover for a particular site can be forecast. But the retailer also requires to know what sort of return on the investment he or she is likely to receive. The first step in this is to estimate the gross profit (net sales minus cost of goods sold) likely to flow from the new outlet. This can be worked out by examining the following factors:

(a) The product mix. Although many multiple retailers try to achieve a standard product mix in each of their branches by taking prime locations in towns of a minimum size, the volume sales from each section or department in various branches may differ from one town to the next. This may be due to a variety of things such as the age and socio-economic groupings of families in the town, local ethnic or regional factors, which may affect tastes and therefore consumption patterns, the strength of local competition from other shops and shopping centres and so on.

(b) Gross margins. In order to estimate an average gross margin for a store, not only does the product mix have to be estimated (often this is done by comparison with other similar stores in comparable locations), but the average gross margin per section (if not per line) must be worked out.

Table 9.1 Gross profit contributions for the sections of a newsagent's shop

Section	Product mix (% of total sales)	Annual sales (£)	Gross margin (%)	Gross profit (£)
News/magazines	20	60,000	33⅓	20,000
Paperbacks	15	45,000	33⅓	15,000
Stationery	25	75,000	30	22,500
Greeting cards	10	30,000	40	12,000
Toys	10	30,000	35	10,500
Confectionery	10	30,000	27	8,100
Tobacco	10	30,000	10	3,000
	100	300,000		91,100

Example

A small newsagent and stationery shop has a current turnover of £300,000 per annum; the gross profit contributions from each of seven main sections might look as shown in Table 9.1.

The average gross margin for the shop is

$$\frac{91,100}{300,000} \times 100 = 30.4 \text{ per cent}$$

Assuming a combined markdown and shrinkage loss of 3 per cent of turnover the gross profit is reduced by £9,000 to give a realized gross margin of 27.4 per cent.

30. Capital costs

The capital cost of a new outlet must also be worked out with reference to:

(a) Freehold or leasehold purchase

(b) Building costs, if any

(c) Fitting-out costs.

For example, assuming that there were no building works but shopfitting cost £25,000, total capital outlay including legal fees, estate agent's fees, initial stock and working capital could easily reach £100,000.

31. Operating expenses and net profit

The running costs of the unit must be taken into account in order to work out the net profitability of the operation. These costs come under headings such as:

(a) Wages and salaries

(b) Rent and rates

(c) Other accommodation costs (including heating, lighting and telephone)

(d) Other expenses including depreciation.

The following is a cost breakdown for the store under consideration (with annual sales of £300,000) at the same time summarizing the information so far:

	£	£
Gross profit	91,100	
Less: Markdown, shrinkages etc.	9,000	
		82,100
Wages and salaries	33,000	
Rent and rates	21,000	
Other accommodation costs	7,500	
Other expenses	9,000	
		70,500
Net profit		11,600

The net profit after all expenses have been paid is £11,600, showing a net margin on sales of 3.9 per cent. Taking the capital outlay of £100,000 this net profit gives a return on capital employed (ROCE) of 11.6 per cent. Whether this figure is an attractive return or not will largely depend on the prevailing interest rates at the time. For example, would the £100,000 produce a similar or better return in a deposit account with a bank or building society.

Figure 9.4 Retail branch break-even chart

32. Forecasting for the future

Whilst it is very important to estimate sales and profitability for the first year of an outlet's operation, estimates must be made for the future so that these can be incorporated in the company's total budget projections. It is notoriously difficult to forecast but it is usual to produce figures for a five-year planning period. A future cash flow estimate can thus be made to produce a long-term return on capital figure, using discounted cash flow techniques. These estimates are often made on the basis of 'today's' prices and therefore do not take inflation into account.

It is useful to illustrate the planned progress of an investment project by constructing a break-even chart. Figure 9.4 shows the projected sales over a given period of time, with costs broken down into the fixed element (e.g. rent), variable costs (e.g. wages) and showing the difference between total costs and sales revenue. The resultant earnings should progress from a loss situation through a break-even point to a steadily increasing net profit.

Progress test 9

1. What is the major determinant of the ideal store location?

2. Describe the three steps in determining the general area in which to locate.

3. What are the main influences on catchment area size and shape?

4. How can the sales potential of different catchment areas be determined?

5. Describe three types of shopping centres.

6. List the factors to be taken into account when choosing a specific site.

7. How can the turnover and profitability of a new retail outlet be estimated?

8. What is a break-even chart? Why is it useful?

9. 'The three keys to success in retailing are location, location and location.' What did the writer mean? Discuss the merits of the location of a local retail store in relation to its target market.

10. Discuss the merits of, and problems with, using price, merchandise or promotion to compensate for poor location.

10

PRODUCT DECISIONS

MERCHANDISE

The most important element of the retail mix according to most retailers is the product. This is what customers require, why they visit a retailer and what generates profit. However, it is appropriate to consider the points below.

1. What is a product?

A product is anything that can be offered to a market that might satisfy a need or a want. Therefore, our definition includes not only physical objects, such as washing machines and toothpaste, but also services, for example a haircut, a cleaning service, insurance, etc.

2. Benefits

The retailer must ask: what products should I offer? what benefits will these products offer my customers? do these benefits match the requirements of the customer?

3. Terminology

Retailing has developed its own terminology and thus it is more usual to speak of merchandise rather than product, and of a merchandise philosophy as embracing such elements as variety, price/quality, branding and stock turnover. Similarly, the term merchandising is often used in retailing but is a rather ill-defined term. To some it is simply the display of merchandise, whilst to others it is much broader. The most quoted definition of merchandising, attributed to Gordon Selfridge, is to have the 'right goods at the right time, in the right place, in the right quantity, at the right price.' Many readers will recognize this definition as also being one definition of marketing.

4. The aspects of merchandising

To most retailers the merchandising process covers the selection, purchase, stock-management and display of a range of products whose successful sale will achieve the marketing objectives of the business in terms of the so-called six 'rights' of merchandising, namely:

Type
Quantity
Price
Quality
Time
Place.

Broadly, then, merchandising relates to the problems concerned with maximizing sales and profits of products and services.

5. Types of merchandise

The type of merchandise offered by a retailer is probably the major determinant of the business the retailer is in, and the variety of merchandise will have a major impact on how the customer perceives the store. Thus a retailer may adopt a specialized merchandise policy and carry only a few related product lines (e.g. a shoeshop), or the retailer may choose a scrambled merchandise policy and offer a wide range of product lines (e.g. Boots).

6. Polarization

Retail polarization has occurred over the last few years with more stores pursuing each of the above policies and resulting in one-stop shopping on the one hand and highly specialized stores such as Sock Shop and Tie Rack on the other.

7. Quantity of merchandise

Obviously the amount of merchandise ordered at any particular time must be related to the demand for it. Seasonal factors will thus be very important along with whether the item is a 'staple' or a fashion good and an eye must also be kept on the line's own stockturn related to the overall stockturn. Some multiple chains still order only a few hundred of a particular line and distribute two or three to each branch 'to see how it goes'. This often results in very fast sales in some branches and nil sales in others, making costly stock transfers or mark-downs necessary. Successful chains like Marks & Spencer use, say, 20 'pilot' stores in busy locations for new lines and extend allocation to other stores if and when the merchandise is successful.

8. Pricing merchandise

Prices have not only to be appropriate to the market segment aimed for, but must also produce sufficient gross profit overall to pay all selling costs and leave an acceptable net margin. A much fuller discussion of pricing policy is contained in Chapter 13.

9. Merchandise quality

Again, quality of merchandise (of which price is very much a function) must be related to the target market. The Harrods' merchandise mix could well be unrepeatable away from Brompton Road, whilst a cut-price food retailer would not necessarily flourish in the Knightsbridge area.

10. Timing

The timing of the arrival of merchandise is largely related to seasonal factors, although there is no use in, say, a baker's shop receiving a supply of cream cakes at 3 o'clock on a Saturday afternoon.

11. Placing of merchandise

The concept of 'place' has two aspects in merchandise theory. Firstly, the correct branches of a chain should be fed with the appropriate goods. Most multiples, for instance, grade their stores into five or six sizes which determines the merchandise ranges they are able to carry in normal circumstances. One retail chain sent a supply of paper panties to the Highlands of Scotland one autumn and, not surprisingly, the stock was all returned unused some months later. Secondly, the location of the stock within a store is often crucial (*see* Chapter 17).

12. Ranging policy

The mix of merchandise required can be looked at in two ways:

(a) **Depth**. A 'deep' stock assortment describes a comprehensive selection of brands, sizes, styles, colours and prices within a *particular* generic class of product, e.g. specialist shops such as 'Just Jeans' concentrate on providing a deep assortment within narrow merchandise variety. In-depth stocking leads to lower stockturns, compensated for by higher margins.

(b) **Breadth**. A 'broad' or wide stock variety describes a wide selection of *different* generic classes of product but with little choice in brands, styles, etc. within an individual line, e.g. an audio shop may begin stocking a few 'white' goods (refrigerators, washing machines, etc.) in order to broaden variety and increase sales. Stockturn may well be higher from a broad merchandise variety, but margins could be slimmer. Most retailers find it necessary to compromise in their ranging policy by optimizing both the 'depth' (assortment) and 'breadth' (variety) factors in order to maximize their profitability.

13. New products

Existing lines of merchandise would be selected on an on-going basis. New lines would be appraised by their:

(a) Appropriateness and compatibility with other existing lines and ranges

(b) Growth potential (bearing in mind the life cycles of products)

(c) Availability and competitive conditions (including exclusivity)

(d) Profitability (including a monitoring of current sales trends of similar lines presently carried and their gross profitability).

14. Range rationalization

The objective of any progressive retailer should be to keep as far as possible an optimum range of product lines for sale. Points to note in this connection are:

(a) The Pareto Rule is a mathematical calculation which shows that, for instance, roughly 20 per cent of the lines carried by a retailer account for about 80 per cent of the sales and/or gross profit. This is important for display purposes, but the slower moving lines must be carried in order to offer a comprehensive range which will attract shoppers, by allowing choice and facilitating comparisons.

(b) As new lines are introduced there should necessarily be a parallel policy to reduce the numbers of old, less profitable lines.

(c) When slow-moving lines are cut out, more space is available for extending better-selling products (true not only of shelf space but stockroom area as well, which all helps to reduce costs).

(d) Not only can lines be pruned, but suppliers, too.

OWN BRANDING

15. Types of own branding

Own branding occurs when products are sold under a retail organization's house brand-name and are sold exclusively through their retail organization's outlets. There are two basic types of own branding (or own labelling) which are as follows:

(a) Integrated. Here the retailer is integrated with his or her own manufacturing capability, e.g. in menswear, audio products, and the retailer has a greater control over quality, delivery, etc.

(b) Independent contracting. Here the retailer contracts a manufacturer to supply products labelled with the name of the retail company. This situation is particularly relevant in food products where companies manufacture to specification very large ranges for the major food retailers.

16. Significance of own branding

The market share of grocery own-brands in the UK is in the range of 25–30 per cent. Most UK multiples regard 25 per cent of sales under their own name as about right, although Sainsbury has carried it much further and Marks & Spencer is almost totally committed to a premium-priced own-brand policy.

17. Advantages of own branding

(a) **To the manufacturer**. Overheads are more easily covered when production of regular brands has fallen off because of seasonal factors. Own-brand production can be slotted in to fit in with production schedules.

(b) **To the retailer**.

(*i*) Purchase prices can be significantly lower and therefore either margins can be increased or lower prices can be passed on to the consumer to stimulate sales.
(*ii*) It allows the offer of a better price choice.
(*iii*) It may allow better space utilization either through the rationalization of minor manufacturers' brands or by producing an improved stockturn.
(*iv*) It allows better control over price, delivery and quality.
(*v*) The retailer's own corporate identity can be strongly reinforced by a broad ranging and aggressive own-brand strategy.

18. Disadvantages of own branding

(a) The strength of manufacturer's brands may be so strong through heavy advertising that the own brand may not be able to establish its own consumer appeal through its lower price.

(b) Carrying an extra line in a range may increase stock investment and, without minor brand rationalization, it could actually lower the stockturn. (For the electrical appliance retailer this could mean the extra problems of spares and service and for all retailers it could mean extra paperwork.)

(c) Minimum order sizes may be prohibitive for the smaller retailers.

(d) The success of own brands may squeeze out the smaller specialist brand thus reducing consumer choice.

(e) The pressure on margins due to the price competition from own brands may force manufacturers to reduce investment in research and development and thus lead to fewer new products coming to the market.

STOCK TURNOVER/GROSS MARGINS

19. Definition

Stock turnover is defined as sales in a given period divided by the average stock, and thus is a measure of how fast merchandise is sold and replaced (*see* Table

Table 10.1 Average stockturns for various retail sectors

Trade	Average number of times stock is turned per annum
Food retailers	
Large grocers	16
Dairies	69
Butchers, poulterers	61
Fishmongers	140
Clothing and footwear retailers	
Footwear	4
Men's and boyswear	5
Women's and girlswear	6
Durable goods retailers	
Furniture	4
Radio and electrical	6
DIY	6
Other kinds of retailers	
Bookshops	5
Chemists	8
Jewellery	2
Confectioners/tobacconist/newsagent (CTNs)	12

Source: Business Monitor SDA 25, Retailing

10.1). For instance, if sales in a particular period were £200,000 and average stock held was £25,000, the stockturn would be 8, i.e. 200,000/25,000.

The calculation may be done in cash terms or unit terms, i.e.

$$\frac{\text{Unit sales}}{\text{Average unit stock}}$$

20. Methods of averaging stock

Stock levels can vary enormously from one month to another so it may be very important to average out stock. There are three methods of getting to a figure that will, when divided into sales, give a reasonably accurate stockturn figure. These are as follows:

(a) The average opening stock and closing stock over a particular trading period, e.g. if opening stock was £17,000 and closing stock £23,000, average stock would be £20,000.

(b) The addition of opening, middle-period and closing stock divided by three.

(c) Stock at the first of each month divided by 13 if the year is broken down into four-weekly periods.

21. Turnover philosophy

The retail organization may adopt a high volume, low price merchandise philosophy which yields low margins but results in high stock turnover. The major multiple grocers work along these lines. Alternatively, a decision may be made to offer exclusive merchandise which would result in high prices, low volume and high margins but low stock turnover. The specialty delicatessen stores would be in this latter category.

22. Advantages of rapid stockturn

(a) It increases sales due to the rapid flow of new merchandise.

(b) It increases the return on the merchandise investment and allows the cash released to be invested if required, in further stock. Some food retailing companies sell a great deal of stock within a few days of its receipt; if they take 30 days' credit from suppliers this means that they are getting further stock investment 'free', i.e. it is being financed by their suppliers and this investment situation is known as 'nil capital'.

(c) It reduces expenses like:

(*i*) depreciation
(*ii*) interest on working capital
(*iii*) insurance
(*iv*) space

(d) It reduces the possibility of mark-downs.

(e) It reduces the incidence of returns out.

(f) It keeps stock clean and fresh and therefore more attractive to customers.

23. Limitations of rapid stockturn

(a) Possibility of lost sales due to out-of-stock position, particularly in fast-moving lines.

(b) Increased cost of purchases particularly in:

(*i*) carriage inwards
(*ii*) discounts receivable (which are effectively deducted from cost of sales) because possibly smaller average purchases are being made.

(c) Increase in certain expenses such as:

(*i*) correspondence
(*ii*) goods handling
(*iii*) clerical.

24. Methods of increasing stockturn

(a) The increase of sales without increasing average stock assortment proportionately.

(b) The decrease of stocks without interfering with sales.

(c) The increase of sales and at the same time reducing stock.

The need is to keep the inventory low in order to reduce stock-holding costs and increase the return on capital tied up in stock by:

(a) The reduction in the number of lines carried.

(b) A concentration on key stock items, e.g. the most popular.

(c) A reduction in size or colour assortments to meet only the most popular demands.

SALES FORECASTING

The sales forecast is an essential part of the planning process. Management requires an idea of the scale of the operation and predicted market developments in order to estimate the resources needed to capitalize on the opportunities presented and whether these resources will be available from profit.

25. The method

One method of producing a sales forecast is as follows:

(a) Construct a graph of sales for the corresponding periods over the last three to five years.

(b) Use a suitable statistical technique to establish a trend line.

(c) The basic assumption is that the trend will continue and a first approximation to the new seasons or annual total is arrived at by extrapolation.

(d) An estimate is made of the extent to which external factors, i.e. those over which the firm has no control, are likely to affect the initial forecast in step **(c)**. External factors include:

(*i*) government intervention, e.g. tax, hire-purchase changes
(*ii*) changes in economic conditions, e.g. structural changes in demand which bring about factory closures or lay-offs and 'dumping' of cheap foreign imports
(*iii*) changes in competition, e.g. opening, extension or closure of competitors' branches within various catchment areas or important competitive national sales promotions.

(e) Internal factors are those over which the business has control; they are now carefully considered and the forecast further modified in the light of a careful evaluation of their profitable effect. These include:

(*i*) changes in promotional support
(*ii*) changes in staffing or in selling methods

(*iii*) refitting or redecorating

(*iv*) any changes in the policy of the firm towards the expansion or restriction of sales not expressed in terms of (i) to (iii) above. It is clear that the effect of internal factors can be much more accurately estimated than that of the external factors in step **(d)**.

(f) The result is now a total figure for the store, possibly broken down by areas, reached from the best information available.

(g) Total the sales of each month over the comparative period, e.g. all April figures, all May and so on.

(h) Express monthly sales total **(g)** as a percentage of the grand total of all the three years or so studied. This will give the percentage of each year's sales for which each month is normally responsible. (It may be necessary to make some allowances for inflation over a three-year period.)

(i) Apply the monthly percentages thus calculated to the forecast for the total for the year to give the monthly estimates.

26. Sales adjustment

Sales estimates are treated as budgets and revised often at monthly or fortnightly intervals as the year and its component seasons progress. Any major revision will have important effects on the merchandise plan, affecting both the level of stock to be carried and the allocation of purchasing power.

Progress test 10

1. What is a product?

2. What is merchandising? What are the main aspects of the merchandising process?

3. Define 'depth' and 'breadth' in the merchandise mix and give examples of retailers operating each of these ranging policies.

4. What is the significance of the Pareto Rule in relation to ranging policy?

5. What are the advantages and disadvantages of offering own brands?

6. What is the significance of stockturn and how can it be increased?

7. How can sales be forecast? Is it necessary to adjust these throughout the year – why?

8. 'Goods well bought are goods well sold' is an old retailing adage. Compare and contrast the alternative merchandise ranging policies for retailers of Sports goods.

9. Explain the importance of width, depth and consistency of merchandise mix to merchandise strategy decisions.

11

BUYING

MERCHANDISE BUYING

Buying is the process of implementing the decisions dictated by the merchandise philosophy (*see* 10:**3**), There are five major areas to consider: who buys; what to buy; how much to buy; from whom to buy; and when to buy.

1. The importance of buying

The vital significance of good merchandise buying in the retail context cannot be overstated. Stock is one of the largest forms of investment made by the retailer. Good stock selection is important for it:

(a) ties up the optimum amount of capital

(b) reduces the amount of space taken up by stock

(c) provides an adequate choice for the customer

(d) enhances the image of the business and encourages repeat purchases

(e) increases the overall profitability of the business.

WHO BUYS?

2. One individual or specialists

The buyer may be responsible for the purchase of a comparatively small range of merchandise or for several complete departments, depending on the size and type of the retail organization. The advantage of having one individual responsible for buying for the entire store is that consistency within the merchandise mix will be maximized. However, buying for larger stores will usually require specialists in order to do the job properly. By using specialist buyers' greater knowledge and control of merchandise can be developed and maintained.

3. Attributes of the buyer

A successful buyer *should* be able to:

(a) Recognize customer needs, even though customers themselves are unaware of them

(b) Know thoroughly the merchandise he or she deals with, keeping a balanced stock assortment

(c) Be a good judge of quality

(d) Be a good judge of resaleability

(e) Be up to date in his or her knowledge so that he or she can pick up ideas for new and profitable lines quickly ('flair' is required particularly in textiles, toys and other fashion goods)

(f) Liaise effectively with suppliers, store management and other sections of the merchandising and marketing departments, e.g. advertising, sales promotion

(g) Plan effectively in numerate terms.

4. Types of buying organization

Because of the way they are structured to service their chosen markets, different types of *retail* organization have developed their own modes of buying.

(a) Department stores. In the department store the buying and selling functions are often merged. A buyer/manager will not only control the sales operation in his or her chosen department but will buy stock for it as well. However, in some department store groups the responsibilities of buying and selling are divided between a central buyer and departmental (sales) managers.

(b) Multiples. The multiple chain invariably buys centrally with only rarely the branch manager being able to select lines for the local market.

(c) Co-operatives. Buying can be done at as many as four levels in the retail co-ops. The CWS buys centrally some 60 per cent of merchandise sold in the retail stores, whilst the balance is made up by buying by the local society and buying through consortia. For example, in London the four large societies operate inter-group buying committees. Again, the local branch manager may also be allowed to buy for his or her own market.

5. Separating the buying and selling functions

Most large multiple groups have set up quite separate buying and selling organizations, but partly through historical accident some department store groups still rely on departmental buyer/managers who carry out both functions. The advantages and disadvantages of separating these two functions are as follows:

(a) Advantages

(*i*) The duties of buying and selling call for different qualities not always found in one manager.

(*ii*) A manager cannot effectively carry out both functions and delegation is not always the answer.

(*iii*) The buyer who is released from routine can travel further, study the market and sources of supply, visit trade fairs, etc.

(*iv*) Selling departments need no longer necessarily conform to arbitrary divisions of merchandise as purchased, but can develop and spread into related ranges. Range rationalization may be encouraged.

(*v*) Competent buyers are scarce and a buyer with no departmental duties can buy a wider range of merchandise to the benefit of store and customer.

(*vi*) Buyers can be centralized in buying offices where team work and liaison with the merchandise manager is helped.

(*vii*) Segregation of buyers eradicates the wasted time sometimes spent in protracted dealings with customers.

(b) Disadvantages

(*i*) It is difficult to ensure that the buyer will retain a really responsible attitude to the purchase of 'risk' merchandise.

(*ii*) Friction is likely to arise between the buyer and the sales manager, particularly where lines are unpopular or turnover declines.

(*iii*) To apportion responsibility, criticism or congratulation for results is difficult and may appear to be invidious.

(*iv*) The store may become too unwieldy in the proportion of managers to selling staff.

(*v*) Remoteness between buyer and sales staff can ensue, firsthand customer reactions being irretrievably lost.

(*vi*) Valuable local purchasing arrangements may be overlooked by central buyers.

6. Central buying

(a) Advantages

(*i*) Better terms may be gained as a result of the very large orders placed with suppliers.

(*ii*) The central buyer is a full-time specialist; he or she should therefore be able to place the best possible orders and obtain the best possible merchandise.

(*iii*) Because of increased buying efficiency there should be a greater proportion of fast-selling lines and stock should be turned over more quickly.

(*iv*) The central buyer is in continuous contact with the market and is in the best position to purchase new lines quickly.

(*v*) Merchandise can be transferred from one store, where sales for a particular line are disappointing, to another where demand is heavier.

(*vi*) Under centralized buying there are no travelling costs incurred by buyers from stores in going to visit suppliers.

(*vii*) Store selling can be organized by specialist department sales managers.

(b) Disadvantages

(*i*) There is some danger that local needs may be ignored, since merchandise is bought in bulk for the group or chain as a whole. Although local differences are small they do exist, for example in food and some fashion merchandise.

(*ii*) There are additional costs of warehousing and distribution as well as maintaining the central buying office.

(*iii*) Sales staff may be unenthusiastic about selling merchandise which they know is not quite what their particular customers need.

THE BUYING PLAN

7. Importance of the plan

Any buying plan must be firmly based on the company's plans for the ensuing period. Most buying plans are broken into monthly periods that accurately reflect seasonal changes and are easily comparable with similar periods in previous years. The plan must, however, be flexible enough to take into account the purchase of new lines and any unforeseen changes which may occur in the trading pattern. The major problems for the buyers are to know:

(a) What to buy
(b) How much to buy
(c) From whom to buy
(d) When to buy.

WHAT TO BUY

8. What to buy

For the buying of particular items the general guidelines are as follows:

(a) Past experience. With staple merchandise (non-fashion long-term sellers) the majority of sales will be made in the most successful lines of the recent past. With merchandise whose sales change markedly with shifts in consumer taste, e.g. fashion items, past experience is less useful. Buyers have to rely largely on their flair for knowing what customers will purchase. Buyers usually have to order in advance and, as fashions change very rapidly, they cannot always rely on fill-in orders, as by the time these are delivered the merchandise may be unfashionable. Too much stock and there is unsold merchandise at the end of the season, too little stock results in lost sales.

(b) Current information. A good deal of up-to-date information on customer demands can be gleaned from the normal accounting and control records of a retail business. The following methods are used:

(*i*) Sales bill duplicates

(*ii*) 'Tallies' of sales, particularly of new lines

(*iii*) Kimball (or other type) tag butts; these are tickets that are attached to goods (usually clothing) and give details of stock numbers, so that after swift processing a quick update of the stock position in a branch is possible

(*iv*) EPOS data – electronic data capture at the point of sale is now common and provides extremely detailed information on sales by product, brand, size, etc.

(*v*) 'Wants' slips (recorded customer requests for specific merchandise)

(*vi*) Customer complaints.

(c) **External sources** of merchandise information can be obtained from:

(*i*) Organized comparison-shopping of competitive stores (monitoring of in-store and window displays, plus their advertising)

(*ii*) Suppliers

(*iii*) Consumer research – retailers are becoming more and more involved in consumer surveys. These may be conducted at the store or in the home (*see* Chapter 5).

(*iv*) Trade fairs.

HOW MUCH TO BUY

9. How much to buy

There are two approaches to the quantitative aspect of buying which, as previously stated, should rely on the sales forecast.

(a) **The open-to-buy approach.** This determines in cash the amount of purchases to make for a particular selling period. An authorized order becomes a commitment, and this reduces the available purchasing power (the open-to-buy or OTB) for the period for which it is timed. Continuous monitoring of current OTB and future commitments ensures that warning is given of overbought positions. This type of stock budgeting is called 'top-down' and forms an integral part of a company's financial stock control.

There are various ways to increase open-to-buy and these are as follows:

(*i*) increase planned sales

(*ii*) increase planned mark-downs

(*iii*) reduce stock on hand by return or transfer

(*iv*) postpone outstanding orders to a later month

(*v*) cancel outstanding orders

(*vi*) increase planned closing stock.

Example

Assuming that the trading year ends on 31 January, the sales forecast for the ensuing six months is £1.6 million, the required stockturn is eight times per annum and the anticipated gross margin is 25 per cent of selling price, the open-to-buy figure would be as in Table 11.1.

Table 11.1 Open-to-buy method

	Feb £000	Mar £000	Apr £000	May £000	June £000	July £000	Total £000
Sales forecast (at selling prices)	160	200	330	350	280	280	1,600
Planned closing stocks (at selling price)	400	600	500	450	300	250	
	560	800	830	800	580	530	
Deduct planned opening stock (at selling prices)	300	400	600	500	450	300	
	260	400	230	300	130	230	
Deduct average margin 25%	65	100	57.5	75	32.5	57.5	
Open-to-buy (at cost price)	195 +	300 +	172.5 +	225 +	97.5 +	172.5 +	

An average stock of £400,000 at selling value is planned to ensure required stockturn rate of four in six months (4 × £400,000 = £1.6 million).

This table shows the total of estimated sales (£1.6 million) has been broken down into monthly targets so that the peak sales are planned for April and May and peak stocks are built up in March and April. The breakdown should be based on an examination of previous years' performances – the average contribution made by each month to the year's total. For example, total the February sales for the past five years and express as a percentage of the five year total. Then determine the contribution to be expected from February (in this case it is 10 per cent of the six months' forecast).

(b) The assortment planning approach. Here stock requirements are calculated on a *unit* rather than a *cash* basis. This system of calculating buying requirements is called 'bottom-up' because, unlike OTB, which deals with a blanket cash figure, assortment planning tries to build up the cash budget from the total value of all stock items budgeted for. Model stock plans can help assortment planning to some extent.

10. Model stock plans

This aspect of stock planning is particularly important in clothing and fashion stores where customers naturally buy most in the middle sizes in the popular colours and in the medium price ranges. By careful sales monitoring it is possible to calculate what percentage of sales each size, colour or price is responsible for. Model stocking is a quantitative method of planning to buy which provides general guidelines on the size and composition of stock but does not specify the exact nature of the merchandise.

11. Bulk-buying

Buying large amounts of stock has certain advantages for the larger retail store or chain able to afford it but it also produces problems.

(a) Advantages

(*i*) Less possibility of run-outs at times of unexpectedly heavy demand.

(*ii*) Minimum quantity discounts are possible, with higher discounts as the purchases become larger.

(*iii*) Clerical work per unit ordered is reduced (i.e. it costs the same in clerical terms to buy one unit as it does to buy 1,000 units).

(b) Disadvantages

(*i*) Higher sales and stockturn are required to keep 'in balance'.

(*ii*) Deterioration and pilferage may increase.

(*iii*) Valuable storage space is tied up.

(*iv*) Cash can be over-committed.

(*v*) Price markdowns tend to occur with stock which is out of date.

FROM WHOM TO BUY

12. Types of supplier

(a) Manufacturers and primary producers. These will normally tend to be limited in the range of goods they produce and to vary considerably in the nature and extent of distributive services which they provide.

(b) Wholesalers. These carry stock at their own risk in either wide (general) or more limited (specialist) assortments. This category would include voluntary group wholesalers such as Spar and cash and carry operators like Nurdin and Peacock.

(c) Importers. These are usually linked in the range of merchandise carried and the extent of the services provided. They may specialize by type of goods wherever produced or by the products of a particular country or area.

(d) Agents. These intermediaries do not carry stock at their own risk. They include food brokers who look after the marketing of a manufacturer's or importer's products through grocery, chemist and CTN outlets. Some agents do not handle the goods at all and others may carry sample ranges but do not hold stock at their own risk. The range of merchandise carried and the services provided depend largely on their principals.

(e) Other retailers. The three main ways in which retailers act as sources of supply are

(*i*) for 'specials'

(*ii*) for finished goods which themselves form part of a more complex product
(*iii*) for bankrupt, damaged or discontinued stock.

(f) Manufacturer-owned retail chains. The problems of supply are somewhat reduced for companies like Thornton's confectionery because substantial percentages of the product ranges are self-supplied.

(g) Government and semi-government sources. A very broad spectrum of products comes from this source, examples being BBC and government publications, railway antiquities, 'forces' surplus clothing, etc.

(h) The public. In merchandise fields such as antiques and second-hand items, the public remains an important source of supply.

In addition, sources of *ideas* for products can be obtained from exhibitions, trade journals, members of the public and so on.

13. Supplier selection

Existing suppliers may be retained because they have given particularly good service in the past, or because there is no identifiable competition. The factors taken into account when selecting a new supplier are:

(a) Prices – including extra trade discount for bulk purchases

(b) Terms, e.g. length of credit, size of cash discount

(c) Deliveries – fast and prompt delivery may be vital for retailers in high volume sales situations

(d) Service – general co-operation.

New suppliers may be found as a result of sales representatives calls or from the supplier catalogues that are mailed to retail buyers. However, a good buyer should be actively seeking suppliers who can do a better job than current suppliers.
   A list of suppliers should be available and kept fully up to date, showing lines supplied by each.

Continuous comparison should be made between suppliers under the headings:

(a) Price comparisons, including discounts

(b) Efficiency of delivery back-up

(c) Level of service

(d) Introduction of new lines.

This will aid the process of review of suppliers and lines, which should be a rolling process, so that strong suppliers may be rewarded with larger orders and weaker support discarded (unless sole sources of supply are involved).

WHEN TO BUY

Merchandise should be purchased so that there will be sufficient in stock to meet consumer demand, bearing in mind seasonal factors and the need to keep down inventory levels to acceptable levels.

14. Ordering

Frequency and size of orders are matters influenced to a great extent by the type of merchandise concerned, i.e. whether staple or fashion merchandise. Important aspects of ordering are as follows:

(a) **Price**. Although a buyer may be searching initially for the most competitive price available, any final price is likely to be affected by quantity discounts of various kinds.

(b) **Terms**. These largely involve discounts of two basic kinds as follows:

(*i*) Trade discounts are discounts allowed by suppliers from their catalogue price to trade customers only and may be quite substantial, perhaps 25 per cent. They provide a means whereby the retailer can cover costs and by which he or she can obtain a reasonable profit without too large an addition to suppliers' prices.

(*ii*) Payment for goods made promptly often ranks for a cash discount. Many retail firms require all orders to be placed at a standard 2½ per cent. Thirty to sixty days' credit is usual.

(c) **Deliveries**. It is important for a retail buyer to set and insist upon precise delivery dates. Where delivery is to be made in more than one consignment, the order should specify:

(*i*) the date on which the delivery is to commence
(*ii*) the date by which the delivery is to be complete
(*iii*) the proportions of the order that are to be delivered within stated intervals, e.g. 30 per cent in September, 40 per cent in October, 30 per cent in November, where necessary or desirable.

Other delivery instructions may include:

(*i*) method of shipment
(*ii*) address (for branch, etc. deliveries)
(*iii*) agreed variations from standard carriage-paid terms
(*iv*) method of charging or returning containers.

15. Progressing the order

Once the details of price, terms and delivery have been agreed the following factors are also important from the buyer's viewpoint:

(a) The order details should be written up as fully as possible immediately.

(b) If the order cannot be completely finalized on the spot it should be marked 'await confirmation', with the agreement of the supplier.

(c) It is good retail practice to require suppliers to acknowledge orders placed with them, especially those for forward delivery.

(d) Some form of follow-up should succeed this to see that delivery promises are being kept.

16. Buying control

The order, once authorized, is a commitment to buy. Commitments are either:

(a) Current, i.e. for delivery during the current period; or

(b) Future, i.e. for delivery in a subsequent period.

When a commitment is delivered and changed into stock it ceases to be a commitment and becomes a purchase. Open-to-buy means the balance of stock between that already committed to or purchased and the budget for purchases for the period. Open-to-buy for the current period is therefore: planned purchases for the period, minus deliveries to date in the period, minus current commitments. For any future period it is: planned purchases for that period, minus future commitments for that period.

17. Buying adjustments

The adjusting of buying operations to the plan becomes automatic with the OTB system. As long as the OTB for any period is positive, the buyer may place orders for delivery in that period. When the purchase plan is fulfilled the OTB automatically cuts off. If deliveries are delayed a check in the system should make allowances for the extra time that this will take.

18. The catalogue

Many retail firms have constructed a catalogue listing all the lines they purchase and from whom they are supplied. The catalogue can be used in the following ways:

(a) as an order form (for head office or for the individual branch)

(b) as a stocktaking list

(c) for range control.

Progress test 11

1. Why is the buying function important?

2. What attributes does a successful buyer need?

3. What are the advantages and disadvantages of separating the buying and selling functions?

4. What are the advantages and disadvantages of central buying?

5. How does the buyer decide (a) what to buy, and (b) how much to buy?

6. Describe the open-to-buy method.

7. How does the buyer decide (a) from whom to buy, and (b) when to buy?

8. According to some retail analysts, it is essential for retailers to develop uniqueness in order to be successful in the 1990s. Many retailers have already established policies to achieve this aim. For example chain store boutiques and department stores rely on nationally promoted products to draw customers into their stores. Calvin Klein, Pierre Cardin, Yves Saint Laurent, and many other UK and European designer products are sold at these stores. When designer labels were first introduced, they were found on distinctive products that offered the stores that carried them a competitive edge. Recently, however this edge has begun to evaporate because of the proliferation of outlets that sell designer labels at prices significantly lower than those of the larger stores.

   In the face of increased competition, how large a part should designer labels play in the merchandise mix of fashion image speciality chains and department stores? (Assume the role of consultant.)

12

STOCK MANAGEMENT

1. Introduction

The purpose of a stock management system is to provide information on the amount of merchandise in stock and its condition. EPOS systems have significantly improved the retailer's ability to operate tighter and more rational stock control.

STOCK CONTROL

2. Aims

The importance of controlling merchandise has already been made clear. It involves the maintenance of a correct balance between the range carried and the sales to which it gives rise. The aim is to obtain as big a turnover as possible with the most economic inventory level. There is a clear indication that the rate of stockturn has a decisive effect on the net profitability of a retail business. If correct stock levels are not kept the problems which arise are as follows:

(a) Too little stock. The merchandise will not generate the full potential sales volume. The gross margin (and therefore the net profit) of the business will be restricted in the short run and in the long run the customer's perception of the business will change for the worse.

(b) Too much stock. Interest chargeable on the stock investment (which is part of the business's working capital) will reduce gross and thus net margins. In the longer term further reductions in gross margin may occur due to mark-downs.

The three main systems of controlling stock are unit control, financial control and combination control.

3. Unit stock control

This is a method of controlling stocks by physical units of merchandise rather than by cash investment. The merchandise characteristics of the stock are compared with those of the products bought by the public in the period under review. The advantage this method has over others is that it can be used to monitor changes in the characteristics of merchandise being sold and is usefully allied to range creation (model stock-building). The stock is physically counted and often merchandise sub-groups are stock-taken on a rotated basis. This is not a full stock control system because:

(a) It cannot control the profitability of the inventory held

(b) It therefore requires back-up by financial systems of control

(c) It loses some of its usefulness if not screened by some system of market monitoring.

4. Financial stock control

As its title suggests, such a system uses cash limits for monitoring stock levels and may be used as an alternative or a back-up to a unit stock control system. This value approach works by comparing the total value of the stock from time to time with the value of the sales it has produced. It is still a common form of stock control particularly amongst small retailers and has two advantages, as follows:

(a) It is cheap to operate since the figures it uses are produced by the normal accounting operations of the business.

(b) Because it deals in money figures it can be used to regulate the gross margin attained or to be aimed at.

5. Combination control

As the name implies, this method is a combination of unit and financial control, and although it is more complex, most retailers would benefit from controlling both the financial investment in stock and the units in inventory.

Items that generate high profits or items that customers expect to be in stock should be controlled by the combination method because stock-outs will substantially reduce profits. Equally, very expensive items overstocked could create financial problems.

6. Periodic and perpetual inventory control

Inventory control may be carried out periodically (*see* **7** below) or on a continuous basis (*see* **14** below).

7. Periodic inventory

One method of keeping track of inventory is to count the stock on hand once, twice or more times per year on a specific date. It is a costly and time-consuming procedure and, although suitable for accounting purposes, periodic inventory control is rarely sufficient for decision-making purposes.

8. Methods

The three main ways by which stock may be observed and recorded are:

(1) Stocktaking

(2) Stock check

(3) Stock calculation.

Although all three methods lay different emphasis on particular aspects of observation and recording, the objective is the same: the maintenance of a correct balance between stock levels and sales. Too much cash unnecessarily tied up in stock can severely reduce the profitability of a business.

9. Stocktaking

This process involves the counting and valuing of every item of stock at a given time. It is therefore the most comprehensive and, if properly carried out, the most accurate of the three methods mentioned above. Physical stocktaking is initially done for strictly merchandise control reasons and consists of:

(a) The breakdown of stock into component parts of the range (i.e. lines and merchandise sub-groups relating to size, style, colour, price line, etc.) to assess its composition

(b) Stock rating by age to find how long products have been in stock in order to depreciate them

(c) Current valuation – the taking of the cost or market value whichever is the lower – irrespective of the original cost.

Other reasons for stocktaking include:

(a) Valuing the stock asset for final accounts purposes, including depreciation and tax

(b) Finding true stockturn rates

(c) Isolating fast and slow-selling lines

(d) Finding true stock losses

(e) Finding the true gross margin

(f) Ascertaining agreed figures for insurance purposes.

Physical stocktaking by staff has the additional benefit of familiarizing staff with the merchandise.

10. Preparation for stocktaking

By preparing for a stocktake the interference with customer service can be minimized to a great extent by:

119

(a) Re-sorting the stock by sub-categories of merchandise to aid counting

(b) Checking goods for missing tickets or other information sources

(c) Clearing up all outstanding queries from suppliers, including debits

(d) Locating and identifying all goods allocated to the department that are, for whatever reason, not physically present

(e) Making appropriate arrangements for dealing with customers' own goods

(f) Fixing cut-off dates for invoices, transfers, price changes, etc. that affect the value of stock

(g) Briefing staff

(h) Requisitioning supplies and equipment

(i) Pre-counting case lots and similar quantities which are then 'frozen' until after the take

(j) Preparing a layout plan showing how the stocktake is to be operated.

11. Main methods of stocktaking

(a) Cost-price method. For goods that have a short shelf-life and consequently low stocks, like produce, items are counted at buying (cost) price. This method is a very accurate trend recorder. The disadvantages of this method are:

(*i*) It may involve searching through many old invoices which can be time consuming
(*ii*) Because the gross margin cannot be calculated in this way there is no way of estimating unknown stock losses, e.g. through pilferage.

(b) Selling-price method. Current retail selling prices are used here and this method is popular in trades where large stock variety makes control difficult, e.g. DIY. The advantages of this method are:

(*i*) It points out both high and low profit lines
(*ii*) It is a good indicator of unrecorded stock losses because *known* stock losses, e.g. breakages, can be built in; the largest cause of hidden stock loss is, of course, pilferage
(*iii*) It allows an interim gross profit percentage to be estimated without taking physical stock.

The main disadvantage is that, because individual invoices are not consulted, the margin used is an *average*.

(c) Cost and selling methods. By using the modifying factors described previously to obtain 'cost or market value', we find the difference between current selling prices and the true cost value of the stock to the company, thus giving a book figure for current stock at selling prices. Therefore the stock can be stated both at current selling and true cost values. The advantages of the cost and selling method are:

(*i*) Accuracy – the only limitation on the accuracy of the book stock figures is the amount of the shortage. This leads to (*ii*) below

(*ii*) Shortage control – any shortage found after an accurate calculation must be due to shrinkage (here it has advantages over the estimated gross margin system)

(*iii*) Pricing control – all initial prices and subsequent changes must be recorded, yielding valuable data for pricing and mark down control

(*iv*) Margin control – initial margins are calculable, therefore controllable.

12. Stock check

This is a simplified or less comprehensive form of stocktaking that has as its object an assessment of the selling qualities of the stock rather than its true value. It is frequently confined to quantities, price lines and the qualities of the assortment, e.g. colour, size, style, etc.

13. Stock calculation

This method can give a very close approximation to the value of stock carried at any given time by a consideration of the stock actually found at the last stocktaking and the additions thereto and deductions therefrom which have subsequently been made (*see* cost and selling method in **11(c)** above).

14. Perpetual inventory

The perpetual inventory system aims to provide information on a continuous basis by monitoring merchandise movements into the store (deliveries) and out of the store (sales).

The perpetual method provides up-to-date information which can be used both for accounting and managerial purposes. The main disadvantage is the cost of operating such a system due to its complexity.

Although it is possible to operate such a system by hand using documents it is the introduction of computerization, particularly EPOS, which has really made the method feasible (*see* Table 12.1).

15. By hand

The tag system has been used for some time mainly by clothing retailers whereby a tag attached to the garment contains information of product, style, size, colour, etc. This information is read from the tag which is removed when the item is sold, the computer then producing the appropriate inventory reports.

16. Computers

Perpetual inventory is one of the advantages of introducing electronic point-of-sale (EPOS) equipment. One of the best methods currently in use for data capture at point of sale is the use of optical scanning to read bar codes. Very detailed

Table 12.1 Stock movement printout

Movement code	Movement	Quantity
00	Opening stock	1,572
01	Purchases	370
02	Purchases returns	−55
03	Part exchange purchases	37
04	Transfers in	15
	Total in	367
10	Sales	412
11	Sales returns	−43
12	Transfers out	27
13	Free replacements	56
14	Stock written off	13
	Total out	465
00	Closing stock	1,474

information on the item can thus be held by the computer to produce many different reports including the amount of inventory for that item at any time, the disclosure of slow-moving lines and those items which fall below a pre-set re-order level. The store computer can also be programmed to phone through orders every night to a central warehouse computer for delivery the following day.

17. Stock valuation

Where possible financial stock control should be linked to unit control so that both commercial and financial management enjoy the benefits. On introducing computerized stock control the opportunity should be taken to value stocks at cost rather than retail price. The latter is the traditional method of bookkeeping in retail companies, but where variable gross margins apply (either as a result of different mark-ups or selective price cutting) stock valuation at purchase cost price is the only way of determining the true margin earned on each item sold. As each new delivery of a stock item is made its new value at cost is added to the value of existing stock and a *new average* cost price is struck. This is known as weighted average cost value of stock, because the cost price used to value stock is being successively weighted by the size and purchase price of each new delivery. This method is probably the best type of stock valuation because it shows the up-to-date earned margin on sales.

Two other stock valuation methods are commonly used. These are LIFO and FIFO.

18. LIFO

With LIFO (last in, first out) the cost of the last merchandise bought is used to calculate the cost of goods sold. However, in periods of high inflation where prices are rising rapidly this method would result in calculated profits lower than those actually achieved.

19. FIFO

With FIFO (first in, first out) the cost of the first merchandise bought is used to calculate the cost of goods sold. This system tends to lead to calculated profits higher than actually achieved which of course could be disastrous if the discrepancy was large.

STOCK SHORTAGES

When the total value of stock found at physical stocktaking is less than the book value (calculated for the same date expressed on the same basis) there is a stock shortage, i.e. an excess of book stock over physical stock. Stock shortages are of two kinds – real (physical) or apparent (clerical).

20. Physical shortages

Real shortages occur when goods are lost to the business in one of a number of ways:

(a) **Theft**. This may take the form of shoplifting (thieving by the public), pilfering (thieving by the staff) or 'sweet hearting' (thieving by the collusion of a member of staff and a member of the public; for example, when goods are sold by staff to their friends at below the true retail price).

(b) **Loss**. When stock is loaned or transferred it sometimes 'disappears'. Although this can often be attributed to negligence rather than dishonesty, the result is the same.

(c) **Breakage or spoilage**. Glass and china may be accidentally broken, textiles may be ruined by children's sweets and so on. If the damage is detected it is possible to make an adjustment, possibly through obtaining a supplier's credit.

(d) **Physical shrinkage**. Some merchandise normally sold by volume, length or weight tends to lose some fraction of these properties, sometimes under good storage conditions if kept too long. For instance, bacon loses moisture and thus weight (additionally, during the cutting and preparation of provisions, small pieces are often lost), perfume evaporates and textiles may shrink.

(e) **Over-issue**. Goods which have to be weighed or measured and small articles which have to be counted at the point of sale are subject to this form of shortage through carelessness or inexpertise. The growth of pre-packs has reduced this shortage factor somewhat.

(f) **Under-supply**. When, through faulty checking at goods reception, a smaller quantity of goods is accepted than is actually invoiced and paid for, a shortage is created.

Unexpected physical shortages are popularly known as either 'shrinkage' or 'leakage'.

21. Clerical shortages

Apparent shortages arise from any one, or a combination, of the following causes:

(a) Error in the count or valuation at physical stocktaking

(b) Error in the extension or totalling of stock sheets

(c) Error in the elements entering into the book-stock calculation, e.g. failure to credit sales or add back in customer returns

(d) Error in the book-stock calculation itself.

22. Minimizing shrinkage

Shrinkage, as a percentage of sales, is typically 1 to 3 per cent. This is a huge loss – often approaching the level of net profit on sales. Internal losses can be minimized by better recruitment procedures, i.e. ensuring that staff are trustworthy, whilst shoplifting is minimized by prosecution of all shoplifters and tight surveillance and security systems.

MERCHANDISE RECEIPT AND RETURN

23. Centralized and decentralized receiving

Multiple retailers must decide whether they require suppliers to deliver goods to their branches (direct delivery) or to a central warehouse operated by the retail organization. This decision will depend on many factors but there is a strong trend toward centralized receiving with the retailer carrying out much more of the delivery to branches formerly carried out by suppliers or third-party carriers.

24. Direct delivery

Some multiple chains still have suppliers' invoices routed to a central accounts section at head office and have goods delivered direct to their branches from manufacturers. Copies of buyers' orders are sent to each branch, giving allocation and the delivery data. The branch keeps these outstanding orders on file and checks the detailed description on receipt. The endorsed order is sent to the head office accounts department. The sum of all such copy orders confirming receipt should agree with total invoice (debited at selling price). Of course, many independent shops still receive direct deliveries from confectionery and other food firms, but this is at the instigation of the supplier rather than (as in the multiple's case) of the retailer.

25. The advantages and disadvantages of direct delivery

(a) Advantages

(*i*) Elimination of central warehouse costs.
(*ii*) Saving valuable time in unpacking, marking, repacking and transport of goods to branches.
(*iii*) Lessens the risk of deterioration of goods by double-packing.

(b) Disadvantages

(*i*) The retailer could lose substantial quantity discounts for bulk purchase and delivery to a single warehouse address.
(*ii*) A less balanced and less up-to-date allocation to branches is possible if manufacturers deliver direct.
(*iii*) Good quality control is more difficult outside the central warehouse system.
(*iv*) Each branch must have its own price marking machines, with the extra cost that entails.
(*v*) Returnable cartons and other empties may remain in branches for too long.
(*vi*) The need for confirmation of deliveries in different parts of the country can slow up invoice processing.
(*vii*) A central warehouse can keep back a certain proportion of a delivery to answer subsequent calls from branches to replenish depleted stocks.

26. Incoming merchandise

The receiving process is concerned with record keeping, inspection, marking and storage. The important points concerning the receiving section organization are as follows:

(a) Admittance only of properly authorized consignments.

(b) Speedy notification of the arrival of goods.

(c) Preliminary inspection of containers and outers for apparent signs of damage or pilferage (at this stage an internal check is impossible and carriers' notes should be marked 'damaged' or 'unexamined').

(d) Facilities for the collating of consignment documents and invoices with copy orders so that correct payment can be made.

(e) Facilities for the inspection of the merchandise itself, possibly by the buyer.

(f) Protection of the merchandise from loss or damage whilst it is under reception control.

(g) Return of chargeable containers.

(h) Prompt forwarding or handling of claims for loss or damage in transit.

(i) In appropriate cases, transport to the marking area, stockrooms or the selling area.

(j) Accuracy and speed at all times (goods in the pipeline cannot earn money).

The above list is particularly applicable to large stores that often have a receiving department. In a multiple's branch, although the bulk of this procedure might be followed, reception is made in the stock room itself.

27. Receiving goods

The basic principles behind organization for the receipt of goods are the same for every establishment and are:

(a) to ensure that the goods conform to the buyer's order

(b) to ensure that the goods conform with the charge made for them (copy order and invoice must be compared at the same stage)

(c) to expedite the speedy transmission of goods to the point of sale.

28. Inspection

Packages should be opened quickly after receipt for the following reasons:

(a) If the goods are in any way short or damaged, the notification of a claim on the carriers must be made within three days followed by a fully detailed claim within ten days of receipt.

(b) The goods may be perishable or fragile.

(c) In order to maintain a steady flow through the marking process and to avoid bottlenecks.

(d) To expedite passing the invoice for prompt payment and full discount.

(e) Selling departments are probably awaiting the goods.

29. Stock checking

There are three methods of checking merchandise. These are:

(a) **Direct check.** Comparison of contents with the delivery note.

(b) **Spot check.** Random sampling.

(c) **Blind check.** Listing and checking without the benefit of a consignment note.

30. Rejection of incoming merchandise

The legal position with regard to the acceptance or rejection of merchandise is given in the Sale of Goods Act. In retailing terms, legitimate grounds for rejecting incoming merchandise and recovering damages if a loss has been suffered are as follows:

(a) Where goods have been bought by sample, failure to come up to the sample.

(b) Where goods have been produced to a written specification, failure to meet that specification.

(c) Where goods have been bought as complying with a minimum specification, e.g. a British Standard, failure to comply with that specification.

(d) Where general standards exist, the supplying of imperfect or sub-standard goods.

(e) When the price, style, colour or any other merchandising characteristic is 'not as ordered', provided that the requirements have been clearly stated.

(f) When there is the wrong quantity or the goods are incomplete (as in the case of goods bought in sets).

(g) If there is a late delivery, provided that a definite delivery date has been specified and agreed to by the supplier.

MARKING

31. Object and methods

The object of marking is to record merchandise information on the article itself or on its immediate container. The information may be for the use of:

(a) Staff (e.g. when stock control information is needed)

(b) The customer (e.g. when the price is marked on the items displayed).

The type of merchandise, the information to be recorded and the method of presentation will all determine the method and media of marking. Standard methods include:

(a) Swing tickets

(b) Pin and clip-on tickets

(c) Gum tabs (often automatically stuck on)

(d) Pressure and heat-adhesive labels

(e) Direct marking media, e.g. rubber stamps, fibre-tip markers.

Marking can be done centrally or in the branch.

32. Centralized marking

Centralized marking, as done by some manufacturers for clients or in central food preparation plants, has the following advantages and disadvantages:

(a) Advantages

(*i*) There is increased efficiency from specialist workers.

127

(*ii*) Opportunities for use of mechanization (speed, accuracy) are available.

(*iii*) Close control over operation is made possible.

(b) Disadvantages

(*i*) Problems occur with matching the peaks and troughs of receiving activities.

(*ii*) A certain inflexibility creeps in.

33. Decentralized marketing

The advantages and disadvantages of decentralized marking are as follows:

(a) Advantages

(*i*) Goods are got quickly to the point of sale.

(*ii*) Processing can be undertaken piecemeal in cases of urgent demand.

(*iii*) Idle staff are utilized during slack periods.

(b) Disadvantages

(*i*) Legibility may be poor without mechanical aids.

(*ii*) Unauthorized or unreported price changes are possible.

Once again the widespread use of EPOS systems has led to a decline in individual item price marking with the consequent saving of time and costs.

STORAGE

34. Requirements

The need for stockroom space varies from one retail trade to another and between various methods of retailing. Normally goods cannot all be sold as soon as they are received or be kept on display from the time they come in until the time they are sold. The need for this kind of space would be determined by:

(a) Seasonal peaks in sales, e.g. Christmas

(b) Frequency of deliveries

(c) Receiving and checking areas

(d) Goods awaiting customer collection or return to suppliers.

35. Design

Stockrooms should be as conveniently located as possible to selling areas but should not take up valuable selling space. The following aspects should be taken into consideration:

(a) Location. Whether this is behind, above or below the sales area depends on the type of building and the type of retail organization concerned. The larger the store, the more important the location.

(b) **Size**. The dimensions should be determined by the rate of the stockturn, the sales level and the bulkiness of the goods merchandized.

(c) **Space ratios**. The ratio of stock space to selling space depends on the type of trade and the method of retailing, and will vary from below 1:10 to 50:50. The introduction of new systems such as Just In Time (JIT) is reducing this yet further.

36. Layout

A stockroom should be used as efficiently and as infrequently as possible. The important factors in layout are:

(a) **Use of space**. Wall areas should be used to the maximum, with free-standing racks allowing sufficient aisle width for trolleys and bulky items. Full use of floor-to-ceiling height should be attempted.

(b) **Accessibility**. All stock should be as accessible as possible and the faster-selling items should be nearest to the sales area.

(c) **Grouping**. Lines should be stacked so that they follow the same pattern and layout as the store. This will naturally involve grouping allied products together (the only exception may be the really bulky or fast-selling lines).

(d) **Space allocation**. Enough space should be allowed, and kept, for the usual stock level of each line.

(e) **Identification**. As far as possible, lines should be kept in outer packs or cases, each properly marked with the contents.

(f) **Rotation**. Old stock should be moved into the sales area before new stock. This reduces deterioration and good stock-keeping can quickly identify the causes and take action.

(g) **Reception**. An adequate space for handling, checking and unpacking the goods as they are delivered is required so that the new goods are kept apart from the old stock until the reception procedure is completed.

(h) **Security**. All lines should be placed in visible positions if possible and lighting should be adequate. For high value items, like tobacco and small electrical appliances, some form of cage or lockfast store may be necessary.

(i) **Stocktaking**. Many of the points outlined above will aid the counting of lines during stocktaking.

Progress test 12

1. What is the primary aim of a stock control system?

2. What are the three main ways of controlling stock?

3. Describe the three ways of observing and recording stock, (a) stocktaking, (b) stock check, and (c) stock calculation.

4. What are the advantages and disadvantages of the perpetual inventory system?

5. What are the main reasons for stock shortages and what procedures can be used for dealing with them?

6. Describe the advantages and disadvantages of direct delivery.

7. What are the advantages and disadvantages of centralized and decentralized price marking?

8. What are the main requirements for the design and layout of a stockroom?

9. The price of EPOS equipment has fallen sharply recently. Many small retailers are now beginning to think about the possibilities of introducing it to aid with stock management. How would the use of EPOS equipment aid the small retailers' decision making? Are there disadvantages other than the cost?

13

PRICING

1. Introduction

Price is for some retailers the most important element of the retail mix. For others, such as convenience stores, the main customer benefit is not the low prices but the convenience both in terms of location and hours of trading. Price has traditionally been determined by the cost of goods and then adding a bit to cover profit. This however is no longer a reasonable approach in today's highly competitive market. Pricing terminology is loose; below are definitions of various terms.

TERMINOLOGY

2. Cost of goods sold

The cost of goods sold is the amount which the retailer has paid the suppliers for goods actually resold. It is by far the largest expense incurred by a retailer who makes a profit by adding on the margin from which all expenses may be paid and the net profit left must be large enough to service and replace the capital and thus keep him or her in business. Cost of goods sold includes:

(a) The invoice cost of all the goods which have moved out of stock in the period whether by sale, transfer or such shrinkage as theft, loss or breakage. This cost figure includes trade or quantity discount but not normally settlement discount.

(b) Value added tax, which is passed on at each stage of the transaction to the final consumer.

(c) Certain expenses involved in bringing the goods to the point of sale or into saleable condition. These may include:

(*i*) carriage inwards
(*ii*) buyers' travelling expenses directly connected with purchasing the goods
(*iii*) net alteration and workroom costs.

(d) Depreciation on goods remaining in stock at the end of the period.

(e) Transfers from other departments or branches.

The cost of goods-sold formula is therefore as follows:

Opening stock (at cost or market value whichever is the lower)
Add purchases and additions (as detailed above)
Less closing stock (valued on the same basis as opening stock).

3. Gross margin

The difference between net sales and the cost of goods sold. (Also referred to sometimes as gross profit.)

4. Percentage gross margin

The gross margin expressed as a percentage of net sales.

5. Mark-up

The amount added to the cost of goods to give the required retail selling price.

6. Percentage mark-up

The mark-up expressed as a percentage of cost.

7. Net profit

Net sales less net cost of goods sold less operating expenses.

8. Net sales

Gross sales less returns and allowances

9. Mark-down

A reduction on the normal retail selling price. For example, 100 slow-moving items normally selling at £10 each are reduced to £7.50 in order to sell them quickly. The mark-down is £250 for the lot.

10. Margin levels

Gross margins tend to be high on comparison goods like furniture which have a low stockturn, in order to cover stocking costs. Conversely, lower margins are charged on convenience and faster turning products.

FACTORS INFLUENCING PRICING DECISIONS

As suggested earlier, the cost of goods is only one factor influencing the pricing decision; others are discussed below.

11. Target markets

The pricing decision should very closely heed the requirements of the target market. If that need is for the best possible price 'deal' then low prices would be offered. If exclusivity, service and status were required, higher prices would be in order. For example, some exclusive fashion retailers refuse to mark down slow-moving lines for fear of compromising their exclusive image. Instead they might sell their merchandise on to another retailer.

12. Competition

Analysis of the competitions' pricing strategy will determine what pricing strategy a retailer may adopt in order to compete effectively.

13. Company objectives

The pricing decision must be consistent with the overall company objectives. For example, if the company wishes to pursue aggressive market share growth then lower prices may be required (penetration pricing); if on the other hand early cash recovery of investment is required this objective may dictate higher pricing (skimming).

14. The role of price

The role of price in the retailing mix should also be determined. If the price is perceived as a key element in the consumer's purchase decision, then price will be used to establish a differentiating role, e.g. Argos. If on the other hand price is not seen as so important, other elements of the mix may be emphasized, e.g. convenience stores.

15. Other factors

Intermediaries may well influence the pricing decision. Financial institutions may alter rates of interest, suppliers may put up their prices, trade unions may demand higher wages or the government may change the legal framework.

SETTING PRICES

16. Cost-orientated pricing

The most basic method of setting the retail selling price is to add a standard mark-up to the cost of buying in. The problem with this approach is that it takes no account of competitor prices or demand for the product, both of which could be a crucial determinant of whether a line sells or not.

17. Demand-orientated pricing

There are several ways in which retailers may set prices according to the anticipated demand for products or services:

(a) By customer. Price discrimination is determined by the retailer's assessment of what an individual customer might be willing to pay. Typically, the price of a secondhand car can be negotiated and the eventual selling price will depend to some extent on the negotiating skill of the customer.

(b) Version. The price of an item in a line of products will be determined by the demand for that particular model. For example, the mark-up on a small portable colour TV will be considerably less than that on the top of the range large-screen TV.

(c) Place. The retailer needs to serve the needs of his or her local market place. Even the large multiples who operate to a national pricelist will make allowance for local factors such as strong local price competition or historical pricing tradition.

(d) Time. When a product or service is purchased may determine its price. The typical example is hotel accommodation which is more expensive during peak periods.

18. Competition-orientated pricing

Retailers price according to the price charged by the competition. Most stores price at or near competitor prices especially in a homogeneous market. For example, there is a going rate for petrol and thus most retailers of petrol will charge very similar prices. In other areas, particularly where there is considerable product differentiation, the retailer has much greater scope for emphasizing other elements of the retail mix and thus price above the competition. Stores with high volume, low overheads or both are able to price below competition.

19. The multi-stage approach

The recommended method for setting retail prices is to take into account cost, demand and competition in a multi-stage approach as follows:

(a) Select the target market.

(b) Determine the floor price. This would usually be the cost of goods but bearing in mind the promotional value of loss leaders or clearance lines.

(c) Determine the ceiling price. The ceiling price is determined as the price charged for the same item by direct competitors. As stated previously, this price can be increased in order to promote an exclusive image or where additional customer services are offered. However, this ceiling price provides a reasonable upper limit unless the retailer has a retail mix strategy which allows him or her to transcend it.

(d) Mark-up. Having identified a range of possible prices it is now necessary to apply a mark-up to cost of goods which will be consistent with the profit objectives. Thus many retailers have a target mark-up to be achieved within a department or section but which allows some variation of mark-up on individual items.

(e) Adjust and select specific price. Many retailers end the pricing process with the mark-up stage, but it may be necessary to adjust this price – to fine tune to be consistent with store image or policy or to adjust for consumer preference. For example, in determining the specific price the retailer should operate a consistent policy with regard to price lining, odd/even pricing, multiple unit pricing, complementary goods and fixed versus flexible pricing.

PRICING TACTICS

20. Price lining

Price lining is the setting up of a reduced number of distinct selling prices within a line of merchandise, goods being marked at these price points and at no others. The practice is particularly relevant in variety store operations. With many types of merchandise, customers tend to group themselves into fairly narrow buying zones. The lower the unit price and the greater the frequency of purchase, the narrower and more sharply defined will these zones be. Normally one, two or three prices can be incorporated within the zone limits, depending on their breadth. For example, a retailer may decide that ties will be priced at £5.99, £9.99 and £15 even though there are 30 ties in the range and each one has a different buying-in price.

21. The basic price zones

(a) The promotion zone. Promotional merchandise is priced within this low price zone which may be responsible for generating 15–45 percent of the total sales volume.

(b) The volume zone. This mid-price zone is aimed at the typical customer and will produce at least 50 percent of the sales volume.

(c) The prestige zone. Even very price-oriented retailers will carry a few of these higher-priced lines which will be responsible for generating 5–15 percent of the total sales volume of its business.

22. The advantages of price lining

These are as follows:

(a) Sales volume

(*i*) This can be increased by the provision of larger choice at each price point.

(*ii*) More effective block displays and advertising through line concentration.

(*iii*) Less confusion by customers on prices.

(b) Gross margin

(*i*) Increased sales from smaller stocks mean a higher stockturn rate and fewer mark-downs.

(*ii*) More possibilities of bulk-buying with better discounts.

(*iii*) Possible reduction in number of suppliers reducing direct buying expenses.

(c) Buying

(*i*) Starting at the selling price level, price lining trains buyers to 'buy backwards'.

(*ii*) Reduction in numbers of suppliers allows closer relationships to develop with the remainder.

(d) Pricing

(*i*) Restriction of choice between prices makes it easier to determine the optimum selling price for a line.

(*ii*) Price co-ordination between related lines and between associated departments is simplified.

(e) **Control**. With fewer lines to watch the buyer should find it easier to keep stocks balanced to sales on a unit basis.

(f) Expenses

(*i*) In so far as cost-to-sell is a function of time, it will be reduced by quicker selling.

(*ii*) Marking expenses may be reduced.

23. Odd/even pricing

The use of odd prices like £2.99 or £499.95 is said to give the impression of lower prices. Certainly it is widely used in retailing and, despite inconclusive research evidence, it probably works. The opposite, even pricing, e.g. £470, is designed to give the impression that price is not the most important factor when considering the purchase decision; for this particular item prestige would be tarnished by the use of odd pricing methods.

24. Multiple unit pricing

Providing a discount for purchase of two or more units can encourage customers to buy more than they normally would. The technique is therefore useful in helping increase stockturn and in keeping out the competition for longer (whilst the customer has stocks).

25. Complemetary goods

The sale of one item may be related to the demand for another. Thus the sales of normally-priced items may be boosted by a special promotion or price deal on another. For example, the sale of shoes and handbags is related, and shirts and ties are considered complementary goods. Grocers may sell bread at a loss (as a loss leader) to stimulate sales of other related grocery products.

26. Fixed/flexible pricing

Most retailers operate a fixed-price policy when the price marked on an item is the only price acceptable to the retailer. However, in certain sectors it is traditional to operate a flexible pricing policy and for negotiation to take place to determine the final price. Flexible negotiation is typified in the retailing of cars, and most consumers would expect to haggle over 'big ticket' items such as furniture or possibly large electrical goods.

PRICE ADJUSTMENTS

27. Introduction

Although price lining allows some flexibility, in times of rapidly changing prices upward or downward adjustment may be necessary. If the share of sales in the volume zone falls below 50 per cent there is a clear indication that adjustment is required either up into the prestige or down into the promotion zone.

28. Mark-downs

Mark-downs are reductions in price to reflect current values. They help to:

(a) Maintain 'clean stock' and get rid of out-of-date merchandise

(b) Create open-to-buy for fresh flow of merchandise

(c) Foster customer goodwill.

29. Use of mark-downs

Mark-downs are made for various reasons, such as:

(a) Encourage customers to respond more satisfactorily to a line (these are called 'correctional' mark-downs)

(b) Sell off shopworn goods, remnants and broken lots or out-of-date, end-of-season merchandise ('operational' mark-downs)

(c) Increase sales by giving customers the incentive of lower prices ('promotional' mark-downs)

(d) Correct errors in buying, in pricing or in selling (another example of the 'correctional' mark-down).

30. Mark-downs due to buying errors

Various types of errors in buying can be made and often they have to be corrected by price reductions, such as:

(a) Overbuying due to:

(*i*) lack of planning for demand
(*ii*) failure to buy experimentally in small quantities first
(*iii*) buying more than the current stock requirement

(b) Wrong buying, e.g. of styles, colours, sizes, fabrics. Other wrong buys can be of novelty goods or merely through poor recording or analysis of records

(c) Failure to anticipate reductions in wholesale prices

(d) Poor timing, e.g. buying too early or too late or because goods are received too late for sale

(e) Failure to take advice

(f) Individualistic or 'pet' buying

(g) Failure to examine incoming merchandise for defects.

31. Mark-downs due to pricing errors

Namely:

(a) When the initial price has been set too high

(b) When the initial price has been set too low, causing suspicion in customer's minds

(c) Failure to check competitors' prices

(d) Deferring price reductions too long,

(e) Making the initial mark-down too small.

32. Mark-downs due to selling errors

On the sales floor, price reductions may have to be made due to:

(a) Failure to show and display merchandise properly

(b) Merchandise displayed in the wrong location

(c) Failure to inform sales people of the target customer market

(d) Failure to encourage sales people to show old and new lines together

(e) Poor stock-keeping

(f) Careless handling

(g) High pressure or careless selling.

33. Operational and uncontrollable causes of mark-downs

Other reasons for price reductions include:

(a) Lack of 'weeding out' slow and unprofitable lines

(b) 'Display' items kept on display too long, thus becoming discoloured and dirty

(c) Weather conditions, e.g. very wet summers may seriously affect the sale of light summer clothing like T-shirts

(d) Economic conditions, e.g periods of recession hit sales of consumer durables, men's outer clothing and the more expensive foodstuffs.

34. Promotion policies leading to mark-downs

Deliberate promotion policies may also lead to price reductions as when:

(a) Price competition has to be met

(b) There are special sales of regular stock, e.g. to counter low sales during times of economic recession

(c) There are frequent sales of promotional merchandise, e.g. to counter seasonal troughs in demand such as in January and in the summer

(d) Ranges are maintained until later in the season to maintain goodwill,

(e) High initial mark-up policy is coupled with big mark-downs, e.g. as in some boutiques

(f) Mark-downs are taken prematurely, e.g. to move stock out quickly

(g) There is a policy of carry-over to the new season

(h) There are multiple pricing policies, e.g. two for price of one.

35. Timing of mark-downs

Mark-downs may be taken either early or late:

(a) Early price reductions occur when sales slow down or fail to take off, e.g. in speciality stores.

(b) Late price reductions occur, for example due to an end-of-season clearance.

36. Effect of price cutting on gross profit

If a retail company is to expand, gross profit must be increased by generating a greater sales volume or by higher retail prices or by better buying. In terms of sales volume, a price reduction can result in a sufficient increase in unit sales for gross profit *to be increased*. This situation is explained by the concept of *price elasticity of demand*, which is the relationship between the price at which a product is sold and the quantity demanded by shoppers. It is therefore important to permit, indeed to encourage, pricing at those points at which the product of the individual margin and the unit sales volume is greatest, provided that any increase in expenses is less than the increase in margin.

37. Price increases

Much customer dissatisfaction can be caused if prices are increased after the merchandise goes on the shelf. However, when the buying-in price of an item rises rapidly the retailer must consider the replacement cost of inventory. Perhaps the most common reason for price increases is the cancellation of mark-downs. In order to minimize customer dissatisfaction the original price label should be removed completely. Price increases after goods have been put in stock should be the subject of very close control by merchandise management, particularly with regard to the following:

(a) Details of price changes should be submitted in writing for sanction before being put into effect.

(b) Unauthorized re-marking of goods.

MARGINS

38. Control and monitoring of margins

(a) All suppliers' invoices should be extended and totalled at retail price with a record kept of the cost and retail values of each invoice.

(b) All invoices received should be totalled and the initial gross margin calculated. Warning of deviations from the planned overall margin can thus be spotted quickly and either adjustment can be made or, if this is impracticable, some assessment of their effect on the overall result is possible.

39. Improving the gross margin

Because the size of the mark-up may condition the size of the eventual price reduction, it is important to look to ways of improving the gross margin. These methods include:

(a) Selling at higher prices by:

(*i*) the acquisition of exclusive goods so price comparison is difficult
(*ii*) elimination of odd prices
(*iii*) selling a larger proportion of the higher mark-up goods already stocked by advertising, incentives to sales people and better display.

(b) Reducing the price reductions by

    (*i*) reducing mark-down losses
    (*ii*) reducing merchandise shortages
    (*iii*) reducing or eliminating discounts to special groups, e.g. employees.

Progress test 13

1. Define the following terms: (*a*) cost of goods sold, (*b*) gross margin, (*c*) mark-up, and (*d*) net profit.

2. What factors determine the selling price of an item?

3. Describe the steps in the multi-stage approach to pricing.

4. What are the advantages of price lining?

5. Give four reasons for mark-downs.

6. How can price be used to improve margins?

7. Many retailers have adopted the principles of price lining. Evaluate this tactic with particular reference to the current economic climate and the recent success of the discount operators.

8. Discuss the role of price in the retailing mix. Choosing three local retailers as examples, check for consistency with other elements of the retail mix and recommend changes as appropriate.

14

ADVERTISING

COMMUNICATION

A retailer could stock the most attractive merchandise priced very competitively and have a convenient location but still fail to attract customers if he or she did not communicate with them.

1. Retail communication

The process of communicating with the target market is known as retail communication and is accomplished using one or more of the following:

(a) **Advertising** – paid-for non-personal communication to present and promote products, services or ideas.

(b) **Personal selling** – person-to-person communication for the purpose of making sales.

(c) **Sales promotion** – short-term incentives to encourage an earlier or stronger market response and stimulate purchase or sale of a product or service.

(d) **Public relations** – non-paid-for commercially significant news or editorial comment which might stimulate demand for a product or service, or promote understanding of the organization.

2. Retail communication mix

The extent to which each of the above is used will depend on the retailer's objectives. MFI, for example, is heavily involved in advertising to the consumer through newspapers and magazines. Marks & Spencer use little media advertising in its retail communication mix but rely more on word-of-mouth advertising and personal selling (through well-trained sales assistants). It can be argued that other elements such as the merchandise itself, price and location should be included in the definition of the communication mix because they too communicate something to the target audience. Within this broader view we would also include atmosphere and layout and customer services (these will be dealt with later). We will first examine the four conventional promotion elements: advertising, personal selling, sales promotion and public relations.

RETAILING ADVERTISING

3. Objectives

There are two principal objectives in retail advertising:

(a) Short-term. To stimulate 'traffic building' within days of the appearance of an advertisement, usually by means of a specific merchandise or promotional offer. This is called promotional advertising.

(b) Long-term. To increase the number of customers in the target market who automatically think of the advertised store as the right choice for the classes of merchandise that are on sale, i.e. including the store in the 'evoked' set. This is called corporate advertising.

These objectives are achieved by informing, entertaining, persuading, reminding or reassuring as part of the overall communication function of advertising.

4. Promotional advertising

Many retailers use promotional advertising in newspapers, magazines, etc. to sell specific items. The advertising will often incorporate an illustration of the merchandise and the price; however, there has recently been a significant increase in corporate advertising, particularly amongst multiple retailers.

5. Corporate advertising

Corporate advertising is used to project an image of a company and create a favourable impression of it. It has been used for some time outside the retail industry and classic corporate campaigns have been developed by British Airways and Prudential Insurance. More recently Sainsbury have attempted to project a 'quality image' using actors and actresses to extol the quality of food products now available at Sainsbury's. Thus advertising can be used to project an image or 'face' of the company to its various outside contacts whether they be consumers, staff, suppliers, trade associations or government agencies.

6. Trends

Media advertising by retailers has grown remarkably during the 1990s, and at a much faster rate than any other category of advertiser except office equipment. Retailers dominate the top ten of the largest advertisers with Sainsbury, Tesco, Comet, B&Q and MFI spending over £20 million per year.

The key to this growth was the abolition of resale price maintenance in 1964 that stimulated price competition and pushed the retail outlet into the forefront of the marketing battle. In the grocery field in particular, a few large multiple groups dominate sales and compete furiously with each other.

Advertising is the prime weapon in this battle, particularly as suppliers pay much of the advertising costs anyway, because retailer advertising in both food and durables is mainly geared to drawing attention to special offers on individual brands.

The extra money they receive is regarded by retailers as an addition to the discounts and general below-the-line deals they negotiate with suppliers.

HOW MUCH TO SPEND

7. Advertising spend

Large multiple grocers typically spend between 0.2 and 0.4 per cent of retail turnover on advertising. MFI typically spends 5 per cent of turnover on advertising, whereas Marks & Spencer spends very little. How then can the retailer decide on the right advertising appropriation? The recommended method is known as the objective and task method and put simply is the estimation of the cost of achieving the defined advertising objectives. Alternative methods commonly used but not recommended are the percentage of sales method or setting the advertising spend purely on the basis of competitor spend.

8. Objective and task method

Having defined the advertising objectives (for example, to increase awareness of the store by 20 percent), it is necessary to determine the different media strategies available for achieving that objective and costing them out. Thus it may be decided that the objective could be achieved using either local radio or local newspaper advertising or a combination of both. The cost of advertising in various media is obtained either directly or through BRAD (British rate and data). The resulting figure should be checked to determine whether it is reasonable both in terms of a comparison with competitor advertising spends and as a percentage of sales. If the appropriation seems either too high or too low a double check with objectives should be carried out along with a justification for the figure.

WHAT MEDIA TO USE

9. Media

The main types of media used by retailers are TV, newspapers and magazines, commercial radio and posters. Some retailers also make extensive use of catalogues, leaflet drops and mailings. Once again, the decision on which medium is best for a particular retailer will depend upon the objectives.

10. Newspapers

The UK is well served with a large number of local newspapers which are extensively used by retailers to reach a well defined geographic segment.

Alternatively, the national press is available for regional or national coverage and choices can be made on which newspaper to use to reach particular segments (e.g. socio-economic groups). The advantages of newspaper advertising are flexibility, immediacy, selectivity and relatively low cost.

11. Magazines

Once again, the advertiser has a wide choice of magazines aimed at specialist groups, men's magazines, women's magazines or local magazines. The major advantages of magazines for advertisers are very good selectivity, good reproduction (allowing high-quality colour reproduction) and long life. Disadvantages would include longer lead times and higher relative costs (on a cost per thousand readers basis).

12. Commercial radio

Born out of the pirate radio stations of the 1960s, commercial radio is now a mature advertising medium with 60 percent of the UK population listening at some time during the week. The 60 local and three national independent radio stations cover about 95 per cent of the UK population with listening biased towards men and younger people; in terms of class ABs (see Table 8.1) tend to be lighter listeners. The advantages for retailers are selectivity, flexibility and relatively low cost (especially compared to TV). It is flexible in that advertisements can be changed regularly due to low production costs. Also high frequency of ad. transmission can be achieved in a short space of time – especially useful to advertise special events. The main disadvantage is that because the message is audio only it is more difficult to attract the listener's attention and get the message across.

13. Television

Independent commercial television in the UK is controlled by the Independent Television Commission and is available as follows:

(a) Terrestrial television

Channel 3, split into 14 regions
Channel 4
S4C, the Welsh language channel
Breakfast TV
Teletext

(b) Cable television

Reaches just 4% of UK homes.

(c) Direct Broadcasting by Satellite

Predominantly Sky TV, reaches about 15% of UK homes.

Thus it is possible to advertise on a local or national level. As an example of cost, it is possible to have a 30 second advertisement on Border TV for less than £1,000. The same advertisement shown in all ITV areas would cost over £100,000.

Thus commercial television offers a tremendous opportunity for the retailer either at national or local level. The major advantages are the dramatic impact through the use of sight, sound, movement and colour; the large audiences which are instantly and simultaneously accessible and a relatively low cost per thousand; the retailer's prestige and credibility are enhanced and it fosters an image of stability and substantiality. The disadvantages of television are: the high total cost (production costs can be high although the use of video technology has reduced these); it delivers a fleeting message with no chance for the viewer to take in detailed messages; it can be lacking in selectivity – it tends to be a mass medium.

14. Direct mail

This is the sending of advertising messages directly to customers through the mail. The target market is selected by the advertiser through the use of mailing lists and is therefore highly controlled and can result in minimal wastage. It is particularly suitable for new businesses or new merchandise offers especially when linked with the use of coupons or catalogues. The advantages are that it is a personalized medium, flexible and an efficient way of reaching a target audience. Many people do not like direct mail, often throwing it away without reading it, so making the conversion to sales ratio low and thus cost per sale can be high.

15. Posters

Posters are a popular medium with retailers because they can be used to reach a well defined target market (especially a geographic segment).

There are 110,000 stationary roadside poster sites in the UK as well as 9,000 panels available on the London Underground. In addition there is an extensive network of panels available on buses (3,400 in Greater London alone).

16. Cinema

There are approximately 2,000 screens in the UK and advertising can be bought on an individual screen basis or nationally. The medium is particularly effective for reaching the 15-24 age group.

17. Media selection

Having identified the alternative media it is necessary to determine which combination provides the most effective way of delivering the advertising message. This can be an extremely complex process given the many alternative media available. Specialist media planners are employed by advertising agencies to undertake this onerous task but the individual retailer can use a common sense approach to arrive at a decision. Factors to be considered in media selection are as follows:

(a) **Reach**. The number of people to be exposed to an advertisement in a given time period.

(b) **Frequency**. The number of times the advertisement is exposed to an audience – complicated messages may require greater frequency.

(c) **Target audience media habits**. For example, a sports retailer may decide that advertising in the sports section of the local newspaper is an effective way of reaching the target audience.

(d) **Merchandise**. The product itself can affect the selection of media. For example, products requiring demonstration to highlight benefits may be advertised on TV. Similarly, a retailer may feel that the quality of a line of furniture can best be communicated using the better colour reproduction available in magazines rather than newspapers.

(e) **Message**. A complex message or one containing a lot of technical data may not be effectively communicated using the transient media of TV or radio.

(f) **Cost**. Although the cost per thousand may be less using a TV advertisement, the total cost may be prohibitive. Therefore the cost must be related to the retail communications budget.

18. Media scheduling

Deciding *when* the advertisements are to appear is known as media scheduling. This is particularly important for the retailer due to the frequent and dramatic seasonal and weekly sales variations. Many retailers take a high proportion of weekly turnover on Friday and Saturday, thus advertising is often scheduled for Thursdays and Fridays. Similarly, Christmas is a peak selling time and the pre-Christmas advertising burst is typical. The most appropriate method of determining these scheduling decisions is to relate them to the advertising objectives, target market and to ensure consistency with the other elements of the retail mix (it is pointless to advertise goods which are out of stock).

WHAT MESSAGE TO USE

19. Purpose

The purpose of any advertisement is to inform, persuade or remind. However, the primary purpose of a particular advertisement will be determined by the advertising objectives. This should therefore be the starting point for deciding on the content of the advertisement. If, for example, the prime advertising objective is to stimulate potential customers to visit a new retail outlet, then informative advertising would predominate and the content of the advertisement would be heavily biased towards providing information in a straightforward and rational manner.

20. Content

The content of an advertisement is usually a mixture of words (copy) and illustrations in a particular configuration (layout). Occasionally advertisements appear which are entirely copy. They are usually designed to provide information only and to appeal to the rational nature of buyers. However, humans are far from being totally rational creatures and we require sensory, social and ego satisfaction rewards. Thus advertisements will use both copy and illustration to persuade customers that their needs can be satisfied by visiting a particular store or purchasing a particular product. Consider the appeals presented in the following examples:

'Your caring sharing Co-op'
'Everything you want from a store and a little bit more'
'B & Q – nobody's bigger, nobody's better'
'United colours of Benetton'
'Asda-price'

An advertisement should be appealing by being desirable, exclusive and believable: it must generate the desire to act within the reader. If possible, in a highly competitive field, a unique selling proposition (USP) should be stressed as something exclusively available at a particular store; and finally the appeal must be credible.

21. Copy techniques

The following are some techniques which have been found to work:

(a) Headline. Bold headlines create impact and stop readers in their tracks.

(b) Tag lines. Memorable slogans often used at the end of an advertisement, e.g. 'Sainsbury – where good food costs less'.

(c) Repetition. Repetition aids learning and can be used within an advertisement and/or as a repetition of the whole advertisement over a period of time.

(d) Colloquialisms. These help to give warmth or local credibility, e.g. 'Is that alright Fyuz'.

(e) Rhyme. Rhyming words aid recall, e.g. 'The family store where your pound buys more'.

(f) Alliteration. This is another form of repetition – the first letter of sequential words are repeated, e.g. 'The wonder of Woolworths'.

22. Agencies

Retailers have tended in the past to feel that they know their own business best and there has been some suspicion of advertising agencies in the past and the importance of their contribution. It has been suggested that the trend in the future will be for retailers rather than manufacturers to carry out the product advertising so that a distinct type of retail advertising will emerge. Certainly retail advertising is much more like direct marketing than product advertising because its effects can be measured with some immediacy by the till. But generally speaking the trend today is for retailers to use advertising agencies much more intensively and many have already taken on the sophistication of successful manufacturers in their use of central media buying, creative consultancies and so on.

Progress test 14

1. What are the four main methods of retail communication?

2. What is meant by the retail communication mix?

3. Explain the difference between promotional and corporate advertising.

4. How does a retailer decide how much to spend on advertising?

5. Describe the main types of media used by retailers.

6. What are the factors to be considered in media selection?

7. Is the use of advertising agencies by retailers likely to grow? Why?

8. Dixons spend in the order of 4% of turnover on advertising. Marks and Spencer spend virtually nothing. Why should this be so? Marks and Spencer is more profitable than Dixons – does this indicate that Dixons should spend less on advertising?

9. Outline and discuss the key decision areas involved in designing and implementing an advertising campaign for a department store.

15

PERSONAL SELLING

THE SALES FORCE

1. Definition

Personal selling is person-to-person communication for the purpose of explaining, informing and demonstrating in order to make a sale. The personal selling process is designed to help sales staff match merchandise benefits to customer needs. Sales assistants, who form the bulk of the stores work-force, can make a tremendous difference to the customers' image of a store. It is therefore vitally important that the retailer develops an overall sales force strategy.

2. The role of the sales force

The first decision with regard to the sales force is whether to employ one or not. In many retail situations customers prefer either self-service or self-selection. In this way, customers have come to expect, for example, self-service in supermarkets and petrol stations – this method is consistent with the overall image of cutting frills to allow the most competitive prices to be offered. Situations where assistance in making the purchase decision would be expected are when:

(a) The item is made to the customer's particular requirements (e.g. made-to-measure clothes)

(b) The product is technically complex (e.g. cameras)

(c) The product is expensive

(d) Flexible pricing is practised and negotiation on price, etc. is the norm (e.g. cars).

3. Decline of personal selling

In recent years many retail sectors have moved away from personal service towards self-selection and self-service. The reasons given for this are:

(a) High cost of good sales staff

(b) Customer waiting time at peak periods tends to be longer than in a self-service store

(c) Inflexibility of the personal-service mode that makes transfers of staff more difficult

(d) Generally lower-quality staff because of lower level of wages for retail sales assistants

(e) The popularity of the self-service type of store for many other reasons, e.g. greater sales potential.

4. Sales force objectives

Once the role of the sales force and its emphasis within the retail communication mix have been determined, it is necessary to determine specific objectives. Sales force objectives must be set in relation to sales turnover. Salespersons can be responsible for providing information, persuading, accepting payment, wrapping, handling complaints, in-store displays, etc. Alternatively, salespersons may be required only in transaction processing, such as checkout or cashier duty. Although it may be considered that little personal selling is involved here, this final part of the buying process is crucial and a bad experience at the checkout may provoke a customer not to shop at that store again.

5. Sales force size

Determining the size of the sales force to adequately service customer needs should take into account:

(a) The role and objectives of the sales force, i.e. in terms of workload and responsibilities

(b) The customer arrival times – it will be necessary to deploy more sales assistants at peak times

(c) The length of time to service each customer

(d) The average sales to each customer – it may be necessary to balance the cost of using more sales assistants to reduce queues against the value to the customer of doing so. For example, customers may prefer to wait in a queue in order to buy at the most competitive prices, than have no wait but at the cost of higher prices.

The size of the sales force can be critical to retail profitability. Salaries typically run at between 4 and 10 per cent of sales turnover and can account for as much as 60 per cent of operating expenses. Where net margins for some retailers are as low as 4 to 5 per cent (e.g. multiple grocers) it can be seen that mistakes in determining the sales force size can have a dramatic effect on net profits.

CUSTOMERS

Chapter 7 explored consumer buying behaviour in terms of the buying process, the buying participants and the factors affecting choice. Some of these aspects are reconsidered below within the context of the selling process.

6. Why consumers buy

It is useful to know the general motivations that help encourage people to buy: it may help the sale and therefore the shopper. The fundamental motives are as follows:

(a) **The satisfaction of physical needs**. This includes far more, of course, than the basics of food, drink and clothing.

(b) **Recreation and comfort**. Greater discretionary income coupled with increased leisure time have caused a boom in recreational products and services.

(c) **Imitation**. Advertising bases much of its appeal on the need for many consumers to imitate those they admire or whose tastes they consider superior. Cosmetics and clothing are two particular areas of imitation – or 'aspirational marketing'.

(d) **Exclusiveness**. Some consumers require prestige and are willing to pay high prices for durables or clothing to underline their self-proclaimed leadership.

(e) **Family affection**. A good deal of money is spent on children, for instance, in the shape of toys and clothes, and this is part of the general pleasure of giving.

(f) **Other motives**. Consumers are brought into retail shops by motives which include health, habit, curiosity, novelty, possession and pride.

The salesperson who recognizes these motivations can modify the presentation of information to appeal to the motivations of that particular customer.

7. What customers buy

The motives for buying may be constrained by other factors which will influence choice, as follows:

(a) **Source**. Some sources have strong selling appeal, e.g. Swiss watches, Japanese cameras.

(b) **Economy**. Price is almost invariably an important factor and particularly with the lower income groups. Customers balance price with their subjective idea of value.

(c) **Performance**. An article is sold for what it does, as well as for what it is.

(d) **Durability**. Many people are prepared to pay more for articles that are likely to last longer without replacement. This is important in the case of consumer durables but less so for clothing.

(e) **Low running costs**. What may be cheap to buy may be expensive to use, but a total saving can be made over a long period if a customer can be assisted in choosing a quality which is economical to run, even if the cost is a little higher at the outset.

(f) **Maintenance facilities**. An article that is expensive at the outset may be designed for cheapness and ease of maintenance whilst a less expensive article may not. Additionally, a comprehensive after-sales service by the supplier is often a powerful influence on customer choice.

8. Customer types

The points of attraction in goods that appeal to customers must be used by the retailer, keeping in mind that what attracts one shopper may deter another. It is important to 'weigh up' the customer quickly and to recognize their main characteristics so that the right approach can be made. Basic customer 'types' are as follows:

(a) The 'just looking' customer. This type of customer may well be browsing or comparing prices and qualities and should be left alone until signs of interest are shown.

(b) The decisive customer. Such customers present few difficulties to sales staff because they have already made up their minds what they want to buy. They should be served as quickly as possible whilst at the same time ensuring that the product will deliver what the customer requires of it.

(c) The uncertain customer. This type of customer requires lots of reassurance, based on the assistant's extensive product knowledge as required.

(d) The silent customer. Without clues to the customer's opinions about merchandise, demonstration may be necessary, with the customer free to handle merchandise so that his or her intentions can be gauged.

(e) The talkative customer. Time spent in conversation with an assistant could mean lost sales elsewhere. Tact and firmness are required to bring the customer back to the merchandise and its selling points.

(f) The disagreeable customer. This type of customer should be shown the stock available but the customer should otherwise be given the chance to do most of the talking.

(g) The opinionated customer. The opinions offered, even if they are factually incorrect, should rarely be challenged but the correct information merely provided as part of the conversation.

(h) The suspicious customer. Suspicion is sometimes produced by a disappointing purchase made in the store previously. This should be allayed, and the confidence of the customer built up again. This can be achieved by an apology, an offer to exchange a faulty article or, if appropriate, a full refund.

THE PROGRESS OF THE SALE

9. Prospecting and qualifying

The selling process, particularly for expensive items, may actually begin well before the customer comes anywhere near the store. The search for potential

153

customers (prospects) to convert into customers is known as prospecting. This may be achieved through advertising, leaflet drops, recommendation from current customers, obtaining lists of potential customers, etc. This list of prospects must then be filtered to provide a list of definite prospects – this process, known as qualifying, involves trying to determine such things as the individual's financial position: can they afford the item? Does the prospect really require the item and have they authority to buy?

10. The pre-approach

Before the salesperson approaches a potential customer, a good deal of preparation and information gathering is necessary. This includes much information on the products and their particular benefits as well as facts about local competitors, prices, etc. In addition the salesperson should have received sales training to allow customer types and their motivations to be spotted.

11. Making contact

The customer's first impression of the salesperson is important as he or she is received into the branch. A smile is important. The salesperson's attitude should be determined by the customer but he or she should be civil not servile.

The most commonly used approach phrase used by sales personnel is 'Can I help you?' and the most common answer is thus generated automatically 'No, I'm just looking'. To overcome this automatic rejection the approach phrase should be modified by the salesperson commenting on the merchandise the potential customer is viewing, e.g. 'That camera is the latest in the range and is on special introductory offer at present'.

Alternatively, a more specific service approach than 'May I help you?' would be 'Have you seen the special introductory offer on the new cameras . . . ?' With experience salespersons can modify their approach phrases to avoid becoming (and sounding) too mechanized.

12. Finding out customer needs

Sales staff must know customer needs before they know they are selling the right merchandise. Much of the information relating to the customer, such as economic standing, family size, specific reason for purchase, may come out through observing and conversing with the customer.

13. Selling the correct goods

Important points at this stage of the sale are as follows:

(a) If the most appropriate item is not in stock, the salesperson may be able to offer a satisfactory substitute, but this must not be pressed on the customer.

(b) In a substitution situation or where the customer is amenable to purchasing higher-priced items in a range, 'selling up' is a possibility.

(c) One of the key sections of the salesperson's presentation is the selling of the benefits of the article.

(d) It may be that at some point the customer's objections have to be overcome. A clever salesperson can spot the negative response and use it as part of his or her presentation or even turn it into a selling point!

(e) Some positive points for salespersons:

(*i*) Present the facts slowly; they are new to the customer.
(*ii*) Emphasize the selling points of the article that appeal most to the customer.
(*iii*) Encourage questions from the customer; this could lead to a multiple sale.
(*iv*) Give the customer the opportunity to 'try' the merchandise.
(*v*) Handle the merchandise with care; this shows how valuable it is.

(f) Some negative points:

(*i*) Items should never be demonstrated on top of other merchandise.
(*ii*) Technical language should not be over-used.
(*iii*) A salesperson should never mislead a customer. Honesty builds goodwill.
(*iv*) Never criticize any items. This may either lose a sale or reduce the firm's goodwill.

14. Closing the sale

(a) As with the initial approach, timing is essential, e.g. the sale must be concluded before interest wanes.

(b) The customer must feel that the buying decision has been his or her own.

(c) At this point the salesperson may be asked about credit, servicing, alterations and so on; it is essential that he or she is as fully conversant with these matters as with the products.

(d) The goods are wrapped and the money is taken.

(e) The correct time to make a related sale is when the merchandise is being wrapped.

15. Related selling

Once the customer has made a first purchase it may be quite natural for him or her to make a second, complementary one, e.g. the purchase of a car wax may suggest a further purchase of a set of dusters. Suggestions should be specific, however, and not the general 'Do you require anything else?'

16. Customer leaves the store

The customer's visit might finish with the salesperson showing him or her to the door, thanking the customer for his or her custom and expressing the hope that he or she will revisit the branch or store in the near future. This should be done, if possible, whether a sale has been made or not, and is still a goodwill-builder even in these days of impersonal selling. In most cases today, however, this rather leisurely leave-taking is impossible because of the volume of custom successful stores need to attract in order to survive.

IMPORTANCE OF THE SALESPERSON

17. Salesperson's attributes

To be successful in the personal selling situation, the salesperson needs the following attributes:

(a) Retailers aim to recruit staff whose appearance and manner is consistent with the store image, i.e. salespeople with whom the customers can identify.

(b) The salesperson must be a good communicator, who can set up a rapport easily with the customers and has the ability to be flexible.

(c) A pleasant and courteous manner is most important, but avoiding the danger of being obsequious.

Progress test 15

1. Give three examples of retailing situations where personal selling would be expected.

2. What factors should be taken into account when determining the size of the sales force?

3. What is meant by prospecting and qualifying?

4. Does the selling process end with 'closing the sale'? If not, why not?

5. What are the main attributes of a good salesperson?

16

SALES PROMOTION AND PUBLIC RELATIONS

DEFINITION AND OBJECTIVES

1. Meaning of sales promotion

There is often confusion over the term sales promotion because it has been used in the past and still is used by some to mean anything which attempts to increase or promote the level of sales. This definition would include advertising and personal selling so this old definition of sales promotion is very broad indeed. A more narrow and precise definition is preferred and therefore sales promotion is now thought of as those promotional activities other than advertising, personal selling and public relations that stimulate consumer purchase.

Media advertising is often classed as 'above the line' expenditure whilst sales promotion is 'below the line'. Typical sales promotion tools would be coupons, samples, competitions, etc.

2. Objectives of sales promotion

(a) Stop and shop. Customers passing the store, who have no intention of going in, can be encouraged to enter by a sales promotion in-store, e.g. wine tasting.

(b) Shop and buy. Having persuaded customers to enter the shop, they must now be encouraged to buy by presenting the merchandise in such a manner as to create the desire to purchase, e.g. money-off vouchers, trade-in allowances.

(c) Buy bigger. During the buying process customers can be persuaded to buy either a larger quantity of the same goods or to buy other products in addition, e.g. premiums, cash-back offers.

(d) Repeat purchase. The final aim is to persuade customers to return again and again to the store trading on the goodwill and loyalty that previous purchases have, hopefully, instilled, e.g. store 'club' cards, or continuity programmes such as collecting a dinner service.

Therefore sales promotion efforts are usually designed to support other communication activities. For example, advertising may be used to generate awareness and desire but sales promotion may be used tactically to overcome any resistance to purchase by offering a (short-term) incentive to create a quicker sales response.

3. Ways to increase sales using sales promotion

The methods of increasing sales without necessarily incurring extra costs, such as increased staffing or sales area, are as follows:

(a) Increase the number of transactions by:

(*i*) using sales promotion methods to get more people into the store, and
(*ii*) improving point-of-sale incentives to buy.

(b) Increase the size of the average sale by:

(*i*) promotions on high margin goods, and
(*ii*) getting more goods sold by offering incentives to buy more, e.g. (multi-pack) pricing.

Sales promotions can emanate from two sources: suppliers or the retail company itself.

SUPPLIER-ORIGINATED SALES PROMOTIONS

4. In-store activities

There are many types of suppliers' promotions that affect in-store activity:

(a) Price-off pack, e.g. '10p off' printed or banded on the pack.

(b) Premiums, small gifts either in, or occasionally attached to, the pack, e.g. plastic toys.

(c) Self-liquidating premiums, i.e. cheap promotions primarily concerned with obtaining good in-store display. The customer writes to the supplier for the gift, enclosing pack tops plus money. The gifts are likely to be bought in bulk by the supplier, giving him or her the benefit of large discounts, thus making the bought-in unit price low enough to be covered by the profit on all extra sales made.

(d) Personality promotions. Some manufacturers have been using show-business personalities to promote their products, but their appeal may be declining because so many companies now use them. To avoid over-exposure some firms now use personalities selectively, e.g. in certain parts of the country.

(e) Competitions. These are often printed on the packs with the advantage to the supplier that the budget is known in advance with the requisite number of prizes ordered from suppliers.

(f) Co-operative promotions, e.g. two or more branded products sharing (and funding) a joint in-store promotion, say garden peat and packet seeds.

(g) Sampling. The giving-away, often in-store, of product samples sometimes with a demonstrator present, e.g. Swiss cheese, Cyprus Sherry.

(h) Coupons. Price-off coupons are printed on the packs or in store hand-outs, usually allowing a substantial saving on the next purchase of the brand. The effectiveness of this type of promotion can be significantly reduced if the store allows the coupon to be redeemed for quite different goods – this is called 'malredemption'.

(i) Buy one, get one free. Customers have to send pack tops back to the manufacturer and, although initially attractive, may be loath to in practice due to the hassle; this reduces the cost of the promotion, as a result of low 'redemption rate'.

(j) Multi-packs. Here two packs are attached and sold for the price of one at the time of the purchase. Occasionally a 'stretched' version of the pack obviates the extra shelf space required. Popular in toiletries and food.

(k) In-store salespersons. An example would be 'demonstrators' used in the electrical 'white goods' market. To work well there probably has to be a further inducement offered, e.g. reduced prices. This promotion is used selectively, normally in supermarkets, department stores and so on.

It will be seen that the retailer has to be organized for the promotion, e.g. the collection and redemption of coupons, reorganizing shelf displays and store layout.

5. Point-of-sale display material

Most manufacturers produce sales-aid material for placing near the products themselves. Examples of these are:

(a) Special fittings, e.g. paperback publishers' racks, dry-battery stands.

(b) Showcards designed to stand on or fit round the products, e.g. washing machines, pens.

(c) Leaflets and product labels.

(d) Demonstrators. Sometimes – demonstrators are used in this context as are authors in bookshop signing sessions.

Many retailers use the display material from suppliers very selectively due to the danger of producing a cluttered and unco-ordinated retailing environment. In some cases, particularly the large multiple groups, manufacturers and re-tailers will collaborate to produce mutually acceptable point-of-sale display material.

6. Trade incentives

These are normally of the following kinds:

(a) **Cash discounts** or straight cash handouts are given by manufacturers to encourage volume sales, period stock building, display and cut-price offers to consumers.

(b) **Special credit terms**. These support special promotions and are often aimed at the bulk retail buyers.

(c) **Goods in lieu of cash**, e.g. one extra free item for every ten purchased by the retailer.

(d) **Staff incentives**. These are payments made by the manufacturer to store management and staff for reaching particular targets. Obviously these are agreed prior to the start of the promotion by the retail company and may form part of a much larger supplier–retailer promotion package. This type of incentive does offer the promoter an opportunity to motivate the people who actually come into contact with the public.

7. Direct promotion to the public

As part of its below-the-line effort, the manufacturer may make use of direct promotions to consumer's homes such as couponing or free samples.

8. Pack design

Because so many products are prepacked and because there is such a fight for shelf space, pack design is important to the retailer who may decide to accept or reject a pack just on the basis of its design rather than its contents, e.g. because of its dimensions or its 'stackability'.

RETAILER-ORIGINATED SALES PROMOTIONS

9. Window displays

Shop windows today have largely become bigger and backless and show much of what is going on in-store. However, department stores and certain types of multiple chains, like jewellers, booksellers and chemists, keep windows for particular products and seasonal or special event promotions. For example, a new line in toiletries may be given a mass window display to itself; Christmas and Easter displays encourage shoppers to enter the store (*see* Chapter 17), by displaying 'special offers' or items 'on promotion'.

10. In-store displays

These can be of various kinds:

(a) **Mass displays**, e.g. in dump baskets or at ends of gondolas.

(b) **Multiple product promotions**, e.g. when two or more complementary products are sold together in an integrated display.

(c) **Demonstrations**, e.g. sampling, product demonstration, fashion shows.

11. Price promotions

These may occur for short periods on a selected number of lines, e.g. the 'super savers' in supermarkets. Some firms prefer to advertise their 'permanent store-wide discounts'. Many retailers, particularly in the textile trades, have annual or half-yearly (or even more frequent) sales where slow movers, bad buys, cheap 'bought-in' lines and deteriorated stock are sold off.

12. Store loyalty cards/trading stamps

Greenshield stamps were a particularly popular sales promotion device of the 1970s. They were used along with other trading stamps such as those issued by Co-ops to even out trade over a week, e.g. 'double stamps on Tuesdays', or to promote particular lines as well as being a general incentive to shop in that particular store rather than its competitors. Trading stamps have now largely been replaced by the stores' own loyalty cards although a successful version of the trading stamp concept is the 'Air Miles' voucher.

13. Competitions

Many retailers use competitions as a sales promotion device. These can be particularly successful if linked to a promotion theme. For example, Woolworths' 'back to school' competition linked to its back to school leaflet distribution requesting completed entries to be taken to the local Woolworths store and posted in the box provided.

14. Free gifts

Electrical retailers, for example, have offered small electrical appliances such as low saturation items like liquidizers as 'free' gifts to consumers buying large ticket items like cookers and washing machines.

15. In-store display material

Most retail companies produce, or have produced for them, window posters, point-of-sale display material, printed tickets and other 'software'.

16. Personality promotions

Following the lead of the manufacturers, some retail chains have paid personalities to take part in their advertising, store openings and so on.

17. Joint promotions with other retailers

As in the promotion of the food court in managed shopping centres.

18. Incentives to sales staff

These take the form of:

(a) Competitions between salespeople or between branches with cash or merchandise prizes.

(b) Use of 'premium' money or bonuses paid to salespeople for the sale of particular lines, usually high-margin.

PUBLIC RELATIONS

19. Public relations (PR)

Public relations is the deliberate, planned and sustained effort to establish and maintain understanding between an organization and its publics. The role of public relations is to obtain favourable publicity for the organization, build a good image and handle adverse comments, rumours or stories. This is often achieved (in larger companies) by the public relations department who will achieve these aims by planning a campaign to communicate the right message to the right people. It is important to understand the concept of 'publics' in the public relations definition. An organization's publics will consist of customers, shareholders, employees, government, suppliers, the local community and the media. Therefore, it may well be necessary to produce information in different forms to appeal to these different publics or indeed to provide different information for different publics.

20. Example of PR objectives

Examples of information that a large food retailer might wish to project in order to maintain understanding are:

(a) External. This is a group that:

(*i*) is a major and influential force in the food marketing and distribution scene
(*ii*) has substantial financial backing
(*iii*) has considerable buying power
(*iv*) in its commercial operations is aggressive, tough and progressive – but also reliable and fair.

(b) Internal. This is a group that:

(*i*) is a large well-developed business with plenty of opportunities
(*ii*) is interested in personnel development
(*iii*) provides a good total remuneration package
(*iv*) deals firmly but fairly and sympathetically with the staff.

It is interesting to note that a number of small retail groups have recently begun spending on 'financial public relations', which is largely aimed at the City of

London. This has reflected a growing concern by companies as to the performance of their share prices and the consequent value (market capitalization) the City puts on their share issues.

21. Publicity

Publicity may be defined as information appearing in the media concerning products, services or companies and secured as editorial material rather than paid-for space.

22. Purpose

The purpose of publicity is to promote brands, products, people, places, ideas or companies. In providing information through editorial space greater credibility results as the audience is less likely to be sceptical of editorial than space which has been paid for by an advertiser.

23. Forms

The most common forms of publicity are:

(a) Press releases or news items

(b) Photographs

(c) News conferences/speeches

(d) Films/videos.

Publicity is often thought of as free advertising but it is far from this. It is not free because although the cost of space may not be paid for there may be considerable cost in producing publicity material. To be truly effective publicity must be planned and managed professionally.

24. Sponsorship

Retail organizations of all sizes and types are spending increased sums of money on sponsoring sporting and cultural activities. A once minor area of PR, sponsorship is fast becoming an important form of promotion in its own right. Sponsorship does seem to offer the retailer a way of being perceived as giving something back to society and thus fostering a good corporate image. Sainsburys is one of the largest sponsors of the arts in the UK and Benetton are well known as sponsor of a highly successful Formula 1 motor racing team.

Progress test 16

1. What is the meaning of sales promotion? Give four examples of sales promotion tools.

2. What trade incentives are normally provided by manufacturers?

3. Describe three types of retailer-originated sales promotions.

4. What is publicity?

5. What are the most common forms of publicity used by retailers?

6. Describe the advantages of sponsorship as compared to media advertising.

7. In 1992 Tesco launched its Computers for Schools promotion. 13,000 items of equipment including 3,000 computers, 600 printers and 9,400 software packages were given away to 8,000 schools nationwide. The promotion was based on a voucher collection system, with one voucher being given for every £25 spent in a single transaction. The promotion was repeated in 1993 and 1994.

   Evaluate this method of promotion and comment particularly on objectives that it might achieve for Tesco.

8. Ian MacLaurin, Chairman of Tesco, contends that publicity is more important than advertising. Comment on whether you would subscribe to this view in relation to UK retailing.

17

ATMOSPHERE AND LAYOUT

STORE IMAGE AND ATMOSPHERE

1. Store image

This can be defined as the customer's perception of the store and its attributes. As such it is a composite of the following dimensions: merchandise, store location, promotion, pricing policy, service, store clientele and store atmosphere and layout. These dimensions are lumped together by the consumer in order to simplify matters to produce a store image. When asked to describe a store's image, customers will respond using terms such as honest, dependable, exciting, etc. as well as describing the physical facilities such as cleanliness, easy to locate, park, etc.

2. Atmosphere

This is a major component of store image and can be defined as the dominant sensory effect created by the store's design, physical characteristics, and merchandising activities.

The components of the store which collectively produce the store atmosphere are the store exterior, general store interior (e.g. flooring, walls, lighting), layout, and displays. The sensory reaction they produce within an individual can be considered in terms of sight, touch, taste, smell and sound.

3. Design

Design has become increasingly important in retailing in recent years, not only in the development of company logos and graphic styles, but also in developing a total retail concept to appeal to particular target groups. Habitat was the first of a new breed of design-led retailers. Terence Conran opened his first Habitat store in 1964 with the basic philosophy of providing well designed products at reasonable prices and in a comfortable environment. In 1982 he applied the same principle to the retailing of clothes and Next was born, offering stylish collections of co-ordinated clothes exquisitely presented. Since then many retail groups have used design consultancies to redesign stores to create a particular atmosphere and thus achieve a differential competitive advantage.

4. The right atmosphere

The right atmosphere starts with the definition of the target market and identifying their requirements. For example, customers buying expensive ladies fashions would expect an 'expensive' atmosphere – deep pile carpets, top quality fixtures and fittings, etc. The atmosphere of the store should be entirely consistent with the desired store image and the other elements of the retail mix.

STORE EXTERIOR

The first impression a potential customer has of the store is generated by the store exterior. It should therefore be designed to project and be consistent with the desired store image.

5. The store's position

The primary concern with regard to position is how visible the store is. Ideally a store should be positioned so that it is clearly visible from the major routes (pedestrian or vehicular) passing the site. Compatibility with surrounding stores and the surrounding area is desirable as is the provision of easy access to the store either by the provision of car parking facilities and/or the exclusion of vehicular traffic to permit safe convenient conditions for pedestrians.

6. Architecture

Architectural style can indicate the size and prestige of the retailer's operation. The use of certain materials (e.g. marble) can also affect image. The overall size of the outlet is important but width (particularly for window space) is often more important than the height or depth of the building.

7. The store's sign

The fascia serves to identify the store and attract the customers' attention. The store's sign may be used to identify who the retailer is (e.g. McDonalds), what is sold (e.g. Tie Rack), where the retailer is located (e.g. Nottingham Hi-fi) or when they are open (e.g. '7–11').

8. The shop front

The three basic shop-front configurations are:

(a) The straight front. Here the shop front runs parallel to the street or pavement with possibly a small recess for the entrance.

(b) The angled front. This creates a more attractive and interesting front and funnels or directs consumers into the store. It also helps provide a better viewing angle and can reduce glare.

(c) The arcade front. Basically, this is a straight front configuration but with several recessed windows or entrances thus providing the shopper with several protected areas for window shopping and creating an attractive and relaxing atmosphere.

9. The store entrance

The store entrance should be designed to encourage the customer into the store. The major factors to consider are the size of the entrance and flat entry surfaces. Some retailers have dispensed with windows thus opening up the whole of the shop front as an entrance – this is possible in a covered shopping centre but does involve increased security risks.

10. The window

Apart from the overriding aim of image-building the conventional window has functions such as:

(a) to show a representative sample of merchandise sold in the store

(b) to display promotional or seasonal lines

(c) a mixture of **(a)** and **(b)**.

The window, whether it is arcaded or a 'picture', is important in helping to persuade the customer to enter the store initially. Many retailers have dispensed with normal window displays and use the window to allow the customer to view the entire store and its contents. Retailers selling small items such as jewellery, however, still rely on window displays, usually set off against a window back.

11. Basic principles

The basic principles of window display are similar to in-store principles and are as follows:

(a) Like products should be grouped together in the window.

(b) Featured lines should be placed in prominent positions in the windows, just below eye-level.

(c) Window display height in a backless window (and these are preferred by most retailers today except in jewellery and other small item stores) should be between average waist and shoulder level so that customers can see into the store. Tall products, such as upright freezers, should be displayed to the sides.

(d) Window displays should not be too deep. The window should allow potential customers to look into and see the whole store.

(e) Where window space allows, mass displays of individual stock items such as a promoted line are valuable interest catchers.

(f) If windows are used as part of the positive effort of attracting customers into the store, displays should be changed regularly to keep up the customer's interest. This has the added advantage of rotating window stock that might otherwise become faded.

(g) Electrically-driven turntables, which hold stock, can attract attention. The colour of displays should also be eye-catching, e.g. the use of red and green at Christmas time.

(h) All stock and window fittings, such as shelving, should be clean.

(i) Windows should be well lit, particularly for evening window-shopping.

The advantages of window displays are that they can be inspected after the store has closed and, unlike press advertising, actual merchandise is used.

STORE INTERIOR

12. Design

The general design of the store interior must be consistent with that of the exterior, thus the colour and design aspects of floors, walls and ceilings must present the right image. For example, it is common practice for food-selling areas to have marble effect flooring to give the impression of cleanliness, whereas fashion-selling areas will normally be carpeted or have wood flooring to enhance the quality/plush image.

13. Other considerations

The basic objective of the retailer is to minimize costs whilst maximizing sales and customer satisfaction. The store interior can contribute to this objective by providing the appropriate fixtures and equipment, lighting, dressing rooms, lifts or escalators and aisle widths to allow comfortable shopping.

LAYOUT

14. Definition

The layout of a store is the arrangement and location of fixtures, fittings, equipment, merchandise, aisles and non-selling areas such as checkouts and dressing rooms.

15. Grouping of sections

In such retail sectors as DIY, grocery and electrical, stock can be divided into a number of sections which form mini-departments of the store. For example, in

DIY stores such sections could be: gardening, home decoration, kitchenware, etc. In electrical retailing the convention is to split the store into 'brown' (TV/audio) and 'white' (major domestic appliances) goods and then to further subdivide the sections, say, into home laundry, refrigeration, colour/mono TV, videos, etc. This logical approach helps customers and staff to find sections quickly.

16. Allocation of in-store space

The amount of floorspace required for customers will depend on the type of trade, the lines carried and the type of service offered. A balance should be struck between customer, selling and non-selling areas. The amount of customer space required will depend on whether certain factors are present, namely:

(a) Need for customer browsing, e.g. at greeting card racks

(b) High percentage of comparison goods, e.g. furniture that requires a lengthy selling time

(c) Need for chairs and tables for 'signing up' procedures for hire-purchase or rental agreements.

The allocation of space for the different merchandise groups should be based on a profit productivity approach, i.e. providing selling space on the basis of profit per square foot. For example, a merchandise group contributing 5 per cent of total profits could be allocated 5 per cent of the sales floor area. However, this initial calculation may have to be modified in the light of other requirements – e.g. the need to provide variety and choice and a proper assortment of merchandise.

17. Ways to maximize the use of space

(a) Devote as much total space to selling activities as compared to storage or non-selling functions.

(b) In prime shopping locations consider assigning non-selling activities to other areas where rental costs are much lower.

(c) In the designated selling space eliminate all non-selling functions, e.g. clerical work areas.

(d) Use vertical as well as horizontal space (but keeping the store image intact).

(e) Replace inefficient fixtures with modern, open, volume-selling fittings.

(f) Analyse sales and profit per square foot of selling space and re-locate departments taking into account:

(*i*) seasonal changes where appropriate
(*ii*) when there are unprofitable departments these should be cut back or dropped altogether and more promising sections extended
(*iii*) the meeting of set minimum acceptable sales/profits targets per square foot.

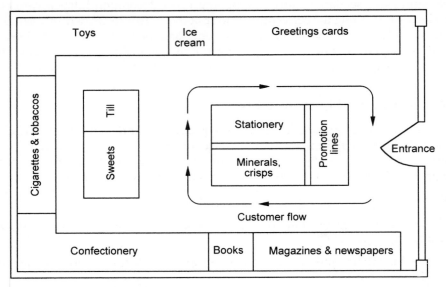

Figure 17.1 Layout of a CTN store

18. Different retail sector approaches

(a) A typical DIY store will place high-demand lines such as nails and screws towards the back of the store so that customers are forced past other high-profit impulse lines such as kitchen utensils and gifts.

(b) In confectioner/tobacconist/newsagent (CTN) stores newspapers are normally located near the door because their sales peak is in the morning and evening and customers shopping only for these items can be served quickly. Rear space is used for 'browsing' lines like toys, whilst impulse lines like sweets are positioned next to the till (*see* Figure 17.1).

(c) Footwear stores, where most of the stock is in the window or round the walls, allow a large part of the space to customers, chairs and fittings.

(d) Stores which sell large consumer durables such as major electrical appliances and furniture display much of their stock so that it is free-standing. Therefore the customer circulation area is the same as the display area.

LAYING OUT A STORE

19. Introduction

The three main factors to be considered here are as follows:

(a) Fixtures and fittings

(b) Merchandise

(c) Customer circulation.

20. Fixtures and fittings

These take four main forms:

(a) Wall fixtures consisting usually of shelving but sometimes made up of hooks (for bagged stationery items), browsers (for records or greeting cards) and other specialist types of fitting, some of which can be used free-standing.

(b) Free-standing gondola (walk-around) or browser units, again with shelving (often adjustable). Many shelves have slotted edges so as to carry price tickets for the merchandise displayed.

(c) Special containers and stands such as wire dump bins and 'spinners' (circular free-standing racks that may be rotatable) for lines displayed as a special promotion, or manufacturers' display units specially designed to carry their own particular product.

(d) Refrigerated cabinets of various designs for the sale of frozen foods, meats, fish, provisions, and produce. These can be placed against the wall or free-standing, and it is important to keep these lines close to their preparation areas.

21. Merchandise

The arrangement of fixtures and fittings will be guided by the type of merchandise sold. The merchandise is positioned in particular ways to aid customer selection and therefore stimulate sales. The following points should be noted:

(a) Principal merchandise sections should be prominently labelled by clear overhead signs.

(b) All merchandise sections should be accessible to the customer.

(c) All merchandise must be clearly and correctly priced (either on the merchandise or on the shelf edge).

(d) The general rule on merchandise location is to use the best selling position for goods providing the greatest profit (i.e. gross margin × rate of sale), not goods carrying the highest profit margins. Best selling positions include ends of gondolas and wall units.

(e) 'Everyday' purchases like canned fruit, vegetables and soups should be placed near the entrance to start the customer buying.

(f) Merchandise can be categorized, by customer intention to buy, into three broad types, and this will radically affect their locations in-store:

(*i*) *Demand lines.* These often consist of staple merchandise that is bought almost automatically, e.g. bread, milk.

171

(*ii*) *Browser lines*. These are products which remind the customer, by their presence on open display, that he or she should buy them, and which need space to allow the customer to make an unhurried selection, e.g. greetings cards.

(*iii*) *Impulse lines*. The customer purchases these lines without any prior intentions, e.g. confectionery.

(g) Careful placing of basic demand lines helps to draw customers to all parts of the shop. High profit margin, impulse purchase lines should be placed alongside them.

(h) Promotional displays should be controlled in size and number so that clutter is avoided, and neither should they be located immediately inside the store entrance nor immediately opposite a fast-moving line. Customers tend to miss badly sited displays.

(i) Heavy and bulky goods, e.g. bread, cereals and drinks, should be placed near the end of the in-store 'journey'. Positioned earlier they could fill the basket too quickly. This is also true of fragile goods which might break.

(j) Displays (except for seasonal lines) should not be changed too often as it tends to annoy the customers.

22. Customer circulation

The following points should be noted:

(a) In self-service stores there is a tendency for customers to 'follow the walls'. Merchandise display techniques mentioned above can encourage wider circulation.

(b) Free-standing units should not be set together in a long line but should show gaps so that customers can move across the store and not be 'forced' round.

(c) Aisle widths should be great enough to allow two trolleys to pass in comfort. Some supermarkets have aisles of up to two or three metres in width. Circulation space at the front of the store should be adequate to avoid congestion.

(d) Research can be used profitably to lay out stores scientifically and to have particular regard to customer circulation behaviour.

Figure 17.2 shows different kinds of layouts. The grid layout, often used in supermarkets, aids and directs customer flow and is designed to enhance efficiency. The boutique layout arranges the sales floor into partially separated areas to create an unusual and interesting shopping experience. The free flow layout encourages browsing and is used most by clothing stores.

DISPLAY

The manner in which merchandise is exhibited or presented to the customer is a vital element of the selling process.

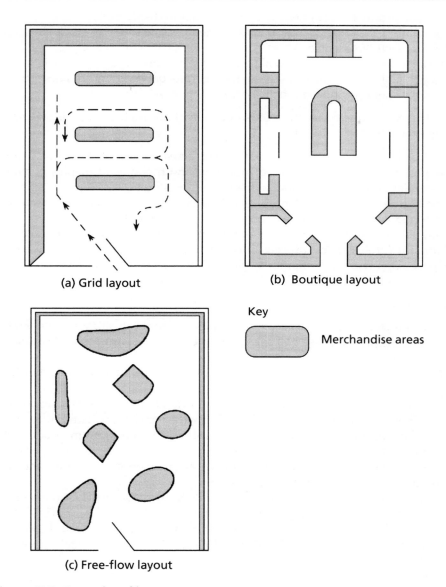

(a) Grid layout

(b) Boutique layout

(c) Free-flow layout

Key

Merchandise areas

Figure 17.2 Examples of layout

23. In-store display

Once the customer is past the window line he or she is usually within the store and the effect of good display continues to be important in catching the customer's eye.

(a) A logical arrangement helps to sell the stock.

173

(*i*) Like products should be grouped together in displays.

(*ii*) Within the store, a logical arrangement of categories of stock should be attempted ('Adjacencies').

(*iii*) The position of stock within the store in some retail sectors is largely dependent on seasonal requirements, e.g. raincoats and umbrellas should be in prominent positions in the winter to encourage impulse buys.

(b) Displays with impact attract customer attention and they may also use space economically.

(*i*) Mass displays of identical products can increase sales substantially. The eye appeal of massed packs can be enormous and this type of display is almost essential for small, promotional lines.

(*ii*) Displays should not be too tidy and symmetrical. A certain amount of planned disarrangement can encourage the customer to buy.

(*iii*) Point-of-sale material can often help increase sales but an excessive amount (of suppliers' messages) can confuse and take up valuable selling space. This type of promotional material also tends to creep over stock and windows, obscuring the real message of the product.

(c) Accessibility of merchandise.

(*i*) Products should be as accessible as possible to the customer: merchandise handled is merchandise half sold. The security aspect must not, of course, be forgotten.

(*ii*) In some stores, like toys and electrical stores, some merchandise should be working and self-demonstrable.

(*iii*) Products should be displayed in proportion to their sales and stockturn.

(*iv*) There is no point in featuring lines for which only a few items are in stock.

(*v*) Main aisle widths in non-food stores should be a minimum of one metre so that two people can pass in comfort.

(*vi*) Stockrooms should be neatly laid out, as far as possible on the same lines as the shop itself. This will speed service.

(*vii*) Best-selling lines on wall fixtures should be displayed just below eye-level, medium sellers on the bottom shelving and slower lines at the top. This is how the human eye travels normally over shop stock – again, block displays of similar items on a shelf should travel vertically, not horizontally ('vertical blocking').

24. Shelving

The methods of displaying goods for maximum accessibility to the customer may vary with the nature of the goods themselves. The basic method is the use of shelving, whether on walls or gondolas, and adapting the shelves within the whole unit to different purposes, rather than using special equipment. Figure 17.3 shows an arrangement typical of a small self-service grocery store, The advantage of this system of arrangement is that a neat orderly presentation of goods is made, which does not create confusion in a customer's mind. At the same time long lines of shelves showing a monotony of cans and packages are

Figure 17.3 Display in self-service grocery store

broken up and become much more interesting for inspection, whilst vertical blocking aids comparison and selection with optimal efficiency.

25. Other in-store checks

Other important factors which the store or department manager should cover, preferably before trading starts each morning, are as follows:

(a) All lines carried by the store should be on display (not just in stock) and correctly ticketed where appropriate.

(b) Damaged goods should never be on normal display but may be sold off at a discount in a 'bargain corner'.

(c) Clutter and the 'bazaar effect' should be avoided.

(d) Stock should be regularly cleaned and dusted along with the shop, its fascia and fittings from window line to the rear of the sales area.

(e) Displays of any product should be built so that they remain steady. Breakages can cost money and lose customers.

26. The objectives of merchandise display

To summarize the importance of window and in-store display we can say that its objectives are:

(a) To interest customers in merchandise and to draw them into the shop to enquire further

(b) In particular to focus the customer's interest on those goods that the company's marketing plans are currently concentrating on selling

(c) To make it as easy as possible for the customer to find and examine the goods he or she wants

(d) To make it as easy as possible for the sales assistants to demonstrate and sell the products

(e) To enhance the company's image and reputation.

Most multiples send out detailed computer-generated 'planograms' to their branches, which provide detailed layouts and illustrate how displays should look. All this helps to standardize the look of a multiple group's stores.

ALLOCATION OF SELLING AREA SPACE

27. Basic practice

Selling area space is at a premium in most retail outlets, particularly those which depend on high sales volumes. In an attempt to optimize the selling area space used with its cost, space for individual lines is allocated as far as possible in line with their contribution to sales and profitability. The extension of space allocated to popular lines will, up to a point, increase their sales and the opposite is often true when space allocation is reduced.

28. Importance of correct shelf allocation

The correct use of limited space within retail outlets is very important because it:

(a) improves profitability (experiments have shown a 20–100 per cent increase in sales and profitability due to correct allocation)

(b) helps to optimize the use of space with its costs

(c) helps give maximum exposure to market leaders

(d) makes adequate use of space on the basis of customer requirements for heavier-demand lines

(e) reduce out-of-stock shelf positions

(f) feeds back information to the buyers as to what lines are fast or slow movers

(g) makes shelf filling more concentrated and less frequent

(h) allows variety reduction with the use of Pareto analysis (the 80:20 rule) and the automatic elimination of slow movers.

29. Some words of caution

(a) Experiments have shown that the effects of varying the number of identical facings (items) on a shelf display affect volume lines only.

(b) The theory and practice of extending display space to increase sale does not work in the case of slow-moving merchandise.

(c) Change in sales can also occur when volume lines are displayed at varying shelf heights.

30. DPP

The allocation of space by computer analysis is now commonplace. The market leading Space Management package is 'Spaceman' which is produced by Nielsen Logistics. This is often linked to the concept of Direct Product Profitability (DPP), that is establishing the individual contribution to profitability of each product by identifying costs of shelf space and transport, overheads and man-hours. The idea is to optimize the return for each type of merchandise as far as possible by matching its profitability against its space allocation. Space is re-allocated by switching space to those products with the highest DPP. Profit for the firm should therefore be maximized. The main problems associated with this type of analysis is that its value in maximizing profit could be severely reduced by the costs of mounting and maintaining such a system, and the need to ensure an adequate choice of merchandise is offered to the customer.

Progress test 17

1. Compare and contrast store image and atmosphere.

2. What should the store's sign communicate?

3. What are the three main types of shop front?

4. What are the important points to note in window display?

5. How should selling space be allocated in order to maximize sales and profitability?

6. What three main factors should be considered in determining store layout?

7. Detail the factors which are important in general in-store display.

8. How should display space be allocated?

9. Over the last few years many specialized design groups have flourished through providing design services to retailers. Equally many retailers believe it is necessary to refurbish stores much more frequently than in the past. Examine why this should be so, and discuss the relationship between store layout and 'atmosphere'.

10. 'Store Image' is a major influence on store selection. Identify those components which go to make up store image and using a local retailer as an example, suggest how atmosphere and layout affect store image.

11. How might an understanding of the following be used by a practising retail manager. Illustrate your answers with examples from current practice.

    (a) Light and colour
    (b) Display technique
    (c) Store movement patterns.

12. Critically assess the application of DPP to merchandise planning decisions with particular reference to assortment and variety.

18

CUSTOMER SERVICE DECISIONS

SERVICE AND LEVEL OF SERVICE

1. Primary and complementary services

Retail organizations offer goods and services to the consumer for personal use. Some organizations concentrate on providing a service; for example, banks, insurance companies and estate agents and they are known as primary service retailers. Many retailers, however, concentrate on physical products and offer services as a back-up. These complementary services such as delivery, credit, installation, alteration, etc. are not essential to the retail operation but are often used strategically to provide a competitive advantage and enhance the retail offering.

2. Level of service

The extent to which a retailer provides consumers with extra help in purchasing a product or service will be determined primarily by the target market (and its expectations) and the retailer's objectives with particular regard to store image. The type of merchandise is also a major determinant of service requirements with bulky or heavy items often requiring the retailer to offer a delivery service. Also to be considered when setting the level of service would be the location of the store, competitors and the resources of the firm.

CREDIT

3. Types of credit

The provision of credit to customers by retail organizations has become very common in recent years, particularly for costly items like large electrical products, furniture, cars and even clothing. In order to compete, most companies in these particular sectors, even discounters, offer some form of credit. The main types are detailed below.

4. Monthly account or charge account

This type of account is operated typically by department stores and normally there is no additional (interest) charge to the customer as long as accounts presented are paid promptly. If they are not, the retailer has to provide the extra credit, which is costly, and therefore effectively reduces gross margins (these tend to be higher to support the normal credit lines).

5. Budget account

Many stores, particularly in the clothing sector, offer this type of account, which enables the customer to buy goods on credit up to the value of perhaps 12 times the monthly payment. These accounts are often of the revolving credit type, so that when payments are made, new credit is increased to the same amount. A small charge is usually made, often a percentage of each purchase value.

6. Payment out of income

Forms of credit of this type are used for the purchase of goods such as clothing and travel goods for which hire-purchase facilities are not usually available. They normally require a down-payment and the balance to be paid over a 6-, 12- or 24-month period, with an appropriate service charge made to cover administration and not infrequently to make an extra profit.

7. Hire-purchase

This is still a popular method of purchasing durable goods on credit. In case of default on payment, the retailer has the right of re-possession under certain conditions because the goods are not sold outright, only hired to the customer until the debt is extinguished (unlike credit sale agreements). The retailer, instead of financing the hire-purchase debt, seeks support from a finance house. Although the customer's total debt may then be funded by an outside organization, the retailer still takes payments, repaying the finance house from this income. For some retail and television rental companies, these repayments can be a substantial form of short-term funds flow, collection costs being minimal.

8. Credit cards

The two best known credit cards are Access and Visa. The latter is promoted by Barclay's Bank, and Access by the other London clearing banks together with the Royal Bank of Scotland. They provide credit facilities to retailers who accept the cards and the retailer normally pays between 2 and 5 per cent of the value of the sale as a service charge. The retailer also pays a sum to join the scheme and the amount depends on how many stores are owned.

Because of the cost to the retailer of offering these third party credit cards, many larger retailers now operate their own in-house credit cards. These operations have uses in addition to the credit facilities. Since much information is gathered on individual customers on the application for credit and subsequent use of the card this may also be used for promotional purposes (e.g. direct mail).

9. Advantages and disadvantages of credit to the retailer

(a) Advantages

(*i*) Turnover is higher.
(*ii*) Higher value purchases are encouraged.
(*iii*) A better defined target market may be attracted.
(*iv*) Customers become 'regulars'.
(*v*) Buying becomes easier, e.g. by telephone.
(*vi*) Goodwill is increased.

(b) Disadvantages

(*i*) Additional capital is needed for funding the debt and this may have to be borrowed when interest will have to be paid.
(*ii*) Extra overhead costs are incurred such as in keeping customers' accounts and preparing monthly statements.
(*iii*) Some losses from bad debts have to be faced.

10. Credit policy

There is no point in operating credit unless it generates a sufficient increase in profits to cover interest charges on borrowed capital, administration costs and bad debts. The retailer has to think whether the capital could be used more profitably in other ways.

11. In-house credit control

The three main aspects to control are as follows:

(a) The application. Customers selected for credit lines should be thoroughly vetted as to their financial standing and ability to pay in full. An application form usually has to be filled in and the vetting of the customer may be carried out by a credit status agency, such as CCN.

(b) Authorization. Identification of authorized customers is made possible by the issue of store credit cards. A system of credit sanction allows customers to purchase further goods on credit if the credit control department finds that their accounts show a credit balance.

(c) Speed of payment. To keep the capital invested to a minimum it is essential to send out accounts regularly, e.g. monthly. Slow payers should be sent polite reminders and if payment is very late (say over three months) without a good reason, the firm may have to threaten (and eventually take, if the threat is not effective) legal action.

12. EFTPOS

In early 1978 the Retail Consortium agreed to set up a joint committee with the clearing banks to study the application of electronic-funds-transfer systems, with customers paying when their personal plastic card is scanned by the in-store terminal; their accounts would then be instantaneously and automatically debited at their branches. In 1987 Barclay's Bank launched its Delta card and the other major banks launched their 'Switch' card which allows electronic funds transfer at the point of sale (EFTPOS). Although the initial impact was small, with many retailers rejecting the scheme due to its high cost compared to cheque clearance, the system is growing in popularity due to the convenience it offered the customer (for example, in simplifying checkout procedures), and is now widely accepted and used.

ALTERNATIVE SERVICE OFFERINGS

13. Hours

There is an increasing tendency for many types of store to stay open longer hours. Once again, this is in response to the customers' requirement for convenience. With more and more women working it has become necessary for grocery stores to stay open longer in the evening. Many DIY operators also operate outside of the traditional nine to five, six days a week in recognition of the fact that their customers want this type of product outside of normal working hours. Ultimately, the retailer's decision on opening hours depends on the target market; for some small communities the store image could be damaged if Sunday trading was operated, due to local social and religious beliefs. On the other hand, many small 'convenience stores' have increased turnover by up to 50 per cent by extending opening hours to the 'eight 'til late' type of format.

14. Delivery

The provision of a delivery service is essential for certain types of merchandise such as furniture or large electrical durables such as washing machines. For others it can provide a competitive advantage and enhance the retail offering by providing time and place convenience. Some fast food operators (e.g. Domino Pizza) have chosen to offer a delivery service as one way of setting themselves apart from the competition.

There can be considerable problems associated with the provision of a delivery service and it is essential to set up a system to handle them. Perhaps the greatest is minimizing cost, particularly in situations of considerable variation in demand. Also, when customers purchase products they want immediate possession. If a delivery service is provided customer dissatisfaction can be caused if delivery is not on time or the product is damaged in transit. Delivery problems are also caused if the customer is not at home on the agreed delivery date – some retailers try to minimize this by phoning the customer before delivery. Certain types of merchandise will require more than delivery and the retailer should determine whether to offer an installation service either free or for a small additional payment.

15. Alteration and repairs

These may be offered either as part of the customer service facility or as an income generating service in their own right. For example, many clothing retailers offer minor alterations at no charge but will also offer to alter garments some time after the initial sale for a fee. Similarly, electrical appliance retailers will arrange for free repair of items within the warranty period and charge outside of warranty on a full profit-making basis. The provisions of extended guarantees can also be a useful way of generating customer satisfaction and increasing revenue. The decision to offer an alteration and repair service does not automatically require an in-house facility to be set up. These services can often be subcontracted to a third party although this may lead to loss of some control and longer service time.

16. Wrapping

It is interesting to note that US consumers expect their purchases to be wrapped whereas in the UK few retailers offer a full wrapping service. Some UK supermarkets offer help with the loading of groceries into the shopper's bag but very few retailers offer the gift wrapping service featuring bows and ribbons which is commonly available for an additional fee in US stores.

HANDLING COMPLAINTS

17. Complaints

Even in the best run establishments there will be occasions when a customer is not completely satisfied and has cause to complain. It is here that the truly successful retailer will stand above the competition by converting a dissatisfied customer to a satisfied one who will return. With the high costs of marketing in today's highly competitive retail scene it is less expensive to resolve a current customer's problem than to win new customers.

18. Causes of complaints

Major causes of complaint are products not being in stock (when advertised), unsatisfactory performance of product or unsatisfactory repair or service. Many complaints are easily resolved but require a procedure to deal with them.

19. Complaint-handling procedure

Minor complaints may be handled by the sales assistants but customers will often appreciate the attention of a higher level of employee. In larger stores a customer service department will handle complaints. Whatever the appropriate complaint-handling procedure, it should be clear to both employees and customer where to go to complain and who to speak to. Standard procedures should be adopted and all employees informed of them.

20. Returns

A customer who returns merchandise which was found to be damaged or broken when unpacked is obviously entitled to return it and demand a replacement or refund. However, there are other circumstances which are not quite as clear cut and require some extra thought by the retailer. If the retailer is offering a high level of customer service a liberal returns policy would be appropriate; for example, offering a replacement because of a customer's 'change of mind' or making a mistake in thinking an item would match or fit in with another product they already own. Marks & Spencer have operated a liberal returns policy for many years which has resulted in a good deal of extra business in the form of buying gifts with customers knowing that if the item is not suitable the recipient of the gift could return it (in perfect condition) for replacement. Returns or refunds are normally offered only on the production of a receipt but here common sense must prevail, e.g. a customer who received an item as a gift will not have a receipt.

21. Product adjustment

Retailers can satisfy most complaints about damaged or unsuitable products by exchanging them but complaints about poor quality should be handled very carefully for fear of damaging the store image. Therefore, higher quality products should be offered as a replacement with an appropriate price adjustment if necessary to protect the reputation of the store as not selling 'shoddy' goods.

Complaints about products not being in stock can be dealt with by agreeing to stock the product, explaining why the product is not stocked and offering an alternative or directing the customer to a store which does stock that product.

22. Price adjustments

Since it is not always possible or practicable to exchange or adjust a product (e.g. an electrical durable delivered to the customer's home), the retailer can often satisfy the customer by offering to reduce the price. A price reduction is often an effective way of demonstrating to the customer that the store is making a special effort to correct a problem, and it is usually possible for the retailer to make a claim upon the manufacturer.

23. New services

Retailers should constantly monitor their service levels and compare them with competitors. Today's sophisticated consumers have moved beyond the search for lowest possible prices and are demanding higher service levels. New services are being introduced, copied by competitors and then replaced, upgraded or abandoned in the constant battle for competitive advantage.

Progress test 18

1. What is the difference between primary and complementary services?

2. What is meant by the level of service?

3. Describe the main types of credit.

4. What are the advantages and disadvantages of credit to the retailer?

5. What is EFTPOS? Why was there resistance to its introduction from retailers?

6. Describe four customer services, other than credit, which many retailers offer.

7. Describe a good complaint-handling procedure.

8. Why should retailers constantly monitor their service levels?

9. Several large retailers such as the John Lewis partnership have their own in-house credit cards but do not accept third party cards such as Access and Visa. Examine the pros and cons of this strategy for the retailer.

10. Provide examples of customer services which retailers have offered in order to gain competitive advantage. Recommend a customer service strategy for a specific department within a department store. Should this service level be higher or lower than operates in other departments?

Part Three

ADMINISTRATION

19

FINANCIAL PLANNING

PROFIT PLANNING

1. Profit

Profit is essential for the survival of any business activity. For some small retailers the profit generated is effectively the salary of the proprietor so it is necessary to set profit objectives or targets to be reached in a particular time period. Generally, profit objectives will be determined in conjunction with sales targets but bearing in mind that the profit generated should be compared to that which might be achieved by investing the capital employed in the business in an alternative (and perhaps less risky) manner.

2. Sales revenue and costs

Since profit is the surplus after deducting the cost of goods sold and expenses from the sales revenue, then a sales forecast is often the starting point for profit planning. Sales forecasting was dealt with in Chapter 9; for a new business the sales forecast is usually calculated by the market share method, but for established businesses it is very much easier since historical data are available for extrapolation. Similarly, costs can be estimated for the given sales volume from historical cost data or industry norms.

3. Improving profit

The profit estimated from the above procedure should be compared with profit objectives and ways of improving profit should be considered. Essentially these will fall into two categories: increasing sales and reducing costs.

4. Increasing sales revenue

This can be achieved by a number of methods; for example, by increasing promotional activity such as advertising or personal selling. Improving customer service helps to stimulate sales as will adding other products or services. Changing prices can also lead to increased sales revenue.

5. Reducing costs

There are many expenses involved in running a retail operation and these need to be carefully monitored and controlled. Wage costs are one of the most significant and may be reduced by better scheduling of staff. Reduction of stock levels can also reduce costs as could a reduction of service level. The relationship between cost, sales and profit should be fully understood. Break-even analysis can be useful to show how the classification of fixed and variable costs helps determine the impact of changes in sales on profits (*see* Figure 9.4).

BUDGETARY CONTROL

6. Meaning of budgetary control

This is the name given to the technique of planning and measuring a firm's operations usually in cash terms for a specific period. Unlike the quarterly, six-monthly and annual financial accounts, which are a historical record of a firm's performance, the budgets attempt to forecast the activity of the firm and to chart progress as it occurs, so that action necessary to deal with the changing situation can be taken. Budgeting shows what is happening in the firm and the management's task is to discover why it is happening and to do something about it.

7. Advantages of budgeting

(a) Helps to ensure the most efficient use of a firm's resources and helps to prevent waste.

(b) Reduces risk and helps ensure profits.

(c) Replaces guesswork, to a large extent, by facts.

(d) Acts as a target-setting agency.

(e) Pinpoints areas for investigation and corrective action in good time.

(f) Permits 'control by exception' so that only variances from the forecast need be brought to the management's attention.

(g) Fixes responsibility within the organization for the achievement of targets.

(h) Engenders co-operation and co-ordination within the firm.

8. Disadvantages of budgeting

(a) May stifle 'over-achievement' that may result in stiffer targets being set in the future.

(b) Over-elaboration or inflexibility can produce a situation where the budget becomes an end in itself and not just another management tool.

9. Types of budget

In retailing there are normally three main types of budget produced:

(a) The operating budget which is made up from three other budgets: the sales budget, the merchandise budget and the expense budget.

(b) The cash budget relating to receipts and payments of money.

(c) The capital budget covering capital expenditure.

These budgets are interrelated and forecasts in one sphere may depend upon what occurs in others.

10. The sales budget

The core of the sales budget is the sales forecast and because it affects other forecasts, such as cash flow, it is important to refine it as much as possible – paying particular regard to the following factors:

(a) Comparability. Exceptional or non-recurring events (e.g. local sales, branch closure for refitting) should be excluded. The calendar year presents a problem (e.g. different numbers of Saturdays in one month compared with the same month in the following year) so that most retail firms work on 13 four-weekly periods or on a quarterly basis (5 weeks + 4 weeks + 4 weeks).

(b) Modifications. Modifications affecting either a single trade (e.g. changes in consumers' tastes for particular types of furniture) or the economy as a whole (e.g. lower volume of consumer offtake due to a recession) or local circumstances (e.g. higher unemployment due to closure of factories).

(c) Data sources. The main data sources are:

(*i*) The internal information on turnover for the past period and a trend of sales over the past three or four years may be taken. The use of moving annual totals and other moving totals and averages will highlight trends. Note should be taken of newly extended or modernized branches.

(*ii*) External sources which include the indices of value and volume sales experienced by broad categories of retail trades, for example Mintel or EIU. These indicate sales levels at current and constant prices as it is most important, particularly in times of high inflation, to make allowances for increased prices that may mask changes in volume. Some sector's Trade Associations produce their own data on product offtake such as in the consumer electrical and car industries.

11. The merchandise budget

This is as realistic a forecast as possible of the cost of goods sold, i.e. the cost of the merchandise for the expected sales volume.

12. The expense budget

This is concerned with expenditure planned for the coming period, specifically in connection with generating the forecast level of sales.

Expenses are classified into fixed, variable and semi-fixed:

(a) Fixed expenses are those that do not vary with the volume of the business, e.g. rent and rates.

(b) Variable expenses are those that alter in proportion to the trading volume, e.g. wrapping materials, commission payments.

(c) Semi-fixed costs are those that contain a fixed element and do not change proportionately to the volume of business, e.g. head office salaries.

13. Expense control

Expenses are inevitably more controllable because of their internal context than other business variables such as sales and gross profit. They can also be used more positively as task-setters for management. The achievement of control depends on these prerequisites:

(a) Adequate degree of analysis of the actual and budgeted expenses. For this to be possible the expenses must be:

(*i*) categorized under homogeneous cost heads, e.g. advertising, so as to make proper comparisons
(*ii*) not over-detailed so that the reasons for variances are hidden.

(b) Divergences. There should be a frequent drawing out of the cost centres and expense sources so that divergences between budget and actual expenses can be quickly spotted. Most retail companies raise detailed expense accounts at least monthly.

(c) Explanation of the variations between actual and budgeted must be rapid, lucid and accurate so that speedy corrective action can be taken by management (for example, some form of exception reporting can be used to aid the scrutiny).

(d) Cost heads. The main cost heads met with in retailing are, roughly in order of magnitude:

(*i*) cost of goods sold
(*ii*) wages and salaries
(*iii*) accommodation costs (rents, rates, lighting, heating, etc.)
(*iv*) general expenses (e.g. transport).

14. The operating budget

This pulls together the sales, merchandise and expense budgets and is usually split into either 13 four-weekly periods or, more commonly, into quarters, each three-monthly period containing five, four and four weeks respectively.

Comparison is made with the previous year's actual sales with expenses and profits shown as percentages (*see* Table 19.1).

15. The cash budget

This is a forecast intended to ensure the maintenance of a satisfactory balance between anticipated income and expenditure. At its simplest level this can be called the 'cash flow' of the business. The regulation of income and expenditure is particularly important where a company is engaged in forms of hire-purchase or credit transactions (e.g. mail order companies), or when it exhibits a highly seasonal sales pattern where there may be low turnover months when losses are unavoidable. The important ratios to be borne in mind here are the cash level (i.e. cash in hand or at bank or other liquid resources), cash and debtors in relation to current liabilities, and cash, debtors and stock in relation to current liabilities (i.e. working capital).

Both the income and expenditure of the business depend on various factors and these are as follows:

(a) The income of the business. This is dependent upon:

(*i*) cash sales (consider the pattern to date and the balance of sales which are made on credit)

(*ii*) interest received (easily predictable)

(*iii*) debtors (these are only likely to be important for the retailer if, like department stores or mail-order houses, they extend a great deal of credit. It is important in these cases to consider the proportion who are likely to pay promptly on arrival of the statement and how many will pay last month's or earlier debts).

Other types of income include interest on investments, proceeds from sale of assets, foreign exchange transactions, etc.

(b) The expenditure of the business. This is dependent upon:

(*i*) purchases as specified in the merchandise budget

(*ii*) creditors (their terms and periods of credit permitted)

(*iii*) wages and salaries

(*iv*) other overheads

(*v*) taxation as and when due for payment

(*vi*) dividends due to shareholders

(*vii*) interest due on debentures or other loans

(*viii*) planned capital expenditure.

16. Cash flow

There are three time-scales which are important when projecting the financing of company activities. These are:

(a) Short-term cash forecast. This involves the day-to-day control of the cash position, detailing each financial movement in stock, expenses, capital expenditure and so on (the time-scale is usually up to four to six weeks). The short-term

Table 19.1 Operating budget

Four-weekly periods →

	Actual 1995 £	%	Period 1 £	%	Period 2 £	%	Period 12 £	%	Period 13 £	%	Budget 1996 £	%
Sales	3,554,207	100.0	388,000	100.0	402,000	100.0					4,851,700	100.0
Gross profit	1,137,104	32.0	128,400	33.1	135,500	33.7					1,666,000	34.3
Expenses:												
Advertising	84,319	2.4	1,000	0.3	2,000	0.5					127,110	2.6
Branch salaries	178,835	5.0	17,600	4.5	18,390	4.6					285,000	5.9
Head office salaries	102,223	2.9	11,900	3.1	11,900	3.0					188,700	3.9
Establishment costs	250,207	7.0	30,770	7.9	30,930	7.6					400,600	8.3
Overheads:												
Financial	9,885	0.3	1,180	0.3	1,180	0.3					15,330	0.3
Legal	8,489	0.2	960	0.2	960	0.2					12,570	0.3
Distribution	35,066	1.0	3,550	0.9	5,400	1.3					54,500	1.1
Others	48,771	1.4	5,780	1.6	5,840	1.6					79,400	1.6
Total expenses	717,795	20.2	72,740	18.8	76,600	19.1					1,163,200	24.0
Net profit before tax	419,309	11.8	55,660	14.3	58,900	14.6					502,800	10.3

forecast also schedules forward commitments and, if necessary, can allow their rearrangement so that temporary shortage of funds can be overcome. The short-term forecast is particularly useful for companies trading to the limit of their overdrafts at any time and also companies with surplus funds where management has been charged with making the best use of these funds, e.g. by placing them on 'overnight call' on the London money market.

(b) The annual cash budget. This highlights periods of strain on liquidity so that budgets can be adjusted accordingly. This type of budgeting is carried out by most retailers but is of particular use to those with marked seasonal changes in volume.

(c) Long-term budget. Here the time-scale is up to five years. It is important because:

(*i*) it will affect the products the company will sell so as to achieve its profitability targets

(*ii*) it will have a bearing on the markets the firm will sell into

(*iii*) it must also help to determine the market share planned by the company

(*iv*) it will affect the size and range of outlets opened by the company. In other words, the long-term cash budget shows the range of expansion that is possible and will help to answer questions like: Can the company finance the rate of expansion on its existing overdraft arrangements? Should some other form of finance be sought to cushion the company against possible poor trading conditions?

17. The capital budget

Capital expenditure is necessary in the longer-term interests of the firm, e.g. the replacement of or addition to existing assets, such as equipment or buildings. The problems of capital expenditure in retailing revolve around four factors:

(a) Investment is often based on property (the location decision for which few alternatives exist).

(b) The time scale is longer in retailing than in manufacturing due partly to the fact that leases tend to be for 20 years and also because many retail companies do not receive an acceptable rate of return for one to three years after the investment has been completed.

(c) As far as multiple retailing is concerned, the company's own corporate strategy may determine the capital cost of the project in terms of branch size, cost of fittings and so on.

(d) The income that the retail unit makes may ultimately be significantly larger than that made on an industrial capital project of the same value.

18. Responsibility for budgeting

The gathering and co-ordination of budgetary information is normally the responsibility of the management and cost accountants whereas the financial accountants are more involved with the historical, end-of-period figures and the construction of the published accounts. In larger companies a budget committee may carry out the co-ordination and represent the buying, selling property development and other functions. Budgeting should always be carried out backed by the expertise of the operational personnel who will obviously be interested in seeing that target setting is fair.

19. Reporting

In order that a budgetary control system is made effective key results must be reported upon at regular intervals. The regularity of reports and detail required will vary according to the type of retail operation. With the advent of EPOS detailed daily reports can be produced comparing actual sales versus budget and previous years' performance. As well as these, a monthly reporting system for senior management is most common.

The components of the monthly report should be the profit-determining variables:

(a) Sales. By outlet, four-weekly and cumulatively, giving actual, budget and variances.

(b) Gross profit. This should at least cover the sales at selling prices and the purchases at cost of all the major merchandise groups and the monthly stock movements of each group.

(c) Expenses. These should cover the major cost heads, e.g. wages, occupation costs.

The tables should be easily digestible showing variances and action to be taken. They should include the minimum of verbal data. The main report should be for top management, with subsidiary reports for departmental heads, e.g. sales, buying. Table 19.2 shows an example of a monthly trading and profit and loss summary.

FINANCIAL STATEMENTS

20. The main accounts

Joint-stock companies are legally obliged to produce final accounts at the end of each trading period. These financial statements should show a 'true and fair' view of the affairs of the company. The most common forms of financial statement are the profit and loss account and the balance sheet. The profit and loss account shows the amount of profit obtained from the use of the assets over a period of time whereas the balance sheet shows the assets of the enterprise and the sources of capital used to finance these assets. (Tables 19.3 and 19.4 show examples of a profit and loss account and balance sheet respectively.)

Table 19.2 Monthly trading and profit and loss summary

| | Period 6 | | | | Cumulative | | | | | | Year-end Position | | | | | |
| | Actual | | Budget | | Actual | | Budget | | Previous year | | Latest forecast | | Budget | | Previous year | |
	£	%	£	%	£	%	£	%	£	%	£	%	£	%	£	%
Sales	382,669	100.0	395,200	100.0	2,622,816	100.0	2,599,700	100.0	1,893,884	100.0	4,930,000	100.0	4,851,700	100.0	3,554,207	100.0
Gross profit	129,775	33.9	130,400	33.0	884,990	33.7	894,500	34.4	616,212	32.5	1,679,000	34.0	1,666,000	34.3	1,137,104	32.0
Expenses:																
Advertising	5,811	1.5	7,800	2.0	95,328	3.6	91,800	3.5	56,506	2.9	130,000	2.6	127,100	2.6	84,319	2.4
Branch salaries	19,693	5.2	20,000	5.1	163,477	6.3	156,600	6.0	85,763	4.5	300,000	6.1	285,000	5.9	178,835	5.0
Head office salaries	15,467	4.0	16,000	4.0	91,175	3.5	88,600	3.4	66,807	3.5	210,000	4.3	188,700	3.9	102,223	2.9
Establishment costs	37,335	9.8	35,000	8.8	178,550	6.8	182,500	7.1	105,540	5.6	385,000	7.8	400,600	8.3	250,207	7.0
Overheads:																
Financial	1,307	0.3	1,250	0.3	7,243	0.3	7,460	0.3	5,442	0.3	15,000	0.3	15,330	0.3	9,885	0.3
Legal	985	0.3	1,000	0.3	5,899	0.2	6,950	0.3	3,907	0.2	11,000	0.2	12,570	0.3	8,489	0.2
Distribution	3,825	1.0	3,600	0.9	31,341	1.2	30,630	1.2	16,638	0.9	56,000	1.1	54,500	1.1	35,066	1.0
Others	5,476	1.4	6,000	1.5	38,777	1.5	40,110	1.5	22,105	1.2	75,000	1.6	79,400	1.6	48,771	1.4
Total expenses	89,899	23.5	90,650	22.9	611,790	23.4	604,650	23.3	362,708	19.1	1,182,000	24.0	1,163,200	24.0	717,795	20.0
Trading profit	39,876	10.4	39,750	10.1	273,200	10.3	289,850	11.1	253,504	13.4	1,497,000	10.0	502,800	10.3	419,309	11.8
HP finance result: Profit/loss on HP charges	2,786	0.7	3,600	0.9	32,604	1.2	35,000	1.3	22,743	1.2	70,000	1.5	72,300	1.5	49,673	1.4
Provision for unrealised profit	(882)	0.2	(1,000)	0.3	(18,212)	0.6	(19,400)	0.7	(15,255)	0.8	(38,000)	0.8	(39,900)	0.8	(27,474)	0.8
Net profit before tax	41,780	10.9	42,350	10.7	287,592	10.9	305,450	11.7	260,992	13.8	529,000	10.7	535,200	11.0	441,507	12.4

Table 19.3 Profit and loss account for the 52 weeks to 31 January 1996

	£
Sales	600,000
Costs of Sales	350,000
Gross profit	250,000
Expenses	190,000
Operating profit	60,000
Interest charges	15,000
Profit before tax	45,000
Taxation	—
Profit after tax	45,000
Dividends	—
Profit retained	45,000

RATIO ANALYSIS

21. Importance of ratio

Although it should be remembered that factual accounting is historical in character, a business can gain much information from a study of the relationships between various values in financial statements. The regular review of significant ratios enables unhealthy trends to be detected and corrective action taken.

22. Return on capital employed (ROCE)

This important relationship establishes how substantial is the return or yield on the money currently invested in the company as measured by the pre-tax profit performance excluding any exceptional profit items, e.g. profit on foreign exchange transactions. The best measure of capital employed is to compute the shareholders' equity at par value (the issued shareholding of the company) plus any reserves (either capital or revenue). All medium and short-term borrowings like debenture issue or bank overdrafts are excluded from this computation. Assuming that shareholders' funds, including reserves, amount to £11.5 million and the pre-tax net profit for the current year is £2.75 million, the return on capital employed is:

$$\frac{£2.75 \text{ million}}{£11.5 \text{ million}} \times 100 = 23.91 \text{ per cent}$$

23. Liquidity ratios

Liquidity determines whether the retailer can meet payment obligations as they arise – there are two commonly used measures:

Table 19.4 Balance sheet as at 31 January 1996

		£
Fixed assets		170,000
Current assets	100,000	
Creditors (amount falling due within one year)	45,000	
Net current assets		55,000
Total assets less current liabilities		225,000
Creditors (amount falling due after more than one year)		100,000
		125,000
Capital and reserves		
Called up share capital		100,000
Unappropriated profits		25,000
		125,000

Note: (*a*) Creditor (amounts due within one year) = current liabilities.
(*b*) Creditors (amount falling due after more than one year) = debentures and other possible items, e.g. tax, HP, etc.

(a) Current ratio: $\dfrac{\text{Current assets}}{\text{Current liabilities}}$

This indicates the retailer's ability to meet current debts with current assets.

(b) Quick ratio or acid test ratio: $\dfrac{\text{Current assets} - \text{Stock}}{\text{Current liabilities}}$

This is a more severe measure of the retailer's liquidity position and measures the ability to meet current debts with assets that can immediately be converted to cash.

24. Cost percentages

Most retail companies express their costs by percentage of turnover both at branch level and overall. This allows comparisons to be made and trends to be monitored. For instance, if a branch's turnover was £400,000 per annum, salaries were £32,000 and rent and rates together were £24,000, the respective cost percentages would be 8 and 6 per cent. (The use of salary percentages, for instance, can help decide branch establishments.) If the achieved gross margin (net sales – net cost of goods sold) was 24 per cent and the planned net contribution was 5 per cent, all the other costs in running the branch could not be more than 19 per cent (these costs might include head office costs, other accommodation costs like lighting and heating and so on).

25. Efficiency of fixed capital utilization

The efficiency of fixed capital utilization can be measured by relating fixed assets to sales, thus giving the speed of fixed capital turnover. Capital development at new and existing outlets unmatched by a corresponding growth in sales volume will be detected by a slowing down in this rate.

OTHER RETAIL PERFORMANCE MEASURES

24. Sales per square foot

This is one of the basic measures of retail performance and is expressed as follows (taking random figures):

$$\frac{\text{£ sales per period}}{\text{Sales floor area}} \quad \text{e.g.} \quad \frac{\text{£1,350,000}}{\text{3000 sq ft}} = \text{£450 per sq ft}$$

The resulting figure is sometimes called the *sales conversion factor*. This performance monitor is very useful for comparing returns in different branch locations. Due to the extra information often now supplied in retail company accounts and statements it is possible to work out sales per square foot for a number of large companies (and thus to compare performance).

A sophistication on this measurement is net profit per square foot, which shows the actual contribution in profit terms that each branch makes.

27. Sales per linear foot

Many stores also measure their sales and profits in relation to the length of wall runs in their stores. This gives a much better indication of the success of in-store display and merchandising in particular sections and brings out the existence of 'hot-spots' (areas of high volume) and 'dead areas'. For example, a 30-foot wall run with sales of £60,000 per annum gives a sale of £2000 per linear foot.

28. Sales per assistant

This is a key measurement in financial analysis of all kinds and forms a useful comparison between the labour productivity of different branches. It may also assist in working out branch establishments, e.g. sales of £3,000,000 and the number of staff being 25 gives sales per assistant of £120,000.

29. Sales per checkout

By dividing the period's sales in a supermarket by the number of checkouts the operator can find out whether he or she is 'under' or 'over-tilled' and make adjustments.

30. Rate of stockturn

This is of crucial importance in the retail context and there is a strong correlation between it and the size of net margins and thus return on capital. In food stores, stockturn rates, which are calculated by dividing average stock into sales, may be as high as 60 times (six days average stock). In non-foods, turns of six to eight times would be considered reasonable.

Progress test 19

1. What is meant by profit planning? Why is it important?

2. What is budgetary control? Describe the advantages and disadvantages of budgeting.

3. Describe the three main types of budget produced by retailers.

4. Why is reporting of results important?

5. What are the two main types of financial statement produced by retailers?

6. What are liquidity ratios? What do they show?

7. Describe four other important measures of retail performance.

20

HUMAN RESOURCES

1. Introduction

The organizing, selecting and training of personnel must be part of the retail planning process. Human assets are of the utmost importance to retail success, but often plans are made with little regard for the people who will carry them out.

ORGANIZATION

2. Definition of organization

A comprehensive definition of organization is as follows:

(a) Determining and providing whatever capital, materials, equipment and personnel may be required in an enterprise in order to achieve its objectives.

(b) Defining the duties and responsibilities of the personnel employed and determining the manner in which their activities are to be interrelated.

3. Types of organization (internal structure)

It will be seen from Chapter 2 that each type of retail company tends to operate its own particular kind of organization to meet its objectives. It is very difficult to identify types of organization in a clear-cut fashion, but they are usually labelled for the sake of convenience as:

(a) Line (or direct) organization. Here the lines of authority and responsibility come direct from the managing director to the junior. This simple system is only workable in practice in smaller stores because it ignores the growth of the business and the need to rely on specialist functions like personnel, merchandising, etc.

(b) Functional organization. This exists where those in charge of specialist activities or functions are responsible for them throughout every unit of the business, e.g. the chief accountant being responsible for the accuracy of every bill in every branch. The removal of functional responsibility from branch managers, however, vastly reduces their job content, undermines team effort and so on. A wholly functional organization is therefore unknown in retailing although some multiples through their highly centralized control systems come near it.

(c) Line-and-staff organization. This is simply an extension or development of the line organization in which one or more of the ancillary services have been functionalized. This structure is that most usually adopted by retail firms and combines the line (usually selling), with support functions like property negotiation broadening the line organization.

> *Note:* It will be observed that in practice, the organization incorporates a measure of each type. Line management has been described as the relationship in which one person gives an instruction or prescription to another from a different line of command, and staff management as the relationship in which the service offered can be accepted or rejected by others.

4. Centralization

Centralization means the retention of responsibilities in sections attached to head office. Many multiple chains display a substantial amount of centralization in their organization structure. The characteristics of such an organization are as follows:

(a) Considerable consistency throughout the concern and a rigid control by head office.

(b) Considerable economies from standardized procedures, e.g. the system of stock control.

(c) Competent handling by specialists in such matters as security services, in-store merchandising, payment of staff salaries and so on.

A problem with highly centralized organizations is that managers with initiative or independence of spirit may well leave after a spell of frustration when the power to use their own judgement has been taken away from them.

5. Decentralization

This means that responsibility and authority to make decisions for certain activities have been delegated to subordinate units that are then given discretionary powers. We find in such an organization the following:

(a) A more dynamic business in which the managers of units are encouraged to show initiative and enterprise, and to think for themselves.

(b) Such a situation nurtures creative management talent for higher posts.

(c) Area or branch managers of a particularly high calibre are usually required which may be costly if not impossible in a multiple chain running many small branches.

(d) A greater need for checks and controls, whether they are used statistically or appraised by inspection and supervision.

(e) Likelihood of higher morale and greater team effort in branches because of closeness to the 'boss'.

(f) A need for greater specification of duties and responsibilities for field managers because of their proportionately more important roles.

(g) Decentralization frees higher management from some routines, allowing more time for determining strategy.

The problem with decentralized control is that many potential economies are lost with much duplication of effort.

6. The preferred situation

The principle usually followed is that policies and procedures have an essentially centralized character, but that most day-to-day decisions are, of necessity, decentralized. For example, the complaints procedure in a multiple may be as follows: a centralized control may be expedient to ensure consistency of dealing with justified complaints; the branch manager may be left, however, to decide which are or are not justified, as they arise.

7. The principles of good organization

Some general principles applicable to organization are as follows:

(a) Objectives. The goals of the company should be clearly defined along with the means of achieving them so that the organizers can determine what type of organization is required.

(b) Flexibility. When planning an organization structure, provision should be made for adjustments caused by changing circumstances or policies.

(c) Responsibility

(*i*) The responsibility attaching to any post should be clearly defined (e.g. by a job specification).
(*ii*) Responsibility invested must be balanced by sufficient authority to carry out the functions of the post.
(*iii*) A person to whom work has been delegated should be responsible to one senior person only (unless the subordinate carries out more than one function).
(*iv*) If several responsibilities are attached to a particular post they should have some common characteristic.
(*v*) There should be no duplication of activity by executives.
(*vi*) Management must ensure that no 'gaps' occur in the organization and that responsibility for each activity or section can be identified with an individual.
(*vii*) The span of control should be limited to a number which is reasonable in the circumstances.

8. Organization charts

An organization chart should present a diagrammatic representation of the structure of a firm or group of firms. Figures 20.1 and 20.2 show examples of

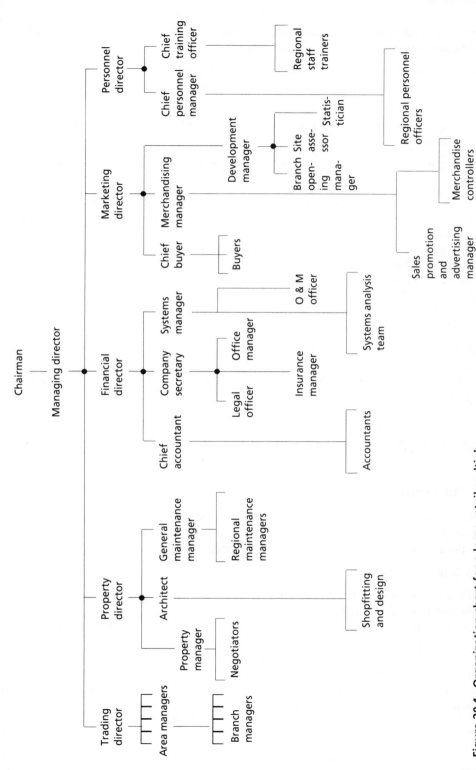

Figure 20.1 Organization chart for a large retail multiple

205

typical organization charts for an individual superstore and a retail multiple company. The functions of an organization chart are:

(a) Relationships, i.e. line, functional and staff, can be clearly illustrated and may assist in defining the levels and status of individuals.

(b) Responsibility is clearly defined and should show each responsible member of the staff to whom he or she is answerable and who are his or her immediate subordinates.

(c) A complete picture of the organization is provided in a graphic way and may help to:

(*i*) pinpoint any bottlenecks or overloading of executives (e.g. span of control)
(*ii*) indicate the character of the organization and the degree to which it is centralized or decentralized
(*iii*) indicate the correct channels of communication for directives, reports and correspondence
(*iv*) indicate anomalies in the relationship between departments
(*v*) secure the introduction of new departments in the right place
(*vi*) help secure the company structure to new staff and delineate promotion ladders.

(d) Grades and levels within the various functions may also be incorporated in the organization chart. Used in this way the chart can provide a basis for the control of staff and ensure the maintenance of an acceptable balance within the various grades.

THE PERSONNEL DEPARTMENT

9. Responsibilities

The personnel department is responsible for maintaining and supporting the human relationships between management and staff. The detailed functions and responsibilities of the personnel department are as follows:

(a) Employment

(*i*) Interviewing or arranging interviews of applicants and dealing with any transfers or dismissals.
(*ii*) Recruitment, including liaison with the Department of Employment and any other appropriate source of labour.
(*iii*) The description of jobs and devising methods of payment and promotion from grade to grade.
(*iv*) Formulating terms and conditions of service and drawing up of redundancy schemes where appropriate.
(*v*) Preparing and maintaining personnel records and statistics.

Figure 20.2 Organization chart for a typical UK superstore

(b) Education, training and development

(*i*) Organizing non-company and external training courses at induction, specialist, supervisor and management levels.
(*ii*) Liaison with appropriate training establishments.
(*iii*) Encouraging further education of all kinds (especially by the provision of financial support).
(*iv*) Dealing with library facilities, the house journal, suggestion schemes, etc. as appropriate.

(c) Wages and salary administration

(*i*) Maintaining the company's accepted wage structure, salary grading, etc. and authorizing rate changes, deductions and special payments.
(*ii*) Consulting management consultants and other specialists concerning proposed incentive schemes.

(d) Health and safety

(*i*) Ensuring compliance with the Offices, Shops and Railway Premises Act and the Health and Safety at Work, etc., Act.
(*ii*) Maintaining working medical services.

(*iii*) Keeping health records.

(*iv*) Supervising arrangements for the prevention of accidents and for investigating them.

(e) Welfare

(*i*) Ensuring compliance with the Shop Acts.

(*ii*) Providing social and sports facilities as appropriate.

(*iii*) Advising employees on their individual personal problems.

(*iv*) Administering pensions and superannuation schemes.

(*v*) Supervising staff canteens as appropriate.

(f) Industrial relations'

(*i*) Serving as negotiating officers with trade unions and other outside bodies.

(*ii*) Keeping a watchful eye on joint consultative procedures.

(*iii*) Ensuring that company policy towards joint consultation is known, both in theory and in practice.

10. Organization of the personnel function

(a) The multiple. Normally a chief personnel officer heads a team that contains a number of travelling branch personnel supervisors. For practical reasons, junior and subordinate staff will be engaged locally by the manager or the staff manager of the branch. Head office will lay down all conditions of service, rates of pay and procedures with regard to sickness and dismissal and may keep a record sheet for all employees which gives a history of their employment. Head office personnel staff should act as final arbiters if field managers are unable to resolve a staff problem themselves.

To sum up, the multiple tends to centralize its personnel function, particularly from a policy point of view, because it allows branch management more time to carry out their main function, which is selling.

(b) The co-operative. In co-operative societies, which are self-contained, there is likely to be a personnel officer and, because the movement has not yet begun to centralize personnel matters, policy is determined by the local management committee.

(c) Department stores. Again a chief personnel manager and assistants are likely to make engagements with departmental managers sitting in. Personnel policy may or may not be made by the personnel manager with the agreement of the board. As in industry generally, personnel management is less likely to be given the accolade of board status, although one director is likely to have responsibility for staff matters.

11. Importance of the personnel function

The importance of the personnel manager has grown in retailing over the past 20 years for the following reasons:

(a) The size of retail business. By organic growth and acquisition, some retail companies have tens of thousands of staff but this has led to greater centralization and a widening gap between management and workers.

(b) Functionalization. The personnel manager is now very much a functional (specialist) member of the management.

(c) Staff problems. The large number of married and part-time staff employed in retailing create domestic and other problems and these require careful handling.

(d) Education and training. Recent reports by the CBI and others have focused on the need for more and better training provision if we are to maintain a competitive position in industrialized society.

TRAINING

12. Introduction

Training is concerned with helping staff to make the best possible use of their talents so as to ensure a high level of business efficiency. Good training is particularly important in retailing because of:

(a) High labour turnover and mobility

(b) Poor recruitment due to:

(*i*) comparatively low wages
(*ii*) long hours (seven-day week trading is now common among bigger companies)
(*iii*) relatively poor working conditions (there are, however, many examples of good conditions, e.g. Marks & Spencer)

The basic requirements of a training system are:

(a) A written company training plan

(b) Assessment of training needs

(c) Appointment of a senior executive to be responsible for training

(d) Appointment of a training officer.

13. Training needs

The training and educational needs of staff in a retail business obviously vary widely. The broad classes of training may be described as for:

(a) New entrants

(b) Established staff

(c) Selected staff, e.g. for promotion

(d) Management.

14. Training new staff

It is vital that training for newcomers to a retail firm is based on a clearly defined, generally understood policy, which is adopted by all members of the firm. Success in training new entrants may be reflected in staff turnover figures. Apart from anything else, confidence should be nurtured in the new recruits as soon as they enter the company. The type of information and training required at this level is as follows:

(a) Induction. The company must be prepared for the arrival of new entrants and start them on a forward plan of training. This plan can be outlined on the first day, much of which will be taken up with looking around and meeting people, one of whom should describe the company and its organization and relate the recruits' jobs to it as a whole.

(b) Information. This may be subdivided into:

(*i*) Essential information, e.g. people and places connected with the newcomers' welfare and work, the company's rules and regulations
(*ii*) General information, e.g. contracts of employment, amenities, safety, accident prevention, personal appearance, security (additionally, details of progress and ability assessment, and specialized training opportunities, may also be given)
(*iii*) Trading information: newcomers, particularly, require the knowledge to help provide the public with a consistent trading identity; everyone, however, needs up-to-date information on the company's basic trading policies.

(c) Customer relations. Because customers do not distinguish between new and established staff, it may be essential that recruits are quickly advised on situations that are outside their knowledge and experience. Avoidance of these 'on-the-job' situations may, however, be thought more beneficial in the interim stages. Customer service training may include:

(*i*) approach to customers, e.g. information offering
(*ii*) customers queries
(*iii*) handling difficult customers
(*iv*) telephone service, e.g. use of the telephone
(*v*) correspondence, e.g. style and content.

(d) Merchandise knowledge. This may involve:

(*i*) stock identification
(*ii*) price and price ranges
(*iii*) colour and size availability
(*iv*) staple and seasonal lines
(*v*) product selling features
(*vi*) uses

(*vii*) advice on care and after-sales service.

(e) Salesmanship. Certain simple sales techniques should be taught in theory and practice and their use supervised until a satisfactory standard is achieved.

(f) Systems and skills. A systems syllabus for selling assistants might include:

(*i*) price labels, e.g. location on the merchandise or shelf edge and their use as a sales record
(*ii*) cash sale recording, e.g. running up on the till and writing sales dockets
(*iii*) cash handling
(*iv*) packing goods and delivery
(*v*) alternative methods of payment and sanctioning, e.g. credit, account, hire-purchase, cash on delivery.

(g) Safety. The recruits should be acquainted with the health and safety hazards within the working environment, e.g. machines and appliances.

(h) Security. Proper systems of checking and surveillance can help prevent dishonesty.

15. Training established staff

Established staff need refresher courses and introduction to new techniques.

(a) Assessing training needs. The methods by which the need is established for particular training for existing staff are:

(*i*) *Systems standards*, i.e. checks on skill and accuracy in using the internal systems.
(*ii*) *Sales ability*. Comparisons of numbers of transactions, average sales, selling staff costs.
(*iii*) *Service standards*, e.g. records and detailed analyses of customer complaints.
(*iv*) *Staff turnover figures*. By expressing the number of staff leaving within say a year as a percentage of the average labour force, the staff turnover ratio can be worked out and used either as a trendspotter or as a comparison between branches or departments.

(b) Topics covered. Areas of knowledge which may need to be restated are:

(*i*) systems
(*ii*) merchandise, i.e. information and assessing customer needs
(*iii*) expenses control, e.g. telephone, lighting
(*iv*) customer relations.

16. Additional training for selected staff

As a company develops it must help its people to develop along with it.

(a) Assessing training needs. In large firms, line and staff managers must advise the personnel and training department as to the job specifications and the qualifications needed to do various types of work so that the recruitment and training of staff produce the right people who are appropriately trained. Training can then continue in individual departments, sections or branches and the personnel department appraised of the results. By co-ordinating these results centrally, training needs can be better identified.

(b) Methods.

(*i*) Job rotation. This involves working for specified periods of time in different departments or branches.

(*ii*) *Planned experience training*. This involves undertaking specific projects or responsibilities in departments whilst working under supervision and reporting on the results.

Both the methods in (*i*) and (*ii*) can be used for staff who have been specially recruited for their academic achievements or for above-average achievements generally.

(*iii*) *Group training*. This is used when some training needs are common to all group members, but it may have to be supplemented by individual training. Group training lends itself more to classroom-type instruction.

17. Management training

(a) Usefulness. A systematic training scheme for management will:

(*i*) enable the business to be run more efficiently and an optimum profit obtained from the investment in premises, equipment, staff and stock

(*ii*) enable individual managers to develop their abilities to full capacity within the firm so that they may be helped to achieve their individual goals and to make a maximum contribution towards the company's goals

(*iii*) ensure a supply of knowledgeable and competent managers to fill future vacancies.

(b) Application to existing managers. Management training is often applied to existing managers in situations of change. Examples of these are:

(*i*) on promotion or preparation for promotion

(*ii*) on the expansion or diversification of the business or other changes affecting the duties and responsibilities of managers

(*iii*) on the introduction of new or different training techniques or policies

(*iv*) on the introduction of new merchandise

(*v*) on the introduction of different management employment policies

(*vi*) on the employment of specialists that requires adjustments in working relationships and communications, e.g. computer systems people or personnel officers

(*vii*) on the availability of new developments in the managers' own and related fields of work.

(c) Management trainees. Reliance on outside sources to fill management vacancies can be expensive and often unsatisfactory and therefore planned career-training for new recruits and promotables is vital to fill future vacancies. The main points to note in connection with these schemes are:

(*i*) Certain preparatory work should be undertaken before training schemes are started.

(*ii*) The company must have a climate that encourages learning and the progress of individuals.

(*iii*) There must be enough suitable line managers and supervisors to help train the trainees.

(*iv*) Individual career-training needs careful planning and communication.

(*v*) The number of trainees at any time should be related to known or anticipated vacancies so that expectations held out to trainees on appointment may be realistic.

(d) Management activities and training needs. Management activity in retailing revolves round four sets of resources and these are as follows:

(*i*) *Finance*. The financial aspects of the business may require training in project appraisal, budgetary control and costing.

(*ii*) *Merchandise*. The merchandise aspect may suggest training in, for example, sales forecasting, stock control, buying and consumer market research.

(*iii*) *People*. The personnel aspect may involve training in interviewing, manpower planning, assessment of training needs and salary administration.

(*iv*) *Premises*. The premises aspect may require training in shop and warehouse site evaluation, planned maintenance or fire practice.

(e) Basis of a sound training scheme.

(*i*) *Assignment of responsibility for training*. Companies with 400–500 employees can find it justifiable to recruit a training officer and in smaller firms one of the directors may take the function over. In any case the scheme must have full support from top management.

(*ii*) *Analysis of managerial functions*. This involves the setting up of job descriptions (i.e. lists of management tasks that are being or should be carried out by the company) and their co-ordination and the production of a control chart that will show the training required to match the management requisite of the company.

(*iii*) *Appraisal of performance*. This is necessary to determine training needs.

(*iv*) *Assessing future management needs*. By the use of detailed availability/ suitability charts an audit of existing management can be produced and matched against future requirements taking into account retirements, known leavings and general expansion.

(*v*) *Design and administration of training*. Training can be either in-company ('on-the-job' and 'off-the-job') or external. It is vital to prepare and maintain personnel records with particular regard to training courses taken, achievement, subsequent promotion and so on.

Progress test 20

1. Define organization and give examples of the various types of internal structure.

2. Discuss the advantages and disadvantages of centralization in retail organizations.

3. What are the functions of organization charts?

4. What are the responsibilities of the personnel department?

5. What are the basic requirements of a training system?

6. Outline the main requirements for training new staff.

7. What methods of training are available to give additional skills to existing staff?

8. What are the advantages of operating a management training scheme?

21

PROPERTY AND LOCATION DEVELOPMENT

THE PROPERTY FUNCTION

1. Importance of the property function

The store premises and other properties owned by a retail company, both freehold and leasehold, may well be its largest asset in value terms. The property department of large multiple retailers serves the trading activity and the company as a whole in a number of important ways, outlined below.

2. Acquisition

Negotiation for the purchase of new property, whether it be new sites or extensions to existing sites, is the life blood of an expanding retail company, provided that the acquisitions fall within the limits of an agreed plan of development and that the new-found premises are capable of profitable use. As part of its development plan the required locations, sites, dimensions and other details will have been sent by the company to estate agents and property developers.

3. Disposals

As a firm rationalizes itself (like many of the multiple food groups have been doing) it will divest itself of the smaller, less profitable branches through estate agents or advertisements in the property press.

4. Surveys

The property department should set up valuation surveys of properties to be acquired to estimate the value to the purchaser as opposed to the rent or price asked. Structural surveys will show defects in the property that would entail expense in reinstatement. It is essential for proper surveys of both types to be carried out before signing a lease or buying a freehold.

5. Scrutiny of conveyancing documents

Although a solicitor is normally retained by a firm when buying or selling properties, leases and title deeds should be examined professionally by the company's property staff. Clauses in short leases are in some cases becoming much more restrictive, for instance in user clauses (restrictions on the use to which a landlord will allow his premises to be put), assignment and subletting rights, right to change the use and right to make alterations, additions and improvements. In addition, length of lease, review clauses, repairing and insurance obligations, service charge, the rent-free period and so on should also be screened on behalf of the company.

6. Planning applications

The property department should make all the necessary approaches to the relevant local authority on planning matters when a new branch or an extension is being developed. This requires the submission of all plans for acceptance by the authority, including shopfronts and fascias, external signs, car parking and so on. The department is also responsible for checking the local plans and the Register of Planning Applications for anything, e.g. road widening, that might affect the site in the future.

7. The Town and Country Planning Act 1990

This Act is the most important successor of the original Town and Country Planning Acts of 1947 and 1971 and it has imposed on each planning authority the duty of preparing a unitary plan.

8. The unitary plan

This is a plan submitted for ministerial approval and is primarily a written statement of policy, accompanied by a diagrammatic structure map for counties and major towns only, designed to expose clearly the broad basic patterns of development and the transport system. Such structure plans form the main link between the policies on a national and regional level and local planning and indicate action areas, i.e. areas where comprehensive development, redevelopment and/or improvement is envisaged in the 10 years after submission. The plan, as far as retailing is concerned, will be able to:

(a) set out the policy and general proposals relating to

   (i) the hierarchy of centres
   (ii) the growth of town centres
   (iii) the creation of new centres
   (iv) the development of district centres
   (v) the relief of congestion in town centres

(b) deal with the quantity of floorspace at significant stages and its distribution

(c) lay out the broad criteria and policies for

(*i*) the location of new development
(*ii*) subsequent local plans
(*iii*) development control
(*iv*) existing development in relation to conservation and conversion

(d) deal with priorities and phasing, particularly in relation to action areas and to deal with implementation, such as the assembly of sites by local authorities and the scope for private development.

9. Project planning and control

When the property department is satisfied that the conditions of a contract are acceptable and that the survey has been competently carried out and is also acceptable, then the actual exchange of contracts takes place (usually through solicitors) and the property is either owned or leased by the retail company. The department then becomes involved in all or some of the following phases:

(a) Rough costing is worked out for project appraisal purposes, probably broken down into shopfitting, shopfront, special equipment (e.g. in-store ovens for a supermarket) and any building costs.

(b) A layout plan is produced by the development department for the shopfitter's use.

(c) Tenders are asked for from two or three shopfitters (although many larger companies have their own shopfitting department). Any building costs may be tendered for separately, along with electrical wiring, air conditioning and so on. Some shopfitting design firms are large enough to take on all aspects of the work but may do some subcontracting themselves. Control of subcontractors is an art and some shopfitting companies have not got it!

(d) A shopfitter is selected and a price is agreed.

(e) A programme of work can then be produced by the department based on the progress charts and other documentary estimates provided by contractors (*see* Figure 21.1). The shopfitter will have produced his own detailed drawing of the site. Although the department will wish to oversee the work in progress it may often ask the main contractor (usually the shopfitter) to oversee the project on its behalf. But the department is still responsible for keeping to dates and should be able to hand over the unit to the trader at the agreed time. Some retail firms employ regional property surveyors to look after company projects in their parts of the country.

(f) All through the project the property department should be checking that work is being kept not only up to date but as per plan in terms of layout, materials used, prices and so on by means of site meetings attended by company development staff and reporting back to the management. At completion the department should inspect the finished product and accept or reject it on behalf on the company. (Incidentally, it is more probable that operating and development

Figure 21.1 A programme of shop fitting work (Gantt chart)

Trade	Week comm. 27 April	Week comm. 4 May	Week comm. 11 May	Week comm. 18 May	Week comm. 25 May	Week comm. 1 June	Week comm. 8 June
Builder and plasterer	Floor screed	Walls, ceiling, back area, and ceiling retail partitions		Frieze and ceiling (back area)			
Shopfitter		All back shop partitions ceilings and frieze groundings		Light trough, shopfront, fascia, back area doors and facings, etc., unit fitting			
Electrician		Wiring installations back shop area		Retail installation ceiling light fittings, etc.			
Heating engineer			Trunking installation		Heating unit installation		
Arcade terrazzo					Terrazzo forecourt ingoes and fascia		
Glazier				Glazing shopfront			
Ceiling fitter					Retail ceiling area		
Painter				Frieze and ceiling retail	All back shop areas and finishings retail		
Polisher						French polisher	
Industrial cleaners						Cleaning	

Note: Site programme will commence 27 April and finish 12 June (i.e. extra week in hand)

218

management have caused modifications to be made to the original plan during the fit; this may, of course, increase the final price.)

(g) Each product, whether it is an acquisition or a refit, should be phased into the total development programme for the year (and in line with the agreed budget) so that the department is not faced with an overload situation at certain periods. It is vital, too, that the number of projects in a budget be kept within the ability of the department to plan and control effectively.

10. Costing, budgeting and accounting

The department should be able to cost out in approximate terms the price of a project so that tender prices, if they are requested, can be compared. This will mean that a schedule of standard costs per unit of fitting or per square metre of sales areas must be worked out. A capital budget can then be formulated and this will be incorporated in the master budget for the company. The department will also be responsible for seeing that all invoices sent in by contractors are correct against estimates or tenders and will authorize payment. The department will also negotiate with contractors if there are any changes in invoice details due to alteration in the design of the project.

11. Design

Many of the very large multiple chains have their own architects department. Whether the drawing up of plans is in-house (where the design team would be part of the property function and responsible to the property manager) or whether outside architects are commissioned, adequate drawings must be dated, described and produced for a building project for the guidance of the company shop planning section, property management, shopfitters, builders, and the local planning authority.

These drawings should be to the accepted scale (e.g. 1 cm = 1 metre) and should show all or most of the following:

(*i*) dimensions, external and internal
(*ii*) position and types of all fittings
(*iii*) lighting
(*iv*) heating
(*v*) floor covering
(*vi*) wall and ceiling finishes
(*vii*) colour schemes
(*viii*) materials
(*ix*) shopfront and fascia
(*x*) stockroom and staffroom facilities
(*xi*) stair positions
(*xii*) any later modifications with dates.

As far as fixtures and fittings are concerned, these may be incorporated later on drawings for internal and shopfitting use (they can, for example, be of help in

219

designing the layout of the branch). The department should produce a catalogue of these fittings, each item being coded and priced. Examples of standard flexible fitments include:

(a) Free-standing wall units

(b) Gondolas

(c) Light-weight merchandisers (a light gondola)

(d) Dress racking

(e) 'Poles' arranged singly or in pairs for bracketing and shelving.

Most proprietary shopfitting systems are today of a modular type. These are standard metric units, which can be run together in sections, that give extraordinary flexibility to shop design possibilities in most trades. Much of the design today is, of course, aimed at the open-plan self-selection type store.

12. Maintenance

The property department should make regular inspections of all properties, preferably on a planned basis and carry out a programme of planned maintenance, which is budgeted for. A maintenance programme will be agreed at head office and initiated both by the latter and by the department.

13. Other statutory duties

(a) Under the Offices, Shops and Railway Premises Act 1963 the retailer's duty to provide proper fire access, sanitation and staffroom accommodation is normally implemented by the department.

(b) If the local authority wishes to purchase a retail property for redevelopment or some other purpose a compulsory purchase order (CPO) is often raised. The department must act on it, particularly in the interests of the retailer so that adequate compensation is possible.

14. Property asset management

One of the most important functions of the department is the control and management of the company's land and buildings. This can mean some or all of the following:

(a) The maintenance of the asset to a level where no loss of value due to dilapidation is incurred.

(b) The collection of sub-tenant's rent.

(c) The manipulation of the property asset to produce the best return for the company, e.g. whether to lease or to buy, whether to sell freehold and arrange to lease it back as a tenant in order to raise further funds for the business or whether to adopt a policy of redevelopment of owned freeholds in order to enhance their values, and so on.

15. Control of stocks

Although the department may not itself physically control stocks of fittings, it often must organize a system whereby stocks are held at convenient points so that they can be quickly transported to project sites. It may be that shopfitters could hold these stocks on the company's behalf.

16. Other functions

(a) **Keeping of plans.** These documents, which should be kept in special plan chests, will comprise drawings of company properties and key plans (of the 'Goad' type) of shopping centres.

(b) **Liaison.** The department creates a link between estate agents, shopfitters, contractors and builders and the company as a whole.

THE COST OF SITES

17. Introduction

Before settling on a particular site the retailer must know something about the cost of shop sites.

18. Definitions

(a) **Value**: the price that a willing seller will accept and a willing buyer will pay. It depends on supply and demand.

(b) **Rental value**: the value as between landlord and tenant.

(c) **Ground rent**: the rent of the site only.

(d) **Rack rent**: the rent of the site improved with buildings. (It is the maximum rent for the value of the property.)

19. Factors relevant to assessment of rack rent

These consist of factual and legal considerations and are as follows:

(a) **Factual considerations**.

(*i*) *The population of the town.* Generally, the greater the population, the greater the rental value in the principal shopping area.
(*ii*) *The classification and type of centre.* Compare a central shopping area in a city such as Glasgow with a main shopping area in a smaller town such as Sevenoaks, Halesowen, Ripon or Penzance.

(*iii*) *Position of the shop in the centre*. The rental value in the part of the area favoured by certain multiples is much greater than at the tail end of the area.
(*iv*) *Side of street*. One side always commands higher rents than the other due to custom, position of shopping magnets, position of the sun, and so on.
(*v*) *Proximity to key traders*. The arrival of a key trader in an indifferent pitch can transform values overnight.
(*vi*) *Pedestrian traffic flows*. Pedestrian crossings, bus stops, and crush barriers all affect the flow of foot traffic. Too wide a pavement is a disadvantage because pedestrians are not forced against shop fronts and could miss them entirely.
(*vii*) *Vehicular traffic flows*. One-way streets are generally unpopular.
(*viii*) *Parking facilities*. The rental value of shopping positions is enhanced by the provision of near-by parking.
(*ix*) *Frontage and depth*. Certain multiple retailers are prepared to pay high prices to secure the precise frontage and depth most suited to their trading needs.
(*x*) *Area*. A rectangular area is worth more than the same area of irregular shape.
(*xi*) *Other accommodation*. Some trades require almost as much storage as retail selling area. Living accommodation above the shop may be essential.

(b) Legal considerations.

(*i*) *Premium*. A capital payment in lieu of whole or part of the rent.
(*ii*) *Length of lease*. A retailer proposing to carry out costly capital improvements requires a long lease to write off the investment.
(*iii*) *Repairing obligations under the lease*. An onerous obligation in respect of a property in bad repair may make the site worthless.
(*iv*) *Rent review clauses*. The effect of such a clause in a lease is to uplift the rent after a stated number of years, to the rental value at that time. The absence of rent review clauses reduces the value of the lease to the landlord.
(*v*) *Insurance provisions in the lease*. These determine who pays for the premiums and thus affects the rent to a small extent.
(*vi*) *Rights set out in the lease*. Rights as to assignment, subletting, to change the use and to make alterations and additions.
(*vii*) *Service charge specified in the lease*. This is the annual amount to be charged by the landlord for providing services, if any, such as lighting, cleaning of yards, porterage, etc.

20. The relationship between rental and capital values

This is measured by a multiplier, called the Years' Purchase, which is applied to the net rent to give capital value. It is the converse of the percentage applied to a capital sum to indicate an income. It is worked out by dividing 100 by the percentage. Therefore 6 per cent = 16.667 YP.

21. Valuers' methods of assessing values

There are various methods, the most usual being:

(a) Comparative. The direct comparison between the price per square metre and per metre frontage of the shop being considered and other similar shops.

(b) Residual. The balance remaining after deducting all the costs of a development from the estimated receipts gives the residual value. If the valuer estimates that a shop and upper part can be sold on completion of a new development for £500,000 and it is going to cost the developer £250,000 to build, including the cost of fees and finance, the developer can afford to pay up to £250,000 as the value of the site.

One method will be used as a check against the other.

22. The points of view of both landlord and tenant in assessing rental values

The rental value is determined by the supply of suitable property and the demand for it.

(a) The minimum rent required by the landlord. The landlord requires the highest profitable return. Consider a new development by a landlord (developer) of a single store. Statutory factors affecting the development are planning as set out under the most recent Town and Country Planning Acts and structure plans provided by Local Planning Authorities, building regulations and road improvement lines. The developer must then estimate the following:

> (*i*) *The cost of the site*. If the developer has recently purchased the site he will have had to pay the value of the most profitable development.
> (*ii*) *Cost of building works*.
> (*iii*) *Cost of fees*. This will include the architect's, quantity surveyor's, solicitor's and letting agents' fees.
> (*iv*) *An amount for contingencies*. This is to allow for unforeseen expenses and rising costs.
> (*v*) *Cost of providing finance*. This is necessary to purchase the site and to meet all the above costs. The cost of finance will depend upon the rate at which it is available at the time at current market rates.

The developer will then know his total estimated costs. To ascertain the minimum rent he must charge he then applies the percentage return to this total estimated cost. If total estimated costs are £2 million, and 10 per cent is regarded as the correct return on a development of this nature, the minimum rent the developer (landlord) can afford to charge before undertaking the development, will be £200,000 per annum. The resultant rent must not be greater than the rent a tenant can be expected to pay. If the resultant rent is lower than the rent a tenant is likely to pay, the difference represents annual profit.

(b) The maximum rent the tenant can afford to pay. The tenant requires to pay the lowest possible rent. He must assess what he can afford to pay by estimating net profit after deduction of all outgoings.

Stages in estimating net profit are as follows:

223

(*i*) Estimate gross profit, i.e. opening stock plus purchases, less sales and closing stock.

(*ii*) Estimate net profit, i.e. gross profit less outgoings. The outgoings must include the cost of capital invested in the business.

(*iii*) Estimate of outgoings. Outgoings will include head office expenses, wages, salaries, national insurance, heating, lighting, insurance, stationery, publicity, telephones, postage, vehicle running expenses, repairs, rates, annual depreciation on costs of shop front, fixtures, fittings and vehicles.

For example, estimates result in a gross profit of £700,000 per annum from which are deducted outgoings of £350,000 per annum leaving a net profit of £350,000 per annum. No deduction has been made for rent. The £350,000 per annum is therefore net profit including rent. The tenant must then estimate what he can afford to pay out of this figure by way of rent and leave sufficient as a reward for running the business. The resultant estimated rent must not be smaller than the minimum rent required by the landlord. If the resultant estimated rent is more than the rental value of the store then the difference represents additional annual profit.

23. Rents based on percentage of profits

Where there is no comparable guide to the property or where the trade is a monopoly, the landlord and tenant may agree on a rent based on a percentage of actual turnover or profits. This type of rent is well known in the USA and is used in several situations in this country, e.g. motorway retail site rents are based on a sliding percentage of turnover. Some shopping centre sites are also let on this basis.

24. Factors affecting choice on whether to lease or to buy

Owing to substantial rises in property value many retailers prefer to buy freeholds. The return on capital employed in the business should, however, exceed the return on the capital invested in bricks and mortar.

The factors affecting the decision as to whether to buy the freehold or take a lease are:

(a) The availability of capital and the cost of borrowing it

(b) The availability of either a freehold interest or a lease whichever is desired in a suitable property. (If a leasehold is required, it is possible to buy a freehold, then to sell the freehold with the benefit of the trader's covenant and the trader takes a lease back at full market rent)

(c) The interest that capital employed in purchase of a property would earn if invested in the business

(d) The possibility of showing a capital increase in the value of the property

(e) Taxation:

224

(*i*) capital gains tax and corporation tax

(*ii*) rent a charge against profits

(*iii*) interest charges on capital borrowed is a charge on profits.

25. Valuation of property assets

Because of rises in property values it is necessary to have periodic independent professional valuations made to assess the correct return on capital employed and the true profit. As a result of the valuation, the real profit arising from the business may be substantially less than supposed. A book value is only of historic interest to a valuer. It has no relation to market value, i.e. what a property will fetch in the market.

26. Some further points

(a) **Reinstatement values for fire insurance**. In the same way that properties must be valued periodically to ascertain true worth, it is essential that properties should also be valued periodically, say every three years, to ascertain cost of replacement in case of fire. The cost of replacing a property asset destroyed by fire bears no relation to the value of the property for sale. For example, the sale value of a freehold store in a prime position will be higher than the fire replacement value. The value of a tenant's short leasehold interest may well be less than the cost of rebuilding the premises after a fire for which the tenant may be liable under his lease.

(b) **Rent review clauses**. The object is to secure to the landlord maintenance of the value of the pound (£) and the enhancement values in the area. The rent is assessed periodically by reference to rental values in the locality at the time, but no account should be taken of the value of improvements made by the tenant. The effect of rent reviews is to remove from the tenant a large part of any appreciation in the value of the property that has taken place.

(c) **Clauses in leases requiring special attention**. The following points should be settled and expressly agreed during negotiations for the lease of a property. It is essential that the solicitors to both sides are advised in detail on what has been agreed in order that they may ensure that the terms of lease truly reflect what has been agreed. The points concerned are:

(*i*) *Assignment rights*. Unless there are special reasons against it the tenant should have the right to assign to a responsible assignee. It would be reasonable for this right not to be given to the tenant where the tenancy is a short one, because it is agreed by both parties at the time of letting that the landlord is to redevelop at the end of the tenancy.

(*ii*) *Subletting rights*. The tenant of a large store capable of being split into several units should have the right to sublet to responsible tenants.

(*iii*) *Right to change the use*. The tenant should have the right to change the use, with consent, which coupled with his right to assign would permit assignment to a tenant of a different trade.

(*iv*) *Right to make alterations, additions and improvements.* The tenant should have these rights to ensure that he is able to trade effectively. He should be made to apply to the landlord for express consent but the landlord should not be able to refuse unless the carrying out of the work concerned is likely to depreciate the value of his interest in reversion.

LOCATION DEVELOPMENT

27. Development management

The development manager, who should be responsible to the marketing or trading director, is in turn responsible for bringing together data so that a plan for the extension and development of a chain is possible. This plan will incorporate some pointers as to the size and type of branches and the general image to be projected.

The main areas of responsibility of the development manager are:

(a) Creating, reviewing, updating the development plan

(b) Finding new sites in conjunction with the property department

(c) Producing viability studies on new projects and meeting viability time-tables and ensuring these are adhered to

(d) Recommending properties to the Board

(e) Organizing regular site visits, in conjunction with the property department and monitoring the progress of work on site

(f) Advising on layouts, lighting, signage, display, systems, colours, etc. of new branches

(g) Co-ordinating and controlling development teams which may comprise representatives from merchandising, architects, surveyors, administration, operations, security, finance, personnel and training

(h) Monitoring the performance of new resited, extended and modernized branches once opened.

In carrying out these functions the development manager and his or her team will use much of the methods and information contained in Chapter 9.

28. Planning retail development

The broad methods by which this part of the company's strategic plan can be framed are as follows:

(a) Possible areas. Determine the geographical areas for possible and profitable retail expansion. This will depend on the minimum acceptable support population to show the desired return on investment and other factors detailed below.

(b) Branch potential. Determine the sales and profit levels and market share which each potential (and existing) outlet can reasonably take as its objective by examining its strengths and weakness and matching these up with a standard store performance profile for the grade of branch being examined. This will produce pointers to extension and modernization needs.

(c) Diversification. Examine the possibilities of diversifying into other market areas by the acquisition of existing businesses. This may also involve diversifying into other product groups or even abroad.

29. Constraints on development

Before producing a development plan as part of the corporate plan, the constraints on extending market coverage must be discussed:

(a) Physical distance. This does not affect the large multiple as much as it might the smaller chain run possibly by one person, the proprietor, who must be readily able to control his or her shops, travelling between them by car. The bigger retail chain normally controls branches on a territory basis, each area being in the charge of an area or regional manager.

(b) Lines of communication. Branches, no matter whether they obtain supplies direct from the manufacturer or from a company warehouse, must be reasonably accessible by road or rail. This is particularly true of stores selling daily lines, e.g. bread and newspapers.

(c) Type of trade. Except in the very largest cities, variety chain stores and other large space users will operate only one branch. The exceptions are some food and convenience stores which, because of the lower support populations required, are able to open more than one branch in many towns, very often in the suburbs.

(d) Existence of market potential. Certain areas offer no scope for development for the following reasons:

(*i*) low catchment populations
(*ii*) over-heavy competition
(*iii*) small, undeveloped or otherwise unsuitable shopping centres
(*iv*) competition from another branch of the same company
(*v*) company image does not fit the socio-economic profile of the area.

(e) Finance. Capital must be available to support an expansion plan. The number of outlets planned, although not necessarily the geographical extent of the development area, may be stultified by high interest rates, lack of self-financing facility or government intervention in capital projects.

(f) Availability of sites. Some shopping centres are highly constricted and the number of sites appearing either in a private sale situation or on the open market may be severely limited. Once on the market the sites must be of a suitable size and shape; variety chains particularly have encountered problems in land

227

assembly in some town centres. High rents are unlikely to deter most big chains these days from seeking and finding representation in prime sites.

(g) Legal and trade restraints. Until fairly recently, supermarket chains had difficulty in securing licences from local courts to incorporate the sale of wines and spirits in their branches. They are still not allowed under the Food and Drugs Act 1963 to dispense ethical drugs except from a separate in-store pharmacy run by a qualified pharmacist. Certain trade restrictions are sometimes enforced. For instance, newspaper publishers and wholesalers will hesitate to grant supplies to a new CTN if they feel the area is adequately covered or if the interests of existing customers are likely to be damaged.

(h) Lack of management. Two limitations could exist here:

(*i*) Training and successions plans in the company may not be advanced enough to provide new branch management quickly.
(*ii*) An expansion plan can be stultified by a lack of professional skills at head office.

(i) Lack of other resources. A big proportional jump in the number of branches operated, perhaps from acquisition, could strain internal departments such as buying, accounting or personnel.

30. Branch profiles

Before a development plan can be implemented a retail chain must have a concrete idea of what sort of units it wishes to operate. Tesco, for example, aims for its stores to be what it calls 'conforming stores'. As part of the pinpointing of the company's strengths and weaknesses for corporate planning purposes, it is essential for the existing stock of branches to be completely appraised. This appraisal is meant to help planners to decide how to improve the current resources and build up for the future. The aspects of the 'profile' examined are as follows:

(a) Layout. This is invaluable in deciding how best to lay out an existing store, how it can be improved in the future (e.g. by extension) and what a standard unit should look like in terms of frontage, depth, etc.

(b) Shopfront and fittings. Again the store layout revolves round fittings, as does the shopfront to some extent (e.g. if the front is arcaded or angled). A chain will aim eventually to standardize in this as in many other areas. Standardization helps reduce the price of fittings and is also instrumental in creating a consistent store image.

(c) Ranging. A retail chain should have some means of finding out in some detail the product mix in each of its branches. This will have implications for gross margin, buying, layout and display, staffing, deliveries, and so on. The idea is to achieve as much standardization in ranging as possible, taking into account local market differences.

(d) Operating costs. As standardization in branch size and staffing continues, standard operating costs can be more easily budgeted for new branches.

(e) Sales. Many multiple retailers categorize branches in particular sales or profit bands.

31. Development lists

At the core of the development plan are the lists of towns and shopping centres within which representation is desired. On the basis of the standard branch profile (or profiles if more than one class or size of branch is envisaged within specific market sizes) and the estimated branch sales, a firm idea of net contribution and therefore return on investment can be gained. If the (apparent) return on investment is acceptable in a particular market, then it will be incorporated in the development plan.

32. Investment and rationalization

After appraising its stock of stores a retail chain will concentrate its development efforts on:

(a) Modernization. Branches are normally refitted every three to five years depending on the trade (fashion stores need a facelift more often). Sometimes strong local competition may speed the process. However, only branches that are likely to benefit should be so treated; they would be expected, as the minimum requirement, not only to be capable, from the extra sales that should flow from the investment, of paying the annual depreciation charge on the new fittings but at least of servicing the capital investment.

(b) Resites. It sometimes occurs that a branch has to relocate within a shopping centre because of changes in the environment, e.g. the movement of a key multiple or a new traffic management scheme. Leases fall due, compulsory purchase orders are tendered, or it is felt that the branch has outgrown its size for the business it is doing and cannot be extended. Resites should be considered very carefully because they occasionally produce a less than satisfactory return if the old branch benefited from cheap rents and other low charges whilst the new branch opens with expensive fittings and at a much higher rent and rates charge. Turnover may have to be consequently much higher.

(c) Extensions. It is often possible to extend branches which have become too small for their sales level. Sometimes it is possible to take over stockrooms or other ancillary accommodation for sales area extension, but may often mean the purchase of flanking shops. When Dixon's took over Curry's, the former was able to expand its branches in this way in several locations.

(d) Acquisition of existing businesses. By buying existing shops owned by competing or even non-competing traders a chain can sometimes not only extend its development area but allow rationalization of its existing spread of shops by closing nearby, less effective units. A list of businesses to be taken over in the future can be framed as part of the acquisition strategy.

(e) **Overseas expansion**. Many UK retailers have expanded abroad with varying results. Important expansion has, for instance, been carried out by Marks &
Spencer in France and the USA (*see* Chapter 3).

Progress test 21

1. Why is the property function so important in retailing and what are its
   main functions?

2. What are the factors relevant to the assessment of rack rent?

3. Describe the points of view of (*a*) the landlord and (*b*) the tenant, in
   assessing retail values.

4. What factors are important when deciding whether to lease or buy?

5. Explain what factors a retailer would consider before embarking on a
   retail development plan.

22

UNIT MANAGEMENT

THE STORE MANAGER

1. Introduction

The task of putting into operation the policies of the organization on a day-to-day basis falls substantially on the store managers. In an independent retail outlet the store manager may well be the proprietor but in multiples a branch manager will be employed. Although much of this chapter will be relevant to the independent trader, it is primarily focused on management of a unit within a multiple retail chain.

2. Duties of branch management

Broadly, the branch manager must put into full and effective operation in the branch at all times the company's policies and procedures. The day-to-day operations of the branch must be organized and directed to its full trading potential within the constraints of position, size of unit, etc. Detailed duties will encompass some or all of the following, in the style of a job specification:

(a) Sales. To achieve budgeted sales for the period.

(b) Costs. To maintain controllable costs within a budget, e.g. lighting, telephones.

(c) Profit. To achieve planned levels of profit, both gross and net for the period.

(d) Stock

(*i*) To maintain a level of stock within the current budget.
(*ii*) To keep stock shortages to a minimum.
(*iii*) To count and record stock in the branch from time to time as required by company policy.

(e) Buying. To ensure that if local buying is permitted, purchases are made only in line with company policy, taking into account the total budgeted stock-holding.

(f) Presentation. To maintain standards of display and presentation that encourage and retain trade and contribute to the identity the company wishes to project. This particularly entails that:

(*i*) Sales areas, windows and shopfronts are maintained in a clean and tidy condition (this applies also to stock areas, rest rooms, toilets, etc.)

(*ii*) All merchandise is displayed in line with company standards, including the open display of all lines appropriate to the grade of branch, the correct price marking and ticketing of products, etc.

(g) Sales promotions. To carry out the company sales promotion policy and to initiate and execute local sales promotions in agreement with the area manager.

(h) Staff

(*i*) To ensure by interview and selection (agreed with the area manager) that the branch is properly staffed to its budgeted establishment with competent section management and assistance.

(*ii*) To train staff in the basic functions of branch operation.

(*iii*) To terminate their employment within the scope of company policy and with regard to legislation such as the Employment Protection (Consolidation) Act.

(i) Premises. To protect and maintain the building, machinery, equipment, fixtures, fittings and vehicles of the branch and to report any action needed to maintain trade assets in good working order and at acceptable safety standards.

(j) Administration

(*i*) To carry out company procedures as published from time to time for the reception and disposition and safe custody of cash, stock and other assets.

(*ii*) To prepare, maintain and submit such records and reports as may from time to time be required by the company.

(*iii*) To observe the large amount of legislation which surrounds retailing today.

(k) Communication

(*i*) To establish and maintain adequate means of communication within the branch of the company's objectives as they affect branch personnel, including in-store meetings.

(*ii*) To keep area management aware as far as possible of local news and developments likely to affect the company's present or future interests.

(*iii*) To play an active part as far as it is feasible in the civic and cultural activities of the locality in which the branch is sited in order to foster confidence and goodwill towards the company.

3. The branch manual

This document lays down the standing orders of the business as far as branch operation is concerned. There should be arrangements in its make-up for additions, amendments and deletions, each of which should be serially numbered and dated for identification and insertion. The manual or bulletin should be signed for, each copy numbered and located (one for each branch) and handed over formally as one manager takes over from another. The wording requires careful consideration as there should be no ambiguity nor misinterpretation between different sections of the business. One criticism of the manual is that, if possible contingencies are legislated for, a deadening effect resulting in some loss of initiative may occur. The quasi-permanent manual may in some businesses be supplemented by such ancillary instructions as the shrinkage manual, the sales promotion plan or the training manual. Many firms send out sales or display memoranda to branches which may then be incorporated in a manual.

4. Responsibility of managers

It will be seen that a number of the unit managers' duties are quantifiable and therefore controllable through budgets. These budgets should, in well-run companies, be agreed with the manager by his or her immediate superior (usually an area manager). Once standards of performance and competence have been published, monitoring can be carried out through exception reports on sales and profit performance and by physical inspections. Breaches of the standards laid down by the company may not, of course, always be the responsibility of the branch manager. For example, an accident occurring to a customer because of the faulty maintenance of fittings would not necessarily rebound on the manager.

MEASURING A MANAGER'S PERFORMANCE

5. Skills

The manager of a retail operation requires two primary skills: trading skills and management skills. Trading skills are based on the ability to spot opportunities within a business environment in order to maximize store profit. Management skills are concerned with maximizing the resources within their control – the major resource which the retail manager has substantial control over is the human resource (see Chapter 20).

6. Store productivity

Productivity involves producing better results with the same mixtures of resources or producing the same results with fewer resources. This means that stocks have to be sufficient to meet (uneven) demand but not excessive leading to the tying up of capital. Similarly, employing too many staff with insufficient work to do is wasteful, whilst employing insufficient staff at peak times causes queues and customer dissatisfaction.

The task of operating management is to balance the load of customers against the capacity (resources) available to it. This means that store management has to generate the best possible performance and results at the least cost from:

(a) Customers

(b) Merchandise

(c) Store human resources

(d) Store physical resources – including space.

7. Measuring store productivity

The most effective way of measuring productivity is to calculate ratios of resource to results, e.g. profit per square metre of selling space, and comparing these ratios with pre-set standards, e.g. budgets. Productivity ratios can also be compared against industry norms, competitor results or even against other company stores or sections within a store.

8. Measures of store productivity

The following is a list of some important measures of store productivity:

(a) Sales per employee

(b) Sales per labour hour

(c) Staff costs as a percentage of sales

(d) Labour costs per activity

(e) Average wage costs per hour

(f) Sales per square metre of selling space

(g) Sales per linear metre of fixture

(h) Sales per customer (by value, number of items or departments)

(i) Customers per time period (e.g. hour)

(j) Items per time period

(k) Sales per checkout

(l) Sales: total assets

(m) Sales: stock

(n) Gross margin return on investment

(o) Gross profit per square metre

(p) Net profit per square metre

(q) Gross and net profit on sales

(r) Shrinkage as a percentage of sales

(s) Wastage as a percentage of sales

(t) Mark-downs as a percentage of sales

(u) Other costs as a percentage of sales.

There are also other qualitative measures such as service to customers and merchandise availability. Unfortunately, these cannot be easily measured but the level of customer complaint may be an indicator. Stock age rating is also important to identify slow-moving stock which unnecessarily ties up capital or requires mark-down, thus reducing profitability.

9. The importance of store productivity

As an example, a typical grocery multiple will have a gross profit on sales of approximately 17 per cent. Staff costs will typically run at 5 to 6 per cent and other operating costs at 2 to 3 per cent of sales. With overhead and allocated costs of 4 to 5 per cent it can be demonstrated that net profits are in the order of 4 to 5 per cent of sales. It is therefore clear that savings in staff or operating costs (i.e. controllable by the operating manager) can have a dramatic effect on the net profit (the 'bottom line').

OTHER ASPECTS OF BRANCH MANAGEMENT

10. Health and safety

The branch manager is responsible for the health and safety of both staff and customers in the store. The two main aspects are the prevention of ill health arising from working conditions and circumstances, and safety – the prevention of accidents.

Branch mangers have to comply with the Offices, Shops and Railway Premises Act 1963, now to some extent update by the Health and Safety at Work Act 1974. The 1963 Act lays down minimum standards on heating, ventilation, lighting, cleanliness and accidents.

11. Heating

Many larger modern stores are fitted with sophisticated ducted heating systems that are often expensive to install and to run. Smaller stores may use convector heaters and in these and larger stores the use of warm-air curtains at entrances keep in much of the internal heat. Heat conservation of this kind is particularly important with open-fronted units in covered air-conditioned shopping centres.

Some points to note on the subject are:

(a) Capital cost and the use of fuel should be economic, particularly in view of today's energy costs (e.g. thermostatic control).

(b) Planned maintenance is needed.

(c) Safety is important, particularly from the point of view of fires.

(d) Equitable distribution of heat is necessary, according to the position and size of the selling or ancillary area.

12. Ventilation

Many larger stores are now fitted with air-conditioning equipment for summer use. Again the capital cost and fuel consumption of air cooling and changing systems can be high. Smaller units are more likely to rely on simpler means of ventilation such as louvres or air extractors. The following points should be considered:

(a) The alternative benefits of natural and mechanical ventilation.

(b) Elimination of draughts is essential.

(c) Spread of clean air is also to be desired.

(d) Unsightly ducting, motors and so on should be eliminated.

13. Lighting

Although expensive, effective lighting is essential to attract customers and enhance the surroundings. The cheapest and most efficient store illumination is still a variation on fluorescent lighting. For example, mercury halide gives as much light as conventional fluorescent lighting but uses 30 per cent less electricity. Spot lights are extensively used in clothing and some durable stores to add atmosphere or to highlight products. Spots, however, can be expensive to run. In larger stores, an emergency lighting system is often installed, powered by a diesel generator. The following points should be noted:

(a) Natural lighting should be used as far as possible.

(b) It is necessary that light diffusors are kept clean.

(c) Spare tubes and spot bulbs should be kept in the branch.

(d) Time switches on window lights can save expense

(e) In summer, some 'starters' should be removed from tubes to reduce the ambient heat.

(f) Different colour tubes can be used for special effects, e.g. meat counter illumination is usually 'pink'.

14. Cleanliness

The multiple organization often leaves it to the branch manager to organize cleaning on a local basis. Most large shopping centres have several professional window cleaners who 'tout' for work as soon as a shop starts fitting-out ready for the opening. Some multiples, however, use national contract cleaning that can bring considerable savings in a large chain. Again, large multiple branches may carry their own heavy-duty vacuum cleaners and polishers that may be operated by the staff or by part-time cleaners.

15. Accidents

Points to note in this connection are:

(a) All accidents to customers and staff should be recorded in an accident book and a report sent to the legal department.

(b) First-aid facilities should be provided in the staffroom.

(c) Staff should be helpful but non-committal in customer accident cases.

(d) Arrangements should be made with the local hospital for treatment in cases of emergency.

SECURITY

16. Pilferage

Pilferage is the theft of cash or stock and contributes much of the 'unknown shrinkage' in retail organizations, of which there are basically two types: shop-lifting (*see* **17**) and staff pilferage (*see* **20**). Depending on the firm and its security management, shrinkage of this kind amounts to between a half and 4 per cent of total turnover. However, about 10 per cent of shrinkage is not deliberate, e.g. inadvertent undercharging or the giving of too much change. In 1995, the UK retail trade was estimated to lose over £2 billion per year in shrinkage, representing approximately 1.5 per cent of turnover.

17. Shoplifting

This is the work of members of the public and is estimated to make up 30 per cent of unknown shrinkage. The methods used to combat shoplifting include the following:

(a) Store detectives. These are either recruited by the retail group or hired from a security organization. Although they tend to be expensive, their success rate is reckoned to be good.

(b) Electronic systems. There are a number of proprietary brands of systems used in the UK, all with tags that are removed at the point of sale. Most potential shoplifters notice the sensitized tags that set off alarm bells at the entrance to the store if taken through a photo-electric curtain and are therefore deterred from stealing. These systems, although expensive, are said to be beneficial, even reducing staff thefts of stock. The tags can also be used for stock control.

(c) Closed-circuit television. Cameras, which are mounted in the store, transmit to monitor screens either in the sales area or the manager's office.

(d) Security mirrors. These convex mirrors, which are available in various diameters, are relatively cheap and therefore more within the range of the smaller retailers. Positioned in blind spots, they act as a deterrent to shoplifting. One-way mirrors are also useful for manager's offices overlooking the shop.

(e) Chains and loop alarms. These are popular in electrical goods stores for smaller audio, kitchen and personal-care items. The simple chain is locked round a number of times, whilst allowing them to be examined individually. Loop alarms are similarly locked and, if broken, send out a high-pitched buzz.

(f) Fitting-room tags. The fitting room is a favourite place for shoplifters to operate and some store groups allow customers to take in a maximum number of items, with hanger tags that have to be returned with the goods.

18. General security

An open display of merchandise undoubtedly increases the risk of shoplifting so other precautions that may be taken could include:

(a) Encouragement of staff alertness

(b) Well lit, properly laid-out sales floor

(c) 'Closed' display of small items such as pocket calculators and electric shavers.

19. Apprehension

A person can be arrested without warrant if he or she is seen stealing or if a theft has occurred and there are 'reasonable grounds' for suspicion of that person. It is usual to give suspected customers the opportunity to pay by asking them if there is anything they wish to pay for. If they decline it is obligatory to wait until they have stepped out of the store before requesting their return to the manager's office for a check of their purchases. A witness to the incident should be present and the local police should be called. All should be done as quickly as possible. Most retail groups now make it a policy to prosecute shoplifters, but it is vital that the staff involved work to a prearranged system of apprehension.

20. Staff pilferage

An estimated 60 per cent of shrinkage is caused by direct staff thefts of stock or cash and collusion with delivery men, salespersons and customers. Super-markets seem to have the worst record here and shrinkage rates of 2 to 3 per cent have been described as workable by supermarket management. Again, super-markets are estimated to have 25 per cent of their losses in the cash system through direct theft from tills and dishonesty with floats, cashing up and banking. One of the 'black spots' for staff pilferage is the goods reception and stockroom areas where security is often lax. For internal security the following precautions should be taken:

(a) Use of security staff for check purchases.

(b) Tills should be spot-checked from the till roll sporadically.

(c) All credit notes and refunds should be signed by the manager.

(d) Employees' handbags, coats and effects should be left in separate cloakrooms or hung well away from stores or in a position where managers can see them.

(e) Reserve stock should be kept either caged in or out of the way of staff with valuable stock like cigarettes and watches locked up.

(f) Staff should be instructed on the correct acceptance of deliveries.

(g) Stock should be kept in sealed outer packing. This minimizes pilferage and helps stocktaking.

(h) There should be a clause in the letter of appointment allowing spot searches of clothing and hand-luggage.

(i) Staff purchases should be isolated from the customer sales system.

It is important that any staff security measures be put out as a precaution for the general good of the majority who are honest.

21. Shopbreaking

Shopbreaking is rarer than customer/staff pilferage but each particular loss is likely to be much greater. The type of theft is of course 'known' and amounts stolen can be checked after the event. Points to observe in this context are:

(a) A strict locking-up procedure should be followed each night and in reverse in the morning.

(b) There should be secure locks on doors and windows at the front, side, rear and on the roof.

(c) Grille and other types of alarm should be set at a low 'sensitivity' because they are liable to be disturbed by heavy traffic – over 90 per cent of alarm calls are false in the UK, due to incorrect setting.

(d) Duplicate keys should be held by the branch manager, security officer and/or the local police station.

(e) A security light should be left on in the branch.

(f) Full audit of stock to be made as soon as possible in the event of a break-in. Many large multiples send out an audit team, including one of the group accountants to check stock units and values.

THE INTRODUCTION OF NEW TECHNOLOGY

22. Electronic point-of-sale systems

A variety of EPOS systems have been developed, all of which utilize micro-processors either 'stand alone' or being connected to an in-store computer. The EPOS systems generally offer three functions, namely:

(a) A price look-up (PLU) facility

(b) The ability to record and store information on the sale of individual items

(c) The capacity to print a till receipt which prints an abbreviated product description and a price.

The most commonly found EPOS system is the 'stand alone' till. This offers a PLU facility, whereby the machine is able to store the price of fast-selling items and, through the application of an appropriate code, checking out is considered speeded up.

The most sophisticated EPOS systems enable the automatic input of a code to the system. This is effected by the application of a machine-readable code to the product, which is then passed over a suitable light scanner (usually a pen-like 'wand') enabling the code to be transmitted to the EPOS computer. These systems are now well established in most retail sectors using a code consisting of bars which enables the speediest checkout by a laser scanner.

The central computer is able to communicate with the in-store computer overnight to gauge total stock levels and to produce individual store order requirements for next-day delivery.

The introduction of EPOS systems offers scope for a degree of automatic re-ordering, when stock falls below certain pre-set levels. This enables overall stock levels to be kept at a minimum, whilst maintaining a maximum service level.

23. Bar coding

The bar code consists of a series of bars which can be read by the laser scanner, in addition to a human-readable number. This coding system, known as the European Article Number (EAN), has been developed on an international basis, enabling compatibility for imported and exported goods.

The human-readable code normally consists of 13 digits known as EAN – 13; a shorter code, EAN – 8, does exist for smaller products. The codes are shown in Figure 22.1.

The first two digits or 'flag characters' identify the nationality of the number-ing authority registering the product. The UK number bank is controlled by the Article Number Association (ANA) and the UK flag characters are 50.

The next five digits are allocated by ANA to the distributor (retailers would have a code for own-label products). The second set of five digits are used by the distributor to *uniquely* identify the product (by price, size, colour, flavour and

EAN−8

Figure 22.1 Bar coding system

pack size). The final digit acts as a check to ensure the product code is correctly composed.

The EAN system also allows for a 'variable weight' code to be used for goods that are weighed in-store (e.g. produce, meat).

24. Advantages of EPOS systems

The hard benefits are:

(a) Higher checkout productivity – up to 15 per cent increase

(b) Labour savings, items do not need to be individually priced

(c) Reduction in 'mis-rings' at the checkout

(d) Price changing is easier since only the computer price-file and shelf-edge label need be changed.

The soft benefits are:

(a) More management information on:

(*i*) customer flows on an hourly basis
(*ii*) product sales, by line and over time
(*iii*) monitoring of checkout operators' productivity
(*iv*) more effective merchandising through knowledge of advertising effects and new product introduction.

(b) Better stock control management

(c) Automatic ordering facility

(d) Closer identification of shrinkage (i.e. theft, breakages, fraud, etc.) points

(e) Better in-store labour scheduling.

The growth of EPOS systems has enabled the instantaneous collation of sales information in a more refined manner. The scanning systems provide detailed sales performance by product and outlet over days and hours. Very detailed market research can thus be quickly produced, which is of invaluable use to the retailers and their suppliers. All the leading grocery operators have now installed scanning systems and have integrated these EPOS systems into existing information networks.

An extension of EPOS is EDI (Electronic Data Interchange) where the scanning of an item at the retailer's checkout provides information not only to the retailer but also is sent directly to the supplier to trigger a replenishment decision in the supplier's warehouse. The overall effect is that inventories decrease and stockouts become less common.

The only significant disadvantage to these systems is the cost, but with this coming down gradually most retailers will find that the need to install them increases.

25. Portable data capture units

The portable data capture unit (PDCU) is a miniature version of the EPOS scanning system and is now widely used in many sectors of the retail trade, largely for stock control purposes. The PDCU consists of a small hand-held computer and an attached fixed light 'pen' or 'wand' for scanning bar codes. The PDCU is used to collect information on stock quantities, which can be entered either manually or by scanning a stock control bar code. Having collected stock information, the PDCU then interfaces with other computerized systems (e.g. buying office, warehouse ordering).

26. Viewdata

With a suitably adapted television set and a computer key pad, it is possible to transmit and receive information via the telephone lines. Such a system has opened the way for communication between the private and commercial sectors.

The UK's main public viewdata network is Prestel, operated by British Telecom, which enables the user to cheaply link into other users' computers. The BBC's Ceefax and ITV's Oracle Teletext services are of a similar nature, but with little scope for communication between users. These systems, plus several privately operated viewdata services, offer significant scope for the transmission of information with tremendous implications for retailing. The technology would appear to be an ideal medium for linking consumers directly to suppliers or retailers, enabling the concept of 'armchair' or teleshopping. There are, however, few examples of significant teleshopping schemes in operation. This is largely due to relatively few consumers possessing viewdata technology and the limited range of products that are presently supplied.

27. Interactive electronic shopping

Recent developments in technology have made it possible for TV users to point and click their way through on-screen catalogues. Viewers can then order goods which are delivered by post. J. Sainsbury has experimented with a virtual reality supermarket. Wearing head sets and holding a handgrip shoppers can 'move' along store aisles and using the handgrip 'take' products from the shelves. They reappear in a shopping basket at the virtual checkout. Such systems are, again, some way away, but Sainsbury has already sold wine on the Internet, the global computer network, using conventional text-based systems, since April 1995.

28. Electronic funds transfer

Electronic funds transfer has operated for some time, and enables the direct transfer of funds from one bank account to another electronically, particularly in the area of personal banking, where auto-teller machines (ATMs) allow the withdrawal of cash, statements and cheque books to be ordered and accounts to be settled at some high street banks and building societies; ATMs are increasingly appearing in stores also.

The wider use of electronic funds transfer at the point of sale (EFTPOS) in retail outlets has required new technology to be installed at the checkout, into which a customer debit card is fed, e.g. Switch. By the use of this card the customer is then able to transfer money to the retailer from his or her bank account.

29. Other applications

As well as the accounting and financial systems that have historically been the reason for installing computers, the following areas are increasingly using new technology:

(a) Space allocation. Knowledge of specific product sales enables the retailer to make the best use of shelf space. Techniques such as direct-product profitability (DPP) identify precise profit contributions for specific products, which naturally affects space allocation.

(b) Energy management. Energy costs for retailers are significant and many are now using computers to monitor and minimize their energy costs (heat, light, refrigeration).

(c) Security. Over £2 billion worth of goods are lost by retailers annually as a result of shrinkage, stock loss, theft or fraud. By tracking individual stock items through the EPOS system such losses can be reduced. Sophisticated electronic surveillance devices are also being used.

30. Implications of the new technology for the manager

Unless management fully understands and is able to operate the new systems, many benefits will be lost. It is therefore important that managers are trained in the capability of the system and how to use it; a broader appreciation of the application of computers is also vital. This might be achieved by short courses on the capabilities of computer systems, keyboard operation, how to read and use print-outs, etc.

As procedures change to meet the requirements of new technology reporting structures also may well change. Management should be aware of these changes and how they will affect the staff. Technology is a management tool and it is vital that managers are aware of the role played by new equipment; they need to fully understand the basic principles and draw on the specific training offered by the equipment suppliers.

Progress test 22

1. Outline the duties of the branch manager.

2. What are the two primary skills required of the retail manager?

3. What is meant by store productivity?

4. List 10 measures of store productivity.

5. Why is the measurement of store productivity important?

6. Describe the main aspects of health and safety for which the retail manager is responsible.

7. Define the terms (a) pilferage, (b) shoplifting, (c) shopbreaking.

8. What are the advantages of EPOS systems?

9. What is a PDCU?

10. What are the implications of the new technology for the manager?

11. With reference to particular examples, examine the contribution, if any, of IT investment to the ability of retailers to survive the current downturn in consumer spending.

23

RETAILING AND THE LAW

1. Development of the law regarding retailing

There have been two main threads in the development of the law affecting retailers. One concerns the sale of goods, regulations for which date back certainly to 1226, whilst the other concerns the status of employees within the industry. In the latter case, specific legislation was not passed until 1912. Legislation of both kinds has been increasing in volume and complexity during the past 10 years and this chapter discusses some of the more important Acts.

2. Some general points

(a) The retailer is legally entitled to demand the exact purchase price for his or her goods, in cash.

(b) Strictly speaking, cheques are not legal tender – payment by cheque is a concession offered to the customer by the retailer.

(c) A deposit paid by a customer in relation to merchandise ordered to the customer's particular specification is not normally returnable to the customer (unless the seller is unwilling or unable to deliver the goods or to pass good title).

(d) There is no obligation for a customer to produce a receipt, and the law allows the customer to prove his or her purchase verbally.

(e) In the absence of any fixed delivery date the retailer must have the goods available for delivery within a reasonable time. The place of delivery depends on what has been agreed.

(f) A retailer commits a criminal offence and may be prosecuted if he or she displays a notice saying 'No money refunded' or 'Sale goods not exchanged or money refunded'.

(g) If a retailer gives the consumer extra rights, e.g. 'Your money will be courteously and promptly refunded if you are not satisfied', then he or she must make it clear that these rights are in addition to the usual statutory rights, by stating, e.g. 'This does not affect your statutory rights'.

CONSUMER PROTECTION

3. The Sale of Goods Act 1979

This Act replaced the Sale of Goods Act 1893 and the Supply of Goods (Implied Terms) Act 1973. It relates to all transactions in which ownership of goods passes in exchange for money – it does not apply to services. But similar provisions apply where goods are transferred under a contract for services, e.g. servicing a car (see the Supply of Goods and Services Act 1982).

The three most important aspects of the Act are:

(a) Goods must be of merchantable quality, i.e. they must be fit for sale, but a customer has no right to reject goods in respect of defects brought to his or her attention before the sale (but they must have been specifically pointed out to the customer), or if the customer examined his goods, he has no right to reject goods because of defects which his examination ought to have revealed.

(b) Goods must be fit for the purpose for which the customer is buying them. However, if the goods are required for a special purpose, the customer must make this known to the retailer, who, if he or she then supplies a particular item, would be liable if it was unfit for this purpose. The retailer would not be liable, however, if the buyer does not rely on the seller's judgement, or if it is unreasonable for him to so rely.

(c) Goods must correspond with their description, e.g. machine-made items should not be described as hand-made.

The retailer must rectify the situation relating to faulty goods by offering a refund. Alternatively, the customer may accept a credit note, repair of goods or a replacement.

It should be noted that the retailer may be liable for consequential loss caused by defective goods, e.g. if a faulty gas oven explodes and ruins the customer's kitchen. The customer has a right to bring a claim against the retailer at any time up to six years from the date of purchase of the product. In the event of a dispute the courts will decide how long a particular component or product ought to last.

4. The supply of services

The provision of a service by the retailer to customers is outside the protection of the Sale of Goods Act 1979, but is covered by similar provisions in the Supply of Goods and Services Act 1982. This Act requires goods supplied under the contract to be of merchantable quality, fit for their purpose and to comply with any description. In addition, services performed under the contract must be completed with reasonable skill and care.

Further protection is available under the Trade Descriptions Act 1968, which makes it a criminal offence for a retailer knowingly or recklessly to make false or misleading statements relating to services.

The law of contract applies, and the customer is entitled to sue the retailer for breach of contract, if something goes wrong. Unless a fixed price has already been agreed between the parties, the customer is entitled to expect that the price for the service will be a reasonable price.

5. Sale and Supply of Goods Act 1994

This Act which came into force in 1995 amends the Sale of Goods Act 1979 and changes the words 'merchantable quality' to 'satisfactory quality' (a more modern phrase) which may include fitness for purpose, appearance and finish, freedom from minor defects, and safety and durability. The customer's rights as outlined in the 1979 Act remain unaltered.

6. Food Act 1984 and Food Safety Act 1990

The purpose of these Acts is to protect the consumer from the sale of inferior food products and the Acts consolidate previous legislation on food, drugs, markets and cold stores. The provisions of the Food Act 1984 have largely been repealed, and are replaced by new provisions in the Food Safety Act 1990 concerning food safety and consumer protection. The 1990 Act makes it an offence to render food injurious to health (e.g. by adding things to it or subjecting it to a process or treatment). It is also an offence to sell food which has been rendered injurious to health, or is unfit for human consumption, or is so contaminated that it cannot reasonably be used for human consumption. It is also an offence to sell food which is not of the nature, substance or quality which is demanded by the purchaser. It is also an offence to falsely describe or present food, e.g. by means of labels or advertisements, or so as to mislead as to the nature, substance or quality of the food. It is also an offence to sell or offer for sale food, the presentation of which is likely to mislead as to its nature, substance or quality.

Food which is suspected of not complying with safety requirements can be seized and condemned, and the use of processes or treatments used in the preparation of food can be prohibited.

Ingredients must be listed in order of weight on jars, and the name or address of the packer or labeller added.

If a food retailer is accused of contravening the Food Safety Act he or she can plead 'due diligence' in defence. This protects traders who can show that they have observed all reasonable precautions to safeguard products and customers.

7. Food Hygiene (General) Regulations 1970 and the Food Hygiene (Amendment) Regulations 1990

The 1970 regulations were originally made under the Food Act 1984, which has been substantially replaced by the Food Safety Act 1990, but the 1970 regulations continue in force as if made under the Food Safety Act 1990. The regulations place certain responsibilities on employees or persons handling food:

(a) Foods must be protected from the risk of contamination.

(b) People handling food must keep the parts of their body which are likely to come into contact with food as clean as is reasonably practicable. Cuts and abrasions must be completely covered with waterproof dressings. The prohibition of smoking and spitting is also included in this regulation. All clothing must be kept clean.

(c) Those handling open food are to use clean (washable) overalls.

(d) Persons suffering from certain infectious diseases must inform the person in charge, who in turn must inform the local authority medical officer (e.g. typhoid fever, salmonella infection or dysentery).

(e) Premises should be clean and in good condition so that food cannot be contaminated directly or indirectly.

(f) Equipment which comes into contact with food must be kept clean to prevent the risk of food contamination.

(g) Certain foods are to be stored at temperatures laid down in the regulations; the foods covered include cheese, cooked products containing meat, fish, eggs, cereals, pulses, smoked fish, prepared salads, sandwiches, pies, etc.

8. Resale Prices Act 1976

This repeals and consolidates the provisions of earlier legislation, e.g. the Resale Prices Act 1964. It is unlawful for individuals as well as collective suppliers to fix minimum prices. A manufacturer can still recommend selling prices for his or her goods but a seller does not have to observe them although in some cases he or she may be bound not to exceed them.

9. Trading Stamps Act 1964

This Act places restrictions on persons carrying on business as promoters of trading stamp schemes. The cash value of the individual stamp must be clearly marked on its face and the Act also makes it possible for retail customers to obtain this cash value rather than 'gifts'. The Act also makes it obligatory for shops operating these schemes to display notices stating the cash value of the stamps and to keep for public inspection a copy of the promoter's current gift catalogue, which must contain the promoter's name and registered office.

10. Trade Descriptions Act 1968

This Act is based on the recommendations of the Molony Committee, which reported in 1962. The Act imposes commercial penalties on any person who:

(a) applies a false trade description (as defined by the Act) to goods

(b) sells goods to which a false trade description has been applied.

It should be noted that a description can be verbal as well as written. The Act gives powers to the Department of Trade and Industry to require information to be marked on goods or to be included in advertisements.

11. Unsolicited Goods and Services Acts 1971 and 1975

These Acts seek to protect people to whom goods are sent or delivered, without being asked for. Section 1 of the 1971 Act provides that in certain circumstances the receiver of unsolicited goods may use, deal with or dispose of them as if they were an unconditional gift to him or her thus extinguishing the sender's rights. It is a criminal offence for the sender to demand payment for what he or she has no reasonable cause to believe there is a right to payment. It is also a criminal offence in such cases to threaten to take legal action, to have the receiver's name put on a list of debtors/defaulters, or to initiate collection procedures.

12. Fair Trading Act 1973

Further strengthening of consumer protection legislation occurred when this Act enabled the setting up of the Office of Fair Trading run by the Director-General of Fair Trading and supported by a Consumer Protection Advisory Committee. The Director-General has powers to investigate both general consumer trade practices and the activities of individual traders and, if there is sufficient evidence, to obtain their discontinuance or modification by a court order or a statutory instrument, which is a type of delegated legislation.

13. The Competition Act 1980

This authorizes the Director-General of Fair Trading to carry out a preliminary investigation to determine whether a course of conduct being pursued amounts to an anti-competitive practice.

If the Director-General identifies the existence of an anti-competitive practice he is empowered to refer the matter to the Monopolies and Mergers Commission for further investigation, and for their report as to whether the practice is against the public interest. If it is against the public interest, the Director-General may ask the parties to undertake to refrain from the practice or take action in order to remedy the defect. The Act's purpose is to encourage competition and prevent anti-competitive practices such as monopoly situations.

The Act defines the existence of a monopoly situation as being when at least one-quarter of the supply of goods or services supplied in the UK are supplied by one person, or one company, or group of inter-connected companies, or where two or more unconnected persons do so, and so conduct their affairs in any way to prevent, restrict or distort competition.

14. Consumer Credit Act 1974

This very important piece of consumer protection legislation is based on the report of the Crowther Committee, which looked into the whole question of credit trading, particularly how it affects the consumer. The Committee suggested important reforms such as the concept of 'truth in lending' so that borrowers can know the exact rate of interest they have to pay. Much of the previous legislation on the subject, such as the Hire-Purchase Acts of 1964 and 1965 and money lending legislation, has been swept away. Nearly every credit trader is affected, from the shop offering 'easy terms' to the department store operating budget accounts and, indeed, to many firms which offer support services or advice to credit users.

Supervision and control of the Act is carried out by the Director-General of Fair Trading. The main provisions of the Act are as follows:

(a) Licensing. The Act requires anyone carrying on a credit or hire business (e.g. TV rental) to obtain a licence from the Director-General. Before granting the licence the Director-General will want to know:

(*i*) the type of activity to be carried out

(*ii*) the type of agreements the trader will want to enter into

(*iii*) whether the person obtaining the licence is 'a fit person to engage in the activities covered by the licence'. (This may be either 'a standard licence' issued to the person named, or a 'group licence' covering a group of persons or a group of activities, e.g. a limited company.)

Note: The fitness to hold a licence may depend on past behaviour as reflected in court records or engagement in business practices which the Director-General feels to be unfair.

(b) Advertising and canvassing. False or misleading advertisements are automatically illegal under the Act and an offence is committed not only by the advertiser but by anybody who publishes the advertisement or even draws it up. The Act seeks to control 'high pressure' doorstep selling by providing that the customer has a right to cancel the agreement where oral representations have been made to him or her in his or her presence, and the agreements was signed anywhere other than the creditor's business premises. This cuts out the risk that consumers will enter into agreements 'on the doorstep'.

(c) Entering into agreements. Important and complicated provisions are set out in the Act regarding the actual form of credit or hiring agreements, particularly to a 'cooling-off period' of five days in order for the prospective debtor to reconsider the matter and, if necessary, get out of the agreement. Specific information must also be supplied before the customer signs, regarding his or her rights (e.g. to cancel the agreement) and duties, the amount and rate of the total charge for the credit, and the protection and remedies available to him or her under the Act.

(d) Default and termination. If the vendor wishes to terminate the agreement for reasons such as non-payment, notice must be given to the debtor with full reasons for termination. With hire-purchase and conditional sale agreements many of the basic provisions of previous legislation are carried on. For instance, a vendor is still prevented from repossessing goods under these types of agreement, other than by means of a court order, once one-third of the total price has been paid. The customer must also have the right to terminate the agreement at any time and his or her maximum liability in such an event is to make the payments up to one-half of the total price (and possibly pay for any damages for failing to keep the goods in proper condition).

(e) Extortionate credit bargains. Where there is an extortionate credit bargain (an agreement requiring grossly exorbitant interest payments, or which is otherwise grossly unfair), the court has power to re-open the credit agreement, and can totally re-write its terms, having regard to the circumstances of the debtor and creditor (the court could, e.g., reduce the rate of interest).

15. The Consumer Credit (Advertisements) Regulations 1989

These regulations provide rules on how the retailer must conduct his or her credit advertising.

At the heart of the legislation is the requirement to define two standard measures of credit cost, namely:

(a) the total charge for credit

(b) the annual percentage rate of charge (APR). The APR must be stated more prominently than any other rate, e.g. annual flat rate or monthly period rate, and at least as prominently as any other piece of credit information.

The regulations also set out the minimum amount of information required in credit advertisements. Also, some expressions may only be used in credit advertisements in restricted circumstances, e.g. words such as 'overdraft', 'interest-free' and 'no deposit' carry special meanings and therefore must not be used loosely.

Where the creditor requires security in the form of a mortgage or charge on the debtor's house, a statement must be made in the advertisement in the form: 'Your home is at risk if you do not keep up repayments on a mortgage or other loan secured on it'.

If the advertisement is for a mortgage or other loan secured on property and repayments are made in a currency other than sterling, a statement is necessary in the form: 'The sterling equivalent of your liability under a foreign currency mortgage may be increased by exchange rate movements'.

16. Unfair Contract Terms Act 1977

This Act reduces the degree to which the liability can be limited or excluded in contracts.

It is not possible to exclude liability for death or personal injury caused by negligence.

Exclusion of liability for breach of contract is also controlled. Where the buyer acts as a consumer the seller cannot exclude or limit the requirements of the Sale of Goods Act (*see* **3**). In other cases exclusion of liability for breach of contract may be allowed if the exclusion clause is reasonable. Ultimately it is up to the courts to define what is or is not reasonable, and this depends on the circumstances in each case, e.g. the relative bargaining positions of the parties; whether there was any inducement for the consumer to enter the contract, e.g. 'low price' (this would make the exclusion more likely to be reasonable); whether the consumer had knowledge of the clause (if so, more likely to be reasonable); whether the consumer could have gone elsewhere and entered into similar contracts without the clause (more likely to be unreasonable as, if other traders do without the clause, then this one should be able to also); and any other circumstances.

17. The Theft Act 1968

This Act allows a store's security officer or other person to arrest a suspected thief.

A person is guilty of theft if he or she dishonestly appropriates property belonging to another with the intention of permanently depriving the other of it.

The use of force is allowed in making an arrest, but only such as is reasonable in the circumstances in the prevention of crime.

Where an arrest is made, the person making the arrest must take the arrested person to a magistrate or to a police station as soon as is reasonably possible, i.e. within a reasonable time.

18. The Consumer Protection Act 1987

This Act introduced the concept of 'product liability', namely that:

(a) A person who puts an 'own brand' mark on goods may be liable to any person who is injured by those goods if they prove defective

(b) A retailer may be liable to any person injured by defective goods supplied by him or her, unless he or she can identify his or her own supplier.

The Act also empowers the Secretary of State to make regulations in respect of certain types of goods, e.g. oil heaters and fireguards, flame-resistant nightwear for children, electrical appliance wiring, colour codes and children's toys. Local authorities are responsible for protecting shoppers. Trading Standards or Consumer Protection Departments see that laws concerning trading are met and investigate complaints.

The Consumer Protection Act repeals Section 11 of the Trade Descriptions Act 1968 (which concerned giving misleading information, e.g. as to the price of goods). Section 20 of the Consumer Protection Act 1987 creates a new offence of giving misleading price indications, and detailed guidance on this new offence is given in the Code of Practice for Traders on Price Indications (*see* **18**).

19. The Consumer Protection (Code of Practice for Traders on Price Indications) Approval Order 1988

This order is made under the Consumer Protection Act 1987, and gives guidance as to what constitutes the offence of giving misleading price indications, and aims to promote desirable practices amongst traders when they are giving price indications. The Code of Practice for Traders on Price Indications is set out as a Schedule to the Order; it states that in general if a trader is making a price comparison he should do so in terms which are clear, and if he is not intending a price comparison, he should not use words which suggest that one is being made.

Price comparisons should always state the higher price as well as the price which is intended to be charged. Statements like 'sale price £5.00' or 'reduced to £39.00' should not be used without quoting the higher price to which they refer.

If expressions like 'usual price', 'normal price' or 'regular price' are used they should make clear whose regular, usual or normal price it is.

If a trader is making a comparison between his present selling price and another price at which he has offered the product in the past, he should state the previous as well as the lower price.

In any comparison with the trader's own previous price:

(a) The previous price should be the last price at which the product was available during the last six months

(b) The product should have been available to consumers at that price for at least 28 consecutive days in the previous six months

(c) The previous price should have been applied at the same shop where the reduced price is now offered.

If any of this is departed from, this is not necessarily a breach of Section 20 of the Consumer Protection Act 1987, so long as the comparison is fair and meaningful, and it should also give a clear and positive explanation of the period in which the higher price applied.

The Code also deals with 'Introductory' and 'Promotional' offers, 'When perfect' comparisons, comparisons with other traders' prices, comparisons with recommended retail prices. Again the comparison must be fair and meaningful, and, for example, an introductory offer should state for how long it applies and should not carry on for so long that it seems to be the permanent price (this could mislead the customer into thinking they are getting a bargain if they buy the item now, whereas the price is not in fact going up for a while yet).

The Code deals with the actual price to the consumer, and this covers things like indicating two different prices, e.g. a lower price shown in the window whilst a higher price is charged at the point of sale (this would be an offence under Section 20 Consumer Protection Act 1987). Also covered is incomplete information given as to price and non-optional extras, postage, packing and delivery charges, VAT and professional fees.

The Code also deals with price indications which become misleading after they have been given (e.g. newspaper and magazine offers), which would happen if:

(a) Consumers could reasonably be expected still to be relying on it; and

(b) The trader does not take reasonable steps to prevent consumers so relying.

If the magazine does not state otherwise, the price should apply for a reasonable period, i.e. at least seven days, or until the next issue.

If the advertisement has become misleading due to, e.g. changes in VAT, the correct price should be indicated to customers who place orders, before they commit themselves to buying the product.

The Code also applies to the sale of 'new homes' and this expression carries a restricted meaning and should not be used loosely.

The Consumer Protection Act 1987 does not require traders to observe the Code – they can still give price indications which do not accord with the Code, provided they are not 'misleading' as defined by Section 21 of the Consumer Protection Act 1987; the definition covers indications about any conditions attached to a price, about what you expect to happen to a price in the future, and what you say about price comparisons, as well as indications about the actual price the consumer will have to pay. It also applies in the same way to any indications you give about the way in which a price will be calculated.

20. Weights and Measures Act 1985

This Act makes it an offence to give short weight, or inadequate quantity, or a wrong indication of amount.

Certain listed foods are required by the Weights and Measures (Miscellaneous Foods) Order 1988, when pre-packed, to be sold in the prescribed quantities. These items include foodstuffs such as salt, sugar, flour, chocolate bars, milk, butter, coffee, pasta, and potatoes.

Pre-packed food stuffs, whether in packets, bottles or tins, must be marked with the weight or quantity, otherwise an offence is committed.

The Weights and Measures Act 1963 (Cheese, Fish, Fresh Fruits and Vegetables, Meat and Poultry) Order 1984 requires that meat, fish, poultry, cheese and fresh fruit and vegetables must have either the weight marked on the packet, or the weight must be made known before purchase, otherwise an offence is committed.

EMPLOYEE LEGISLATION

21. Shops Act 1950

This is aimed very largely at protecting staff from exploitation and long hours. The Act lays down fairly tight controls over three main areas:

(a) General closing hours (i.e. the ordinary week-day closing times). Serving of customers generally must not be later than 8 pm, and 9 pm on a late closing day. To accommodate the special position of confectioners, tobacconists and newsagents (CTN) special differing provisions apply.

(b) Early closing days. There is a statutory requirement for every shop to close at 1 pm for one half-day each week. The local authority can, however, make shops in a particular area exempt from this provision, if that is the wish of the majority of shopkeepers in the area. Such exemptions are common. The early closing day requirement does not apply to shops at certain airports.

(c) Staff employment conditions. The Shops Act also contains many conditions of employment for staff. For example, no more than six hours can be worked by an adult shop assistant without a 20-minute break. Where the hours of employment include the hours 11.30 am to 2.30 pm at least 45 minutes must be allowed for lunch (one hour if lunch is not taken in the shop) and if an assistant works between the hours of 4 pm and 7 pm, a minimum of 30 minutes should be allowed for tea.

These provisions do not apply to a shop if the only persons employed as shop assistants are members of the occupier's family, maintained by him and dwelling in his house. Persons under the age of 18 may not be employed for more than five hours without an interval of at least 20 minutes.

22. Shops (Early Closing Days) Act 1965

This Act allows the occupier of the shop to select the premises' early-closing day. This revokes local authority powers in this respect as laid down under the Shops Act 1950. Occupiers are obliged to display a notice specifying the early-closing day and this notice should be readable from the shop entrance.

23. Offices, Shops and Railway Premises Act 1963

Under this Act, shopkeepers must register with the local authority on a form known as OSR1. The Act lays down certain minimum standards concerning health and safety.

(a) Standards of comfort

(*i*) Cleanliness. All premises, fixtures and fittings must be kept clean including staff-rooms, stairways, exits, halls and lifts.

(*ii*) Overcrowding. Office staff must have at least 400 cubic feet (11 cubic metres) of area each in which to work, but this stipulation does not extend to the public areas of shops or showrooms (although there is still a general responsibility here to avoid overcrowding likely to cause risk of injury to health).

(*iii*) Temperature. Staff are entitled to a reasonable room temperature laid down in the Act as a minimum of 16 degrees Centigrade after the first hour.

(*iv*) Overall comfort. Adequate ventilation, lighting and drinking water must be provided, along with seating and outdoor clothes storage.

(b) Standards of safety. Staff must be able to move around the building in safety. This means that all areas must be soundly constructed, properly maintained and free from obstruction and slippery substances.

(*i*) First aid. A proper first-aid box or cupboard must be provided for each 150 people employed.

(*ii*) Dangerous machinery. Great care must be taken to see that staff are not injured by machinery, such as preparation machines in the butchery section of superstores. All dangerous parts of machinery must be properly fenced in either by a fixed guard, or if this is not possible, by an automatic safety device.

Certain machinery which is prescribed by the Minister as dangerous must be operated by trained staff, who must be supervised.

(c) Hygiene. Adequate washing facilities for staff are required under the Act along with a minimum of one lavatory per 15 members of staff of each sex.

(d) Fire precautions. The Fire Precautions Act 1971 and the Fire Precautions (Factories, Offices, Shops and Railway Premises) Order 1989 apply, and the following requirements are laid down:

(*i*) Fire-fighting equipment, which is suitable and properly maintained, must be kept ready for immediate use on the premises.

(*ii*) Proper means of escape in case of fire, signposted for shoppers as well as for staff, should be available. The fire exits should be kept uncluttered and the fire doors themselves should have panic bars.

(*iii*) Inspection for fire certification is required, and the local authority has a duty to inspect the premises before issuing the certificate.

However, the Fire Precautions (Factories, Offices, Shops and Railway Premises) Order 1989 states that a fire certificate is not required where not more than 20 people work at any one time, or where fewer than 10 people work at any one time in upstairs rooms in the building.

(*iv*) Fire alarms will also be required to have a certificate. The most important point here is that the noise must be heard clearly in all parts of the building.

(*v*) Fire drill is another requirement placed upon the retailer if his or her shop is large enough for fire certification. A set routine in event of fire should be known to all staff and random practices carried out for test purposes.

24. Health and Safety at Work Act 1974

This Act provides a comprehensive and integrated system of law dealing with the safety, health and welfare of people at work and even the health and safety of the public. Employers must tell their employees what the policy of the firm is towards health and safety. Guidance notes are available from the Health and Safety Executive. Local authorities through their inspectorates are responsible for the general enforcement of the Act's provisions which include the serving of two notices, detailed below.

(a) Improvement notices. These state how the Act has been contravened and calls upon the shopkeeper, for example, to put it right within a particular time.

(b) Prohibition notices. If the inspector feels that some activities involve a risk of serious personal injury, he or she may serve a prohibition notice that has an immediate effect and may involve the full or part closure of the store.

The employer's duties under this Act are to:

(a) draw up and publish a safety policy statement

(b) ensure that safety procedures are implemented

(c) keep and publish safety records

(d) advise staff and others of their responsibilities.

Employees are also liable under this Act if they fail to follow safe methods of working.

25. The Equal Pay Act 1970

This Act came into force in 1975 with the purpose of eliminating discrimination between men and women in regard to pay and other terms of employment contracts, i.e. basic rates of pay, overtime, bonus and piece work payments, holiday and sick pay entitlement. Under the Act, an individual woman has the right to equal treatment with a man when she is employed on like work, or on a job which has been given equal status under job evaluation or on work of equal value.

26. The Employment Protection (Consolidation) Act 1978

This Act replaces the Contracts of Employment Act 1972 and the Employment Protection Act 1975. It is a complicated piece of legislation and is subject to periodic modification, e.g. the Employment Acts 1980 and 1982. The following are some important provisions of the Act regarding:

(a) Contracts of employment:

(*i*) A written statement of main terms and conditions of employment must be provided to the employee within 13 weeks of the commencement of employment.
(*ii*) Written notification, within one month, of a change in the name or identity of the employer.
(*iii*) Entitlement to an itemised pay statement for those employees working more than 16 hours per week.

(b) Maternity rights – maternity leave, etc.

(c) Dismissal and redundancy, e.g. redundancy pay, notice of termination of employment, written reasons for dismissal, compensation for 'unfair' dismissal.

27. Sex Discrimination Acts 1975 and 1986

It is unlawful to discriminate in employment, training and education, as well as in the provision of goods and services. Individuals have the right to complain to courts and industrial tribunals. The Equal Opportunities Commission was established to help enforce this legislation promoting sexual equality. The law covers both recruitment and existing employees in matters like appointment and promotion. Firms with fewer than five employees are excluded.

28. Race Relations Act 1976

By this Act discrimination on the grounds of race, colour, creed or religion is unlawful in employment, training and related matters. Individuals have access to industrial tribunals and civil courts. The Race Relations Board was replaced by a new Commission for Racial Equality for the elimination of racial discrimination.

29. The Social Security and Housing Benefits Act 1982

As a result of this Act employers are responsible for paying Statutory Sick Pay (SSP) to their employees for up to eight weeks of sickness absence in one tax year. The retailer is required by law to keep records of:

(a) Dates of sickness absence of at least four consecutive days (including Saturdays and Sundays) reported by employees

(b) Any days within such sickness absences, for which SSP was not paid, with reasons

(c) Details of each employee's qualifying days in each period of incapacity for work.

These records should be kept in such a way that DSS inspectors can have access to them on request.

> *Note:* This chapter on Retailing and the Law is intended for guidance only. The reader is advised to refer to specific texts for more detailed, authoritative and up-to-date information.

Progress test 23

1. Outline the main provisions of the Sale of Goods Act 1979. How has it been updated recently?

2. Explain how the Food Safety Act 1990 protects consumers. What defence can a food retailer offer to an alleged breach of the Act?

3. Describe the general provisions of the Consumer Credit Act 1974? What is the connection with the Fair Trading Act?

4. The Shops Act 1950 lays down fairly tight controls over three main areas. What are they?

5. Briefly discuss the several Acts which try to protect employees from discrimination at work. How effective do you think they are?

APPENDIX 1

BIBLIOGRAPHY

Baron S., Davies B., and Swindley D. (1991), *Macmillan Dictionary of Retailing*, The Macmillan Press.

Brown S. (1992), *Retail Location: a Microscale Perspective*, Avebury.

Christopher M. (1985), *The Strategy of Distribution Management*, Gower.

Collins A. (1992), *Competitive Retail Marketing*, McGraw Hill.

Cook D. and Walters D. (1991), *Retail Marketing: Theory and Practice*, Prentice Hall.

Corstjens J. and Corstjens M. (1995), *Store Wars: the Battle for Mindspace and Shelfspace*, Wiley.

Davies G.J. and Brooks J.M. (1989), *Positioning Strategy in Retailing*, Paul Chapman.

Fernie J. (1990), *Retail Distribution Management*, Kogan Page.

Fitch R. and Knobell L. (1990), *Fitch on Retail Design*, Phaidon Press.

Gardner C. and Sheppard J. (1989), *Consuming Passion*, Unwin Hyman.

Guy C. (1994), *The Retail Development Process*, Routledge.

Harris D. and Walters D. (1992), *Retail Operations Management*, Prentice Hall.

Howe W.S. (1992), *Retailing Management*, Macmillan.

Jones K. and Simmons J. (1990), *The Retail Environment*, Routledge.

Johnson G. (Editor) (1987), *Business Strategy and Retailing*, Wiley.

Kay W. (1989), *Battle for the High Street*, Corgi Books.

Knee D. and Walters D. (1985), *Strategy in Retailing*, Philip Allan.

McDonald M.H.B. and Tideman C.C.S. (1993), *Retail Marketing Plans*, Butterworth Heinemann.

McGoldrick P. (1990), *Retail Marketing*, McGraw Hill.

McGoldrick P. (1994), *Cases in Retail Management*, Pitman.

McGoldrick P. and Davies G. (Editors) (1995), *International Retailing: Trends and Strategies*, Pitman.

Walters D. (1988), *Strategic Retailing Management: a case study approach*, Prentice Hall.

Walters D. (1994), *Retailing Management: Analysis, Planning and Control*, Macmillan.

Walters D. and White D. (1987), *Retail Marketing Management*, Macmillan.

APPENDIX 2

CASE STUDIES

1. PENSENDS

Panarjee Amersan, a young graduate of Indian descent, worked in a large UK department store as a management trainee and undertook evening classes at the local university to add Diplomas in Management Studies and Marketing to his Degree in Economics. When he married at 25 years of age Panarjee was determined to start his own business and had the idea of a small shop specializing in quality pens.

He opened the shop in October 1987 in the centre of a Midlands city with the aid of financial support from his family and a bank loan. Panarjee had previously toured Europe and acquired a considerable collection of high quality speciality pens with up-market styles which he featured in his opening window display. These were backed with high quality pens from the better UK-based suppliers such as Shaeffer, Swan and Parker. Panarjee had also learned the art of engraving and he offered a free engraving service with every purchase, together with an after-sales maintenance and repair service.

A press reception party resulted in favourable editorial publicity in the local paper and local radio. Subsequent Christmas gift shopping led to an initial sales turnover of well above Panarjee's expectations and budgets. However, after Christmas sales were virtually at a standstill until increasingly pen gift receivers began coming in for refills, nib changes and additions.

Panarjee worked long hours and although he was helped part-time by his wife and family, he was finding it difficult to make sufficient profits on retailer margins. In despair he attempted to secure higher discounts but was told these were reserved for wholesalers. Panarjee borrowed more money to open up a wholesale business and at the same time designed and developed special display units to add to the attractiveness of his shop interior. The business thrived and soon Panarjee was supplying other retailers from his wholesale business with both pens and display units.

Encouraged by his success, Panarjee opened retail shops in two other Midland city centres and these were managed by his two brothers. Although these other shops were successful, they did not do as well as his, which Panarjee put down to lack of owner-motivation. Panarjee is considering radical expansion through *Franchise*, a rapidly growing form of distribution in the UK following proven success in America. The form of franchising under consideration is an agreement whereby franchisees in return for an initial payment of £17,500 and a 5 per cent royalty on subsequent sales are allowed and indeed helped to establish their own retail outlets in city centres under the *Pensends* banner. Panarjee would in return train franchisees in his current shops, offer a site location service, provide shop fascias and fittings, advertise and initiate special sales promotions and negotiate with suppliers. Franchisees would be bound to buy stock from Panarjee's wholesale business for a period of at least five years. A major bank has agreed to consider underwriting the arrangement and provide loans to franchisees of up to 80 per cent of the estimated £200,000 business start-up costs, conditional upon a properly drawn-up legal franchise agreement and stringent franchisee selection and control procedures.

It is expected that an average *Pensends* franchise business will turn over £250,000 a year at 40 per cent gross margin with £40,000 rent and rates and need the equivalent of two full-time staff. This franchise offer is expected to appeal to executives recently made redundant who are finding it difficult to regain employment and have some savings and their own houses as collateral (security) for the bank loan. Panarjee is thinking of advertising in the Sunday national newspapers to this target audience and seeking advice from the British Franchise Association with regard to the drawing up of a franchise agreement and operating manual.

Questions

1. Outline the marketing plan which Panarjee will need in order to operate this new venture.
2. What control problems would confront Panarjee in endeavouring to expand up to say 50 outlets by this franchise method?

2. SPORT 'N' STYLE

Sport 'n' Style was owned and managed by Jack Ashley who started in business in sports and leisure retailing in 1991, after spending some 15 years in industry in a variety of senior positions.

Jack Ashley was not a retired footballer, or a disillusioned tennis professional. Indeed, the only sport that Jack had any real affinity for was snooker, preferably being watched from a comfortable armchair! He considered himself first and foremost to be a business-man, and having scoured central England for a good business opening he became increasingly convinced that the sports and leisurewear market offered the opportunity for real business development providing professional retail management practice was deployed.

Before setting up his shop, Jack set out to make a comprehensive examination of retail custom and practice in the sports and leisurewear industry throughout most of the UK. He arranged quite lengthy discussions with retailers (both independent and multiple), suppliers, and other organizations represented in the industry.

After almost five months of research he again re-examined some of the principal conclusions that he had reached. Briefly these were as follows:

(a) Too many of the independent retailers were not professional enough in their business practice, exhibiting little overall competence in key success areas such as marketing, buying, and financial control. A worrying number of owner-managers were more con-cerned with pursuing their own interests in sport and leisure than pursuing policies which increased profitability or maximized return on investment.

Initial conclusion: poor retail management.

(b) The sports and leisurewear markets are strongly interlinked and retail success depended ultimately on understanding the dynamics of what was essentially a volatile, seasonal, and invariably frustrating industry to monitor, but one which exhibited phe-nomenal rates of growth in certain segments.

Second conclusion: opportunities for growth.

(c) The above point was recognized and understood by some of the multiple retail organizations who had seized the opportunity to participate in corporate growth. Many of the independents had failed to re-invest sufficiently, resulting in an under-capitalized, weak retail structure, which for the most part was undisciplined and unprofessional. Furthermore, many independents were under pressure from the multiples in their prime trading positions.

Third conclusion: try to adopt the business and trading policies successfully pursued by the multiples.

(d) Competition among the principal suppliers to the industry was becoming more intense and more sophisticated – *not* based primarily on price. There had been an increase in new products, styles, ranges, brands and colours. Also, new and aggressive market entrants had emerged recently, adopting hard but professional marketing techniques.

Fourth conclusion: understand and appreciate the importance of marketing throughout the industry.

Although these four points were only general in outline, Jack was convinced that they had to be the backbone of his business plan. He was sure that to be a *successful* independent retailer in this industry meant adopting modern business methods and techniques, especially marketing and promotion.

In January 1991, Jack opened his shop in a prime retail position in the new and highly acclaimed shopping centre in central Milton Keynes. He was delighted with his immediate retail neighbours which included John Lewis, Dixons, Habitat, Boots and British Home Stores.

Determined from the start to achieve real success, Jack set the business the following objectives:

(a) to break even by January 1993, and to repay the bank loan of £100,000
(b) to achieve a turnover of two times total stock in year one, and three times total stock in year three.

Jack was well aware of one lesson that many small businesses demonstrated, which could be summarized in the phrase, 'Having lost sight of our objectives, we re-doubled our efforts'.

Furthermore Jack wanted to set marketing objectives for the business by exploiting his excellent retail presence. After negotiating hard for one of the best retail sites, this seemed absolutely imperative.

He decided, therefore, that the following were to be given paramount importance in his business operations:

(a) Customer impression of the shop should be associated with high quality products and professional, courteous service. If any goods should be found to be faulty, the wrong size or colour, or simply not suitable, an immediate replacement would be given to the customer or a full refund. (Jack was not slow to appreciate that customer retention often derived from customer reassurance.)

(b) The shop name, image, colours and logo, should capitalize on the interdependence of sport, leisure, and fashion. The name *Sport 'n Style* was therefore selected as a suitable trading name. (Jack was very much against the conventional retail approach of simply putting the word 'sports' after the owner's name.)

(c) The shop should be seen as selling the best available products – this should be established as quickly as possible.

(d) Finally, Jack appreciated that if the right marketing plan was put together then the business could exploit the benefits associated with stocking the major brands, e.g. Adidas,

Nike, Hi-Tec, etc., and *capitalize on the consumer awareness of such brands*. Jack was therefore keen to see consistency in his approach to the customer when it came to:

(*i*) in-store layout and display;

(*ii*) co-ordinated ranges; and

(*iii*) the identity of the store.

In his own modest but methodical way he wanted to follow the marketing strategy adopted by Olympus which has made them the undisputed leading sports multiple in the UK and Europe.

Jack admired success in any field and saw Olympus as the model to copy in his chosen market. Accordingly, the following promotional features were incorporated:

(a) The *Sport 'n Style* name and logo over the shop fascia was reproduced in miniature on all promotional uses and media, e.g. letterheads and business notepaper, business cards, Yellow Pages advertising, local press advertising, etc.

Also, the three members of staff that Jack employed to serve in the shop were all immediately recognizable because of their similarity of dress and the shop name printed on their jumper or sweatshirt.

(b) Jack installed two TV monitors and two VHS video players showing recorded sporting highlights from athletics, football, tennis, etc. One unit was an integral part of the front window display, the other unit being positioned at the rear of the shop near the changing rooms. Some fifty different recorded sporting highlights together with 40 brand and product advertisements could be shown giving good coverage and variety.

(c) *Sport 'n Style* only sold exclusively branded goods from the principal companies. Jack saw to it that his suppliers and customers were well informed of this policy in order to accord with the image of the store.

As a result, Adidas, Nike and some other leading brands were keen to assist in the success of the store by offering good point-of-sale material, posters and displays.

At the beginning of February 1993, Jack went back to Barclays Bank to meet the loans manager, Mr Childs, and discuss the future of his business. He had managed to pay back the first loan of £100,000 to the delight – and surprise – of the Bank. (The original loan was repayable over three years, and Mr Childs fully expected Jack to keep to the original timetable.)

In his discussion with Mr Childs, Jack drew his attention to various forecasts on the sports and leisurewear markets describing and predicting certain trends which he considered to be generally favourable.

Jack wanted to open a second shop in Stony Stratford, in Northern Milton Keynes, with the aim of achieving two objectives:

(a) to be recognized as the premier sports retailer in the new City;

(b) to attain a 25 per cent share of the local market for sports and related leisurewear.

Mr Childs was impressed by Jack's confidence and commitment and agreed to advance another loan of £100,000 repayable over three years to assist with the fitting out of the new shop, again located in a prime retail position.

In June, a footwear shop some 100 yards from the first *Sport 'n Style* shop ceased trading and the lease was promptly secured by Olympus Sports. Jack was naturally concerned, but not too worried about the threat to his trade. After all, he had been established in that position for over 2 years – his shop was modern and reflected the best retail style, his products were known to be good, and his staff were courteous and professional. Some trade might be lost but both he and his main competitor could gain in the medium and long term as the City developed and population grew. Besides, Jack was a realist and no market, of whatever nature, was without competition. Furthermore, Jack *knew* of the corporate and marketing strategies pursued by Olympus Sports and could therefore plan accordingly.

In August 1993 the second *Sport 'n Style* shop started trading amid a blaze of local promotion and specially discounted lines. It was a carbon copy of the first shop – a testament to Jack's demand for retail consistency and predictability. Any changes that took place were subtle in nature, notably in the product mix, for Jack had decided to include certain 'own label' products, notably in jogging suits, tee-shirts and selected footwear items.

Jack's 'number two', John Stevens, now managed the first shop and was surprised to find that some 30 per cent of Olympus' total sales were own brand – no wonder they were so profitable!

If *Sport 'n Style* could account for just 10 per cent of total turnover in its own brand goods, then total profitability of both shops could be enhanced by 17 per cent – a tremendous financial inducement. Jack had successfully negotiated a deal with a sports-wear manufacturer in Leicester to supply these items substantially cheaper than the branded goods, but of comparable quality and style. The deal also included the *Sport 'n Style* logo *SNS* to be incorporated on all products.

Both Jack and John Stevens were tremendously excited by this development as it would not only increase profits and return on capital, but afford them more control over buying, therefore allowing a greater degree of freedom from the main brand suppliers. Jack was becoming increasingly frustrated with many of the reps who called because they refused to cut prices even when he placed a very large order. Their inability or blatant refusal to reduce prices when their parent companies were spending fortunes on expensive media advertising made Jack annoyed on several occasions. Now Jack had a competitive weapon 'par excellence'. The price of SNS own brands could be set 20 per cent lower than some of the main brands and still produce a gross margin of 60 per cent for the business. At the same time it was decided to increase the advertising budget to consolidate the market position of the new shop and accomplish the following goals:

(a) to inform existing and potential customers of the new shop;

(b) to reinforce the high market image and corporate identify of *Sport 'n Style*;

(c) to promote the new *SNS* range of sports and leisurewear, by introducing the phrase, *High quality at a kind price*;

(d) to preserve and enhance customer loyalty against competitive pressures;

(e) to let Olympus know that *Sport 'n Style* meant business!

It was estimated that both shops could stand a promotional budget of £10,000 over the coming trade year.

For the next four months (which included the Christmas period) business was excellent and Jack told John Stevens how pleased he was with the performance of both shops.

The *SNS* brand sold up to expectations and there were plans to increase its presence further into other lines, perhaps even into sports equipment. Also turnover was up by 10 per cent over the predicted level in both stores.

There were other indications that the business was doing well. For example, Jack was asked if he thought about joining *Intersport*, the buying and marketing group that represented many of the independent retailers in the industry. This was dismissed by Jack; he couldn't see what benefits it would bring.

By February 1994 *SNS* own brands accounted for 20 per cent of total stock with a consequent reduction in certain proprietary brand ranges, notably Adidas, Puma, Lacoste and Nike. Jack still stocked some of their products but was planning to reduce his stock even further to improve profitability.

Towards the end of March it started to become apparent that the numbers of people buying from both shops were falling. Plenty of people would stare at the window displays, watch the videos, and come inside, but fewer sales were actually made (down by 5–6 per cent). Jack was not overly concerned (recognizing the seasonality of certain lines and sports) but thought that a wise move would be to increase the annual advertising budget by £2,000 with immediate effect to arrest this trend.

April and May saw turnover improve slightly, but not in line with the increased promotional expenditure. More worrying was the decline of *SNS* own brands by 6 per cent, whereas proprietary brands remained constant.

Jack discussed these problems with John Stevens and they both agreed that it would make good sense to increase the promotional budget still further to £15,000 pa. Olympus Sports were advertising very heavily both nationally and locally and it was certainly noticeable that the numbers of people entering their Milton Keynes store had increased.

By the beginning of August, turnover for both shops was 15 per cent below target, with most of the reduction being *SNS* brands which now accounted for some 25 per cent of total stock. The rent review on the first shop was due shortly and an increase of at least 10 per cent could be expected. Jack, despite his outward calm, was becoming anxious about a situation that he could not really understand and which he seemed unable to correct. He again discussed the problem with John Stevens and they both agreed to reduce the promotional budget back to its original level in order to reduce costs.

At the end of August sales had risen slightly but only enough to cover the increased fixed costs which the business had to bear.

Jack decided that it was time for action, and compiled a number of alternatives which he would discuss with John Stevens later that day. These were:

(a) to reduce the price of *all SNS* brands by 20 per cent and promote a large summer/end of season sale;

(b) to make discounts on selected main branded items and redirect promotional expenditure accordingly;

(c) to switch all advertising expenditure to local radio in an effort to increase awareness of the business. Jack noticed the increase in the number of retailers who seemed to be using this medium.

What frustrated Jack was that he had been methodical and professional in his approach to entering the sports and leisurewear market unlike so many of his competitors. He had done his research, acted with credibility and for what? – to watch his business losing turnover which he seemed incapable of preventing.

If one of the three above strategies failed to work then Jack was seriously thinking of selling the business and going back to work for his last employer.

Questions

1. What advice would you give Jack? Make recommendations on the objectives and direction of the business, including any aspects of management that you consider particularly important.
2. Comment on the marketing and trading policy that has been pursued so far.

3. WESTERHAMS

Westerhams is a regional grocery chain with 50 stores in the South East and East Anglia stocking merchandise which is designed to appeal to the AB consumer segment.

The company is the result of a series of mergers and acquisitions by Westerhams over the years and branches are, without exception, located in shopping centres. Many of these centres are in prosperous market towns in the south.

The average Westerhams store size is around 500 m^2 (selling areas). During the 1980s the company began to focus on fresh, healthy foods from service counters. Provisions, delicatessen and fresh bread are sold in this way while meat, produce and groceries are merchandised conventionally from self-service sections. The company now boasts a range of over 4,000 grocery and provisions lines with the majority of branches carrying the entire merchandise range. Staff are mainly full-timers with the employment of part-timers on Saturdays in the busier branches. All branches open from 9 am–6 pm, Monday – Friday. All staff work a five-day week and take their days off on a rota basis.

Although the company considers itself to be trading in a satisfactory niche in the market, it suffers from escalating competition from Sainsbury, Safeway, Waitrose and other mid-to-up-scale grocery chains. The recent (1990–92) UK recession has severely affected Westerhams in sales, which have fallen from £149 million in 1989 to £137.5 million in 1992. As a result profits have been seriously affected in spite of the high gross profit margins the chain earns on its merchandise.

Westerhams is a family-owned limited company and old Mr. Westerham (89) as chairman still visits two or three stores a week, while his son, Robert (67), carries out most of the buying.

Mark Stone has just been appointed as sales manager for the chain to replace the other Westerham son, Michael, who recently died. Mark works through four area sales managers, who each supervise about a dozen stores grouped on a geographical basis.

Mark needs to liaise with Robert Westerham, the chief buyer, whilst at the same time motivate his area managers to improve sales and profitability in each of their respective branches.

As part of his learning, Mark has carried out some research into the current operations of the chain and has come up with some unpleasant findings:

- Most branches report frequent out-of-stock positions in a large number of fast-selling lines.
- The length of check-out queues in many branches has produced anecdotal evidence that customers are now deserting the chain to shop at competitors.
- A management trainee who was carrying out a marketing project for his MBA told Mark that, in one store in Kent, customer complaints had risen by 27% over the same period last year.
- According to a local job centre another store in Essex had a staff turnover of 150% in 1992.

Questions

1. What specific sales and related information does Mark need for each of the branches? Explain how he might analyse the information collected.
2. Describe methods which Mark could put into action to reverse the trends currently troubling the retail chain.

INDEX

accidents 237
accompanied shopping 48
accordion theory 6
accounts 196–8
 ratio analysis 198–200
acid test ratio 199
acquisitions 5, 26, 36, 229
advertising
 agencies 148–9
 budgets 144
 corporate 143
 direct response 17–18, 146
 legislation 250, 251
 media 144–7
 media scheduling 147
 messages 147–8
 objectives 143
 promotions 143
 retail communication 142
 trends 143–4
agents 112
alarms 238
Aldi 8, 15, 26
alliances 25, 26–7, 31
ANA (Article Number Association) 240
apprehension of shoplifters 238, 252
architects 219–20
area sales potential 87
Asda 10, 15, 75
assortment planning approach to stock 111
ATMs (auto-teller machines) 243
automatic vending 19

balance sheets 196
bar coding 240–1 •
behaviour segmentation 71–2
Bentalls 13
Body Shop 27, 28, 53
BRAD (British Rate and Data) 144

branch manuals 232–3
brand names 25
 own brands 99–100
break-even analysis 94, 190
budget accounts 180
budgetary control 144, 190–6, 219, 233
bulk-buying 112
buying behaviour
 decision process 58–60, 62
 external factors 65–7
 influencers 61–2
 internal factors 63–5, 152–3
 post-purchase feelings 61
 use behaviour 60–1, 62–3

C & J Clark 27
CACI Market Analysis 85
capital
 costs 93
 expenditure budgets 195
 utilization 199–200
cash budgets 193
cash and carry 21
cash flow 193–5
catchment area analysis 80–4
CCN Systems 85
Census of Distribution 4
Census of Population 85
central buying 108–9
centralized organizations 203
chain stores 4, 10–11, 107, 208
change, see environmental change
charge accounts 180
Charles Good Ltd. 85
cheques 245
cinema advertising 146
city centre sites 88
closed-circuit television 237
club trading 19
co-operative societies 11–13, 107, 208

Comet 15
Competition Act (1980) 249
competition-oriented pricing 133
competitions 158, 161
competitors 53–5
  pricing policy 133
complaint handling 183–5, 204
compulsory purchase orders 220
computers 122
Conran, Terence 165
Consumer Credit Act (1974) 249–50
Consumer Credit (Advertisements)
  Regulations (1989) 251
Consumer Protection Acts (1987/1988)
  252–4
Consumer Protection Advisory
  Committee 249
consumer protection legislation 246–54
consumers, see customers
contracts 251–2
  of employment 257
conveyancing documents 216
copywriting 148
corner shops 89
cost percentages 199
cost-oriented pricing 133
costs
  budgetary control 144, 190–6, 219, 233
  of capital 93
  of goods sold 131–2
  and net profit 93–4, 235
  reducing 190
  rents 221–6
  and sales volume 189
  of staff 235
coupons 159
credit
  control 181
  legislation 249–51
  provisions 179–82
credit cards 180–1
culture 52, 66–7
current ratio 199
customer flows 43–4, 172
customer service 8, 179–85
  complaint handling 183–5, 204
  credit provisions 179–82
  delivery services 124–7, 182–3, 245, 249
  opening hours 182, 254–5
  strategy 38
  training requirements 210

wrapping merchandise 183
customers
  buying motivation 63, 152
  choice of products 152–3
  communicating with 9, 38
  expenditure trends 4
  incomes of 51–2, 70
  as information sources 42
  personal selling to 153–6
  prospecting 153–4
  satisfaction of needs 59, 63, 68–9, 71
  and store location 79
  types of 153
  see also buying behaviour

Debenhams 13
decentralized organizations 203–4
delivery services 124–7, 182–3, 245, 249
demand-oriented pricing 133
demographic factors 51
  and segmentation 69–70
department stores 13–14, 107, 208
deposits 245
diaries 47
direct delivery 124–5
direct organizations 202
Direct Product Profitability (DPP) 177,
  243
direct response advertising 17–18, 146
discount stores 6, 14–15, 89
discounts 136, 160
discrimination 257–8
discussion groups 48
displays 170, 171–6
  in-store 160–1
  point-of-sale 159
  window 160, 167–8
distribution chain 55
district centre sites 88
diversification 36, 227
Dixons 27
door-to-door trading 19
DPP (Direct Product Profitability) 177,
  243

EAN (European Article Number) 240,
  241
economy and retailing 3
EDI (Electronic Data Interchange) 242
EFTPOS (electronic funds transfer at
  point of sale) systems 53, 182, 243

electronic security systems 237
employees
  contracts of employment 257
  and legislation 220, 235, 254–8
Employment Protection Act (1978) 257
employment in retailing 3
environmental change 5–6, 50–6
  macro-environment 51–3
  micro-environment 53–6
environmental issues 53
EPOS (electronic point-of-sale) systems
  42, 53, 121–2, 240–1
Equal Opportunities Commission 52
Equal Pay Act (1970) 257
estate agents 85
European Article Number (EAN) 240,
  241
exit surveys 47
expenses, see costs
experimental research 44

Fair Trading Act (1973) 249
Family Expenditure Surveys 85
family factors 62, 65–6, 70
fascia 166
FIFO (first in, first out) stock valuation
  123
financial planning 189–201
  accounts 196–8
  budgetary control 144, 190–6, 219, 233
  cash flow 193–5
  performance measures 200–1
  profit planning 92–5, 189–90
  ratio analysis 198–200
financial stock control 118
Fire Precautions Act (1971) 256
first aid 255
fitting-room tags 238
fixed/flexible pricing 137
fixtures and fittings 171, 174–6, 219–20
Food Act (1984) 247
Food and Drugs Act (1963) 228
Food Hygiene Regulations (1970/1990)
  247–8
Food Safety Act (1990) 247
franchises 16, 56
free gifts 161
functional organizations 202–3

geodemographic segmentation 69

geographic segmentation 69
government
  buying from 113
  economic policy 52
  and planning applications 216–17
  statistics 43, 85
Granada 29
Grand Metropolitan 28
group training 212
growth strategies 26, 35–6
guarantees 61, 183

Habitat 165
Hanson 28
Harrods 8
health and safety 207–8, 211, 235, 255–6
Health and Safety Executive 52
Health and Safety at Work Act (1974)
  235, 256–7
heating 235, 243
hire-purchase 180
House of Fraser 13
hypermarkets 4–5, 15–16, 24, 89–90, 238

Iceland 28
IKEA 31
image 38, 165
independent traders, see sole traders
induction of staff 210
industrial relations 208
information 40–1
  analysing 46
  collecting techniques 43–8
  sources 41–3, 84–5
  and store location 85–6
insurance 225
interactive electronic shopping 242–3
international retailing
  country preferences 27
  reasons for 23–5
  strategy 26–7
  trends 25–6
  of UK companies 27–9
  of US companies 25, 29–30
interviews 44, 48
investment 195, 229–30

job rotation 212
joint ventures 25, 26–7, 31
joint-stock companies 196

Kingfisher 27

landlords 223
Laura Ashley 27, 28
leases 216, 222, 224–6
legislation 52, 245
  advertising 250, 251
  compulsory purchase orders 220
  consumer protection 246–54
  on credit 249–51
  and employees 220, 235, 254–8
  Food and Drugs Act (1963) 228
  licences
    alcohol 228
    credit 250
  on merchandise 246–7, 248–9
  on prices 252–4
  and rents 222
  Town and Country Planning Act (1990)
    216, 223
licences
  alcohol 228
  credit 250
life cycle stages 69
lifestyle 52, 64
LIFO (last in, first out) stock valuation
  122–3
lighting 236
line organizations 202
line-and-staff organizations 203
liquidity ratios 198–9
local authorities 84
location 8, 24, 37, 79, 166
  area sales potential 87
  catchment area analysis 80–4
  development 226–30
  information needs 84–6
  profit appraisals 92–5
  and rents 221–2
  resites 229
  types of site 88–92
Londis 56
loyalty cards 72, 161

magazine advertising 145
mail order organizations 16–18
management
  of co-operatives 12, 13
  duties 231–2
  function 40
  in international retailing 31

performance measurement 233–5
  of property assets 220–1, 226–30
  responsibilities 233, 235–7
  and technology 243–4
  training 212–13
manuals 232–3
manufacturers 112, 113
mark-downs 132, 137–40
market research, see information
market share 35, 54
market trading 18
marketing, see advertising
markets
  developing 35–6
  entry barriers 24
  identifying 25, 30
  and pricing 133
  saturation 23
  segmentation 37, 68–75
Marks & Spencer 8, 10, 26, 28, 29, 31,
  142, 144, 184
media scheduling 147
merchandise 96–100
  buying 106–15
    quantity 110–12
    suppliers 112–13
    timing 114–15
    what to buy 109–10
  delivery services 124–7, 182–3, 245, 249
  Direct Product Profitability (DPP) 177,
    243
  display 170, 171–2, 172–6
  legislation 246–7, 248–9
  marking 127–8
  new products 35, 98–9
  own brands 99–100
  product liability 252
  quality 98
  quantity 97, 110–12
  range 8, 36, 37, 98, 99, 109–10
  sales forecasting 103–4
  sampling 159
  shortages 123–4
  stock control 117–19
  stock turnover 100–3, 200–1
  stock valuation 122–3
  stocktaking 119–21
  storage 128–9
  training requirements 210–11
  types of 97
mergers 5, 26, 36, 229

MFI 29, 142, 144
mirrors 237–8
mobile shops 19
Monopolies and Mergers Commission 249
monthly accounts 180
multiple stores, *see* chain stores
mystery shopping 47–8

neighbourhood sites 88–9
Nestlé 25
newspapers 85, 144–5
Next 36, 64, 165

odd/even pricing 136
off-centre stores 89
Office of Fair Trading 52, 249
Offices, Shops and Railway Premises Act (1963) 220, 235, 255–6
open-to-buy (OTB) approach to stock 110–11, 115
opening hours 182, 254–5
operating budgets 192–3, 194
organic growth 26
organization charts 204–6
organizations
  centralized 203
  chain stores 4, 10–11, 107, 208
  classification 8–9
  co-operative societies 11–13, 107, 208
  decentralized 203–4
  definition 202
  department stores 13–14, 107, 208
  discount stores 6, 14–15, 89
  franchises 16, 56
  hypermarkets 4–5, 15–16, 24, 89–90, 238
  mail order 16–18
  sole traders 9–10
  structure 8, 202–4
  wholesalers 19–21, 112
  see also stores
out-of-town shopping centres 90–1
own brands 99–100

packaging 160
party selling 19
PDCU (portable data capture units) 242
penetration pricing 133
perceptual map 54, 75
performance measurement 200–1, 233–5

periodic inventories 118
perpetual inventories 121
personal selling 150–1, 153–6
personnel department
  importance 208–9
  organization 208
  responsibilities 206–8
pilferage 237, 238–9
planning 32–4
  buying plans 109
  reviews 38
  stock plans 111
  see also financial planning
planning applications 16, 24, 216–17
PLU (price look-up) facilities 240
point-of-sale displays 159
positioning in the market 74–5
posters 146
price lining 135–6
price zones 135
price-off packs 158
pricing
  of competitors 133
  consumer checks on 47
  discounts 136, 160
  factors influencing 8, 132–3
  fixed/flexible pricing 137
  increases 140
  legislation 252–4
  mark-downs 132, 137–40
  and market segment 97, 133
  penetration pricing 133
  and profit margins 132, 140–1
  setting 133–5
  skimming 133
  strategy 37–8
  tactics 135–7
  terminology 131–2
product liability 252
productivity 36–7, 233–5
products, *see* merchandise
profit and loss accounts 196, 197
profits
  estimating 92–5
  of grocery multiples 235
  improving 189–90
  margins 132, 140–1
  mark-ups 132, 135
  planning 92–5, 189–90
  and pricing 132, 140–1
  and rents 223–4

promotions
  advertising 143
  definition 157
  and mark-downs 139
  objectives 157–8
  retailer-originated 160–2
  supplier-originated 158–60
proof of purchase 245
property
  asset management 220–1
  development 226–30
  see also stores
psychographic segmentation 70–1
public relations 162–3
publications 43, 85
publicity 163

questionnaires 44–5
quick ratio 199

Race Relations Act (1976) 258
rack rent 221–2
radio advertising 145
ratio analysis 198–200
rationalisation 229–30
recessions 24
recruitment 206, 232
redundancy 257
reference groups 66
rents 221–6
Resale Prices Act (1976) 248
research, *see* information
retail parks 24, 91
retail price maintenance 14, 143
returns policy 61, 184
ROCE (Return on Capital Employed) 94,
  198

safety 207–8, 211, 235, 255–6
Safeway 75
Sainsbury 24, 28, 143, 242–3
salary administration 207
Sale of Goods Act (1979) 246
Sale and Supply of Goods Act (1994) 247
sales
  budgets 191
  forecasting 87, 92, 103–4
  increasing 189
  performance measures 200–1
sales forces 150–1, 156
  incentives to 160, 162

training requirements 211
sampling 45–6, 159
security 211, 237–9, 243
segmentation 37, 68–75
  bases for 69–73
  strategy 73–5
self-liquidating premiums 158
Sex Discrimination Acts (1975/1986) 257
shopbreaking 239
shopfitters 217–19
shoplifting 123, 237–8
  apprehending 238, 252
shops, *see* organizations; stores
Shops Acts (1950/1965) 254–5
Signet 28
situation analysis 33–4
skimming 133
social class 66, 70–1
Social Security and Housing Benefits Act
  (1982) 258
sole traders 9–10
'Spacemon' 177
Spar 56
sponsorship 163
staff costs 235
staff pilferage 238–9
staff turnover 211
Statutory Sick Pay (SSP) 258
stock control 117–23
stock shortages 123–4
stock turnover 100–3, 200–1
stock valuation 122–3
stockrooms 128–9
stocktaking 119–21
store audits 47
store detectives 237
Storehouse 26, 29
stores
  atmosphere 165, 166
  branch profiles 228–9
  cleanliness 236, 255, 256
  customer flows 43–4, 172
  design 165, 168, 219–20
  exterior 166–8, 228
  fixtures and fittings 171, 174–6, 219–20
  heating 235, 243
  image 38, 165
  layout 168–72, 228
  lighting 236
  merchandise display 170, 171–6
  modernization 229

numbers in Britain 4–5
opening hours 182, 254–5
planning applications 16, 24, 216–17
purchasing 215–16
rents 221–6
security 237–9
selling area 169, 176–7
shopfitting work 217–19
size 9
valuations 222–3, 225
ventilation 236
window displays 160, 167–8
see also location; organizations
strategy 32, 34–8, 55
structural surveys 215
subculture 66–7
subletting 216, 225
superstores, *see* hypermarkets
suppliers 112–13
  promotions 158–60
  strategies of 25
Supply of Goods and Services Act (1982)
  246
surveys of customers 44–5, 47
surveys of property 215
SWOT (Strengths, Weaknesses,
  Opportunities and Threats) analysis
  33

technology 53, 240–4
  bar coding 240–1
  EFTPOS (electronic funds transfer at
    point of sale) systems 53, 182, 243
  EPOS (electronic point-of-sale) systems
    42, 53, 121–2, 240–1
  interactive electronic shopping 242–3
  and management 243–4
  PDCU (portable data capture units)
    242
  security systems 237–8, 243

and space allocation 243
  viewdata 242
telephone surveys 44
teleshopping 53
television advertising 145–6
Tesco 27, 29, 228
Theft Act (1968) 252
Thorn EMI 28, 29
Tie Rack 29
Town and Country Planning Act (1990)
  216, 223
Toys 'R' Us 29, 30
Trade Descriptions Act (1968) 246, 248–9
trade discounts 114
trading stamps 161
Trading Stamps Act (1964) 248
training 206–7, 209–13
turnover, *see* sales

Unfair Contract Terms Act (1977) 251–2
Unilever 25
unit stock control 117–18
Unsolicited Goods and Services Acts
  (1971/1975) 249
USP (unique selling proposition) 148

valuation of property 222–3, 225
ventilation 236
vertical marketing systems (VMS) 55–6
viewdata 242

wages administration 207
Weights and Measures Act (1985) 254
W.H. Smith 28
wheel of retailing 6
wholesalers 19–21, 112
Wickes 27, 29
window displays 160, 167–8
Woolworths 29, 30
wrapping merchandise 183